S0-BAH-512

New York Presbyterianism at the Founding of the General Assembly, 1788

(apart from a few upstate churches)

☐ Founded Presbyterian
△ Founded Congregational
○ Anglican Appropriation Attempted

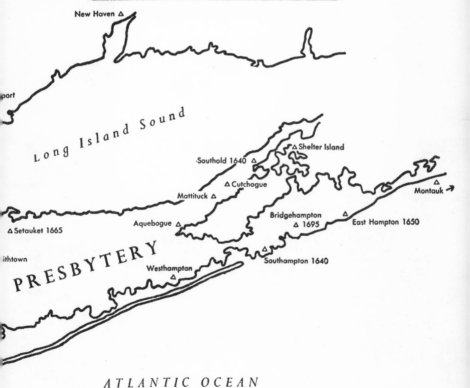

New Haven △

port

Long Island Sound

△ Shelter Island
Southold 1640 △
△ Cutchogue
Mattituck △
Montauk →

△ Setauket 1665
Aquebogue △
Bridgehampton △ 1695
East Hampton 1650

ithtown

PRESBYTERY
Westhampton △
Southampton 1640

ATLANTIC OCEAN

285,147
N518

THE GENERAL THEOLOGICAL
SEMINARY LIBRARY
CHELSEA SQUARE, NEW YORK II, N. Y.

Society for Promoting Religion
and Learning

Presbyterianism
in
New York State

PRESBYTERIAN HISTORICAL SOCIETY

STUDIES IN PRESBYTERIAN HISTORY

Published by The Westminster Press

The Presbyterian Enterprise: Sources of American Presbyterian History, edited by Maurice W. Armstrong, Lefferts A. Loetscher, and Charles A. Anderson. (1956.)

The Presbyterian Ministry in American Culture: A Study in Changing Concepts, 1700–1900, by Elwyn A. Smith. (1962.)

Presbyterianism in New York State, A History of the Synod and Its Predecessors, by Robert Hastings Nichols, edited and completed by James Hastings Nichols

Published by Pennsylvania State University Press

Journals of Charles Beatty, 1762–1769, edited by Guy S. Klett. (1962.)

Published by The Yale University Press

Hoosier Zion: The Presbyterians in Early Indiana, by L. C. Rudolph. (1963.)

PRESBYTERIANISM IN NEW YORK STATE

A History of the Synod and Its Predecessors

by

ROBERT HASTINGS NICHOLS

Edited and Completed by

JAMES HASTINGS NICHOLS

Published for the Presbyterian Historical Society
by
THE WESTMINSTER PRESS
PHILADELPHIA

COPYRIGHT © MCMLXIII W. L. JENKINS

All rights reserved — no part of this book may be reproduced in any form without permission in writing from the publisher, except by a reviewer who wishes to quote brief passages in connection with a review in magazine or newspaper.

LIBRARY OF CONGRESS CATALOG CARD No. 63–8820

PUBLISHED BY THE WESTMINSTER PRESS ®

PHILADELPHIA 7, PENNSYLVANIA

PRINTED IN THE UNITED STATES OF AMERICA

Contents

Preface

This history has been three quarters of a century in the writing. Four years after the Synod of New York was consolidated in its present bounds in 1882 a committee was appointed "to prepare a history of this synod." Dr. T. Ralston Smith, the stated clerk, had received the records of all the merging synods, but apparently the intended writer was Dr. Charles W. Baird, of the Rye Church, author of *Eutaxia, or the Presbyterian Liturgies* and *The History of the Huguenot Emigration to America*. Dr. Baird did publish several valuable works on Presbyterian history in the Westchester region, which are cited in the footnotes and bibliography of this present work, but his death in 1887 cut short the projected history of the synod.

At the end of the century the Presbyterian Historical Society was apparently responsible for prodding the synod again to gather materials on its history. Dr. T. Ralston Smith was appointed historian in 1894 and given a committee in 1902 to help him assemble and collate materials. This committee recommended that a writer be assigned to compose a history. Dr. Frederick E. Shearer was elected in 1903 but apparently never brought book to press.

The prospect of the fiftieth anniversay of the synod in 1932 revived the project. The synod of 1930 requested Prof. Robert Hastings Nichols, of Auburn Seminary, stated clerk, to prepare and publish a history. The work was well advanced, but the synod decided that the time was not favorable for marketing such a production and it was not completed.

After the war Dr. Nichols resumed his work, but was slowed by illness and died before it was finished. He left complete drafts of Chapters I, II, III, IV, and VIII, extensive notes for the remainder, and outlines for all but the last chapter. Chapters V, VI, VII, and IX have been written so far as possible according to his outlines, utilizing his notes. It proved possible in almost every case to supply footnotes for the citations made in his completed chapters.

It seemed best to devote the space for bibliography to a relatively full list of local Presbyterian histories within the bounds of synod, while referring the reader to N. Burr's *Critical Bibliography of Religion in America* for more general works. For the churches of New York City there is adequate guidance in the W.P.A. Historical Records Survey, *Inventory of the Church Archives in New York City, Presbyterian Church in the United States of America.*

The Rev. Robert Beach and his staff in the library of Union Theological Seminary, where are deposited the historical materials owned by the synod as well as the largest collection of works about New York State Presbyterianism, have been helpful well beyond the call of duty in assisting in the completion of this study.

Without the generous assistance of the Presbyterian Historical Society, the history could not have been published in its present form. It is the fruit of a joint effort by the Synod of New York, the Presbyterian Historical Society, and The Westminster Press.

J. H. N.

I : *Congregations Prior to the First Presbyteries and Synod, 1640–1717,*

1. THE SEVENTEENTH-CENTURY FOUNDATIONS

Presbyterianism first appeared within the bounds of New York State in the seventeenth century in independent churches on Long Island and in Westchester County. Independent they had to be, for the first American presbytery and the earliest general Presbyterian organization in New York, the Presbytery of Long Island, began their lives in the next century, in 1706 and 1717.

Eastern Long Island. The two oldest churches now belonging to The United Presbyterian Church in the United States of America are Southampton and Southold. These originated in 1640 before the English Civil War or the Westminster Assembly, but not as Presbyterian churches. The people of Lynn, Massachusetts, "finding themselves straitened, looked out for a new plantation," says John Winthrop. About forty families called to go with them Abraham Pierson, "a godly learned man," a Puritan clergyman of the Church of England, and "he with some seven or eight more gathered into a Church body at

9

Lynn before they went." [1] They settled far out on the southern shore of Long Island, after having been repelled by the Dutch from the western part, and at Southampton in 1640 they established their church. Southold, on the north shore, was settled by people from New Haven, the principal company being led by the Rev. John Youngs, from Southwold, Suffolk. With him as minister, a church was formed in 1640, and recognized by a council of churches of New Haven and the neighborhood.

Further migration across the Sound in the seventeenth and eighteenth centuries caused an extension of New England to grow up in eastern Long Island. Connecticut influence naturally was strong. The church life that was integral to New England appeared on the island almost as soon as the settlement of the towns, with New England ministers in charge of the churches. Down to 1717, five churches besides Southampton and Southold came into being. In East Hampton, Thomas James began in 1650, two years after the settlement, his ministry of forty-six years. This grew to be one of the strongest churches on the island, and in 1717 had the largest church building. Setauket (Brookhaven) had in 1665 as its first settled minister Nathaniel Brewster, who stayed till 1690. His successor from 1697 to 1730 was George Phillips, one of the first members of the Presbytery of Long Island. To Huntington, on the western edge of eastern Long Island, there came as minister in 1658 William Leverich, who had been a missionary to the Indians on Cape Cod and at Oyster Bay. After him began in 1676 the very long ministry of Eliphalet Jones. Of Bridgehampton, the first minister was Ebenezer White, who was settled in 1695 and served fifty-three years. At Mattituck, where settlement began about 1650, the church was not organized until 1715, and Joseph Lamb was installed as pastor in 1717. At Southampton and Southold, meanwhile, church life proceeded vigorously. Each of them by 1711 had its third building. Abraham Pierson left Southampton after three years with a part of

---

[1] *Winthrop's Journal*, ed. by J. K. Hosmer (New York, Charles Scribner's Sons, 1908), II, 4–5.

his congregation because a change in law allowed nonchurch members to vote, and they went to Branford, Connecticut. (From there they were to migrate again in 1667 and found Newark and its church.) But by 1716 there had been two ministries each of about thirty years. At Southold, John Youngs ministered from the foundation to 1672 and Joshua Hobart from 1674 to 1717. This eastern Long Island was a prosperous region, inhabited largely by strong people, and the length of ministries attests a stable church life.

All these churches were ultimately to be Presbyterian. But, composed originally of New England Puritans, Congregationalists by preference, in their early life they were Congregational. A fact about them which favored this independent polity was that, as often in New England, especially in Connecticut, they were town churches. The civil society, the town, acted in church affairs, calling the minister, erecting church buildings, levying church taxes, sometimes exercising church discipline. Thus the religious character of the community was expressed, its civic and church life being one.

But New England Puritanism had in itself Presbyterianism. Both Puritan groups that developed in England — Independents or Congregationalists, and Presbyterians — were represented in New England. The fundamental difference was in the theory of the church. In strict Congregational thought the church was the local congregation, and the word " church" was not applied to any larger organization on earth. In Presbyterian thought the church was the whole company of Christians, the one body of Christ, locally manifested. This difference expressed itself in several practical matters. Most important, in the Congregational way, church government was a function of the local congregation, and there was no authority beyond it. In the Presbyterian way, church government belonged to the whole body, exercising authority through local and higher judicatories.

In Connecticut the Presbyterian tendency in Puritanism asserted itself in the latter part of the seventeenth century, es-

pecially after the ejection of many Presbyterian Anglicans
from English parishes in 1662. This went on to a climax in
1708, in the adoption of the Saybrook Platform. This ecclesiastical constitution of Connecticut, influenced by the London
Heads of Agreement between Presbyterians and Congregationalists, set up "consociations" of churches, which were virtual
presbyteries. The Connecticut churches thereafter often called
themselves Presbyterian. In Long Island, most of whose
churches had Connecticut origins, naturally Presbyterianism
appeared. As in New Jersey and Westchester County, Connecticut people leaving home showed Presbyterian leanings. A
deed of 1707 granted land to "the church or congregation of
Presbyterians at Southampton," [2] showing the earlier use of the
name. The town of Southampton in 1712 assigned land to
Bridgehampton "for the use of a Presbyterian ministry and
noe other," [3] a stipulation also laid on the new church building at Setauket in 1714.[4] Evidently in the churches of eastern
Long Island there were Presbyterian tendencies which facili-
tated their entering Presbyterian organization in the eighteenth century. As yet no churches had sessions; there were
New England deacons, not elders. But there were people and
churches who preferred Presbyterian order to Congregational
independency.

Western Long Island. The first Presbyterian minister in western Long Island was Francis Doughty, a Puritan clergyman of
the Church of England who settled in Taunton, Massachusetts.
Thence he was driven because he maintained the doctrine regarding infant baptism then held by many Presbyterians in
England and Scotland, that it should be administered to all
children of baptized persons, contrary to the views of Congre-

[2] A. F. Halsey, "The Early Church" in *First Presbyterian Church,
Southampton, L. I. 1640–1940* (reprint in part from *In Old Southampton*), p. 11.
[3] Halsey, *idem.*
[4] K. W. Strong, *First Presbyterian Church in Brookhaven, at Setauket*
(Bay Shore, 1942), p. 7.

gationalists in Taunton and elsewhere. With some followers, he obtained from the New Netherlands government land at Mespat (Maspath), Long Island, nearly coterminous with the later Newtown. The patent gave "power to . . . erect a church or churches, to exercise the Reformed Christian religion and Church discipline which they profess." [5] Doubtless a Presbyterian church, in keeping with the views of Doughty and his adherents, was intended. A settlement was made in 1642, and worship under Doughty's charge begun. But soon the houses were burned in Indian warfare, and Doughty and his followers fled to Manhattan Island. There he ministered in the years 1643 to 1648, supported by Puritans and some Dutch. He preached also for a short time to a congregation in Flushing, where he had trouble with the people over political matters. Becoming involved in a lawsuit over the Maspath land, he went to Maryland, where he preached to Puritans for years.

Richard Denton, a Presbyterian Puritan who had had a charge at Halifax, Yorkshire, with some of his people went to Watertown, Massachusetts, and later to Stamford, Connecticut. To a minority of the Stamford congregation, led by Denton, land at Hempstead, Long Island, was granted by the Dutch government in 1644, with authority "to build a town or towns . . . with a temple or temples to exercise the Reformed religion." [6] In this year church life in Hempstead began, for then Denton entered on a ministry that lasted until 1658 or 1659, when he returned to England. The town built a church in 1648. Denton encountered dissent from Independents in his congregation who objected to such practice in infant baptism as Doughty taught in Taunton. After Doughty left Manhattan Island, Denton ministered somewhat to the Puritans there, as well as in Hempstead. He was followed in Hempstead by two New England ministers, Josiah Fordham and Jeremiah Ho-

[5] James Riker, *Annals of Newtown* (New York, D. Fanshaw, 1852), p. 18.
[6] Benjamin Thompson, *History of Long Island* (New York, R. H. Dodd, 1918), 3d edition, II, 471.

bart. After Hobart left in 1696 the church seems to have weakened. There was no minister till 1705. Then, with the induction by the governor, Lord Cornbury, of an Anglican minister, a chapter began of his invasion of the New York churches, which will be described later.

Jamaica was settled in 1656 by people from Hempstead, including as leaders two sons of Richard Denton. The town in 1662 arranged for the building of "the minister's house," and early in 1663 there came as minister Zechariah Walker, of Boston, a licentiate, who was "greatly beloved by the people he served." In 1663 also, the town voted that "a meeting house shall be built twenty-six foot square." In 1670, after a vacancy of two years, the town called John Prudden, a recent Harvard graduate. Two years later it agreed "to further the coming into a church way according to the rules of the gospel in this town by Mr. Prudden and such as shall join him." [7] There is documentary evidence that the phrase "the rules of the gospel in this town" signifies Presbyterian order.[8] It follows that a Presbyterian church was formed in 1672. Thus Jamaica "was probably the first permanent Presbyterian church in the new world." [9] Jamaica was also a town church, established by law and maintained by tax monies.

Prudden remained as minister, with two interruptions of his services, until 1692. After two short ministries during which the celebrated Stone Church was finished, the town records in 1700 say that John "Hobbertt" (later called Hubbard) had been minister "some considerable time" and that the town "does show their willingness to continue him still and to have him ordained provided it be according to the rule and way of the presbetterine way." [10] In 1703 his ministry was broken in

[7] James Macdonald, *A Sketch of the History of the Presbyterian Church in Jamaica, L.I.* (New York, Leavitt, Trow & Co., 1847), pp. 16–22.

[8] *Ibid.*, pp. 56–76.

[9] L. J. Trinterud, *The Forming of an American Tradition* (Philadelphia, The Westminster Press, 1949), p. 22.

[10] J. M. Macdonald, *Two Centuries in the History of the Presbyterian Church, Jamaica, L.I.* (New York, R. Carter & Brothers, 1862), p. 95.

upon by the intrusion into his place by Cornbury of an Anglican minister, and then began the long struggle of the Jamaica
Presbyterians for their rights in their church.

One of the first churches of the Presbytery of Long Island
was Newtown. On the land at Mespat, where Francis Doughty
and his associates had met misfortune, a strong company of
New Englanders, having Director Stuyvesant's leave, built a
hamlet in 1652. Its name "Middelberg" became "Newtown"
at the English possession in 1664. At the beginning the settlers
had with them a licentiate, John Moore, who preached until
his death in 1657. Five years later the town called William
Leverich, who had just served four years at Huntington, and
was highly regarded in his churches, "a learned and pious
man." [11] During his ministry, which lasted until his death in
1677, a church, or as these Puritans would have called it, a
"meeting house," was built. After the two short terms of service of Morgan Jones and John Morse, the town secured for its
minister Robert Breck, just out of Harvard. At his departure in
1704 the governor intruded into Newtown the minister William
Urquhart, whom he had just inducted into the Jamaica church.
Newtown was in the same parish with Jamaica.

Westchester County. Five churches in what from 1683 was
Westchester County had in their early history more or less
Presbyterian character. Three became Presbyterian. Concerning the village of Westchester, the famous Dutch minister
Megapolensis wrote in 1657 that "it has been begun over two
years" and that the inhabitants "are Puritans alias Independents." [12] These Puritans came from Connecticut under the leadership of Thomas Pell, of Fairfield, and very soon established
regular Sunday worship conducted by laymen. There was lit-

[11] J. Riker, *op. cit.*, p. 53.
[12] Edmund B. O'Callaghan, *Documentary History of the State of New
York* (Albany, Wee, Parsons and Co., 1853), III, 107 (large edition); 71
(smaller edition). Compare another translation, in Hugh Hastings, ed.,
Ecclesiastical Records, State of New York (Albany, J. B. Lyon, State
printer, 1901–1905), I, 398; hereafter, *Eccles. Records.*

tle ministry until Warham Mather, of Massachusetts, nephew of Increase, served Westchester, Eastchester, and Yonkers for a year in 1684–1685, and in 1695 was called by the town of Westchester. During his time a second church building was erected. In 1701, Colonel Caleb Heathcote, of Scarsdale, whose large activity in establishing Anglican ministers in the churches of the county will be later described, found that Mather was in the way of his plans to "bring the people over to the Church," and accordingly contrived, he said, "ways to gett him out of the county." [13] This opened the way for the induction in Westchester by Cornbury in 1702 of an Anglican minister, John Bartow.

In 1660, land in the region of Rye was bought by people of Greenwich, Connecticut. From this time followed immigration from that colony into the interior of what became Westchester County, and by the latter years of the century several towns had sprung up. As had occurred among the New England settlers on Long Island, the towns from the first contemplated church life, taking steps toward the choice and maintenance of ministers and the building of houses of worship. These Puritans showed that they meant to have a church by setting apart in 1662 three acres for the use of a minister. But despite the urging and commands of the General Court of Connecticut, to which Rye then belonged, they did not get one till Thomas Denham came in 1677, to stay seven years. Then followed two other Puritan ministers, the second of whom, Nathaniel Bowers, served from 1697 to 1700.

During these years it was uncertain whether Rye and Bedford belonged to New York or to Connecticut. They came into the province of New York in 1683 by agreement between the two governments. But from 1685 there were disputes and clashes of authority until, in 1700, William III confirmed the

[13] R. Bolton, *History of the County of Westchester* (New York, Cass, 3d ed., 1905), II, 333. Also, John T. Scharf, *History of Westchester County* (Philadelphia, L. E. Preston & Co., 1886), I, as cited by William J. Cumming, *History of Westchester Presbytery 1660–1889* (Hartford, Conn., Case, Lockwood & Brainard Co., 1889), p. 24.

arrangement of 1683. During this contest, for nearly four years to 1700, the two towns were under Connecticut jurisdiction. In Rye there was activity in church affairs under Bowers' ministry. Plans were made, but not realized, for the building of a "meeting house" and a "house for a minester." [14] The people had been worshiping in the "town house" and so continued until 1705. In the Rye church there was a vacancy after 1700 until in 1704 an Anglican minister, Thomas Pritchard, was inducted by Cornbury.

A company of people of Stamford, having received in 1681 from the General Court of Connecticut "liberty to erect a plantation . . . about 12 miles to the northwards," were at once directed to provide land for "the first minister of the place" and his successors "forever." [15] Next year the Court gave the town the name "Bedford." The first settled minister, Thomas Denham, came from Rye in 1684, to stay five years. From 1689 for ten years Bedford had no minister, but the town cared for religious concerns, providing for worship and building a meetinghouse. After Joseph Morgan's service from 1700 to 1702 in both Bedford and Eastchester, John Jones was called to Bedford. He feared at the time that his ministry would be interfered with; and this came to pass in 1704, in the intrusion by Lord Cornbury of Thomas Pritchard, at the same time inducted in Rye.

Eastchester was settled in 1664 by people from Fairfield County, Connecticut, who at once in Puritan fashion considered themselves a church and provided for the ministry of Nathaniel Brewster. Several Puritan ministers followed for rather short services, including Morgan Jones, much desired of the people, from 1685 to 1692. Finally in 1700 came Joseph Morgan, who ministered also at Bedford for two years. His service at Eastchester in the church just erected by the people

[14] Charles W. Baird, *History of Rye, 1660–1870* (New York, A. D. F. Randolph and Company, 1871), pp. 282–283.
[15] Charles W. Baird, *History of Bedford Church* (New York, Dodd, Mead and Company, 1882), p. 19.

was broken off in 1702 by the intrusion by Cornbury of John Bartow, established that year in Westchester. "Intrusion" is the right word, for Bartow said that he entered the church while Morgan was ministering, and proceeded to hold full service.

These four churches were originally composed of Connecticut Congregationalists. They were town churches, like those of Connecticut. Naturally their ecclesiastical connections were with Connecticut Congregational associations, and they got most of their ministers from Connecticut. But the tendency toward Presbyterianism that appeared in Connecticut in the seventeenth century manifested itself in Westchester, as it had on Long Island. By 1700 the people of the churches were loosely regarded by those without as Congregationalists or Independents, or Presbyterians. While among them there were preferences, Congregational or Presbyterian, like the Long Island people they were not decided denominationalists. Rye and Bedford, especially Bedford, showed the strongest Presbyterian inclinations. Pioneers of Anglicanism in the late seventeenth century found that "dissenters" made up almost all the population.

Among these congregations of Connecticut origins, refugees and exiles of Calvin's tongue now appeared. There had been Huguenots and Waldenses in New Amsterdam and on Staten Island under the Dutch. The great persecution of Louis XIV in the 1680's sent many more into exile, and there were four Huguenot churches in the province by the 1690's. Huguenots came to New Paltz in 1683,[16] and another company to Pelham Manor in 1686 and then to New Rochelle. Probably Pierre Daillé, "apostle of the Huguenots," did pioneer work among them. Daniel de Bonrepos was minister of their church in 1688 and in 1694 went to the French church on Staten Island. Soon after 1695, the New Rochelle church being vacant, Colo-

---

[16] R. LeFevre, "The Huguenots — the First Settlers in the Province of New York" [New Paltz], *New York State Historical Association, Proceedings,* Vol. XIX (1921), 177–185.

nel Heathcote secured the placing in it of Daniel Boudet, a Huguenot who had received Anglican ordination. By 1709 the majority of the French people had conformed to the Church of England, and in 1710 they built a church. But a minority maintained the life of the original church. These Reformed people of course held Presbyterian principles, and the First Presbyterian Church of New Rochelle continues their church.

2. THE CAMPAIGN TO ESTABLISH ANGLICANISM

At the English conquest of 1664, New Netherlands came under the authority of the Duke of York. "The Duke's Laws," promulgated in 1665, required every town or parish to have a church and maintain the ministry, the expense thereof to be raised by tax. There was to be liberty of conscience, and the choice of the minister was to be with the majority of householders.[17] When the Duke became James II, secret instructions were sent in 1686 to Governor Dongan, directing him to require the regular use of *The Book of Common Prayer* and the administration of the Sacrament according to the rites of the Church of England; also ordering that "no minister be preferred by you to any ecclesiastical benefice" unless he have the Archbishop of Canterbury's certificate of his being conformed to the Church of England.[18] These instructions, given by a Roman Catholic king to a Roman Catholic governor, appeared to intend an establishment of the Church of England in a population consisting mostly of Dutch Reformed and English dissenters, with some French Reformed and Lutherans and a few Anglicans — according to the Anglican chaplain of the garrison, 90 families out of 3500 in 1695.[19] In these circumstances Dongan's instructions resulted in no alteration in church life.

Changes came under the Ministry Act passed by the General

[17] *Eccles. Records*, I, 570–572.
[18] *Eccles. Records*, II, 915–916.
[19] J. Miller, *New York Considered and Improved, 1695*, ed. by V. H. Paltsits (Cleveland, The Burrows Brothers Company, 1903), pp. 40, 54.

Assembly of the province in 1693.[20] This provided that within one year "there shall be called, inducted and established a good sufficient Protestant minister" in each of six localities, one in New York City; one in Richmond County (Staten Island); two in Westchester County, one for Westchester, Eastchester, Yonkers, and the Manor of Pelham, the other for Rye, Mamaroneck, and Bedford; two in Queens County, one for Jamaica and the other for Hempstead. In each of these "parishes" there were to be elected ten vestrymen and two churchwardens. They were to call the minister. The vestry and the justice of the peace were to levy taxes for the salary of the minister and other church expenses. Existing arrangements with ministers were to continue.

It has been extensively asserted and believed that the Ministry Act established the Church of England in the province. Plainly this is not the case. The Act applied to only six places in four of the ten counties. It did not mention the Church of England. A resolution of 1695 forbade an exclusively Anglican establishment: "The vestrymen and churchwardens have power to call a dissenting Protestant minister, and he is to be paid and maintained as the law directs." [21] But two royal governors, Fletcher from 1692 and his successor from 1702, Lord Cornbury, wrested the Act to mean that the Church of England was established. Under color of this and of their instructions, the same as those given to Dongan, they claimed authority in the affairs of churches of dissenters.

Cornbury was most active in this line. He inducted Anglican ministers into churches in disregard of the rights of dissenting ministers in office and generally tyrannized over the churches. He was helped in his policy of induction by a supply of Anglican clergymen provided by the Society for the Propagation of the Gospel in Foreign Parts, founded in London in 1701. The Society (known as the SPG) by its missionaries strengthened the ministry of the Church of England

---

20 *Eccles. Records*, II, 1076–1079.
21 *Eccles. Records*, II, 1114–1115.

generally in the colonies. In New York this end was pursued by the supplanting of dissenting ministers and the induction of Anglican ministers into dissenting churches temporarily vacant, under the authority of Cornbury.

This intrusion of Anglicanism into their churches excited among the people opposition in different degrees and forms in different churches, most of all in Bedford. In several places they refused to the incumbent the salaries raised by taxation and instead paid them to " dissenting " ministers of their own choice. The strength of the hostility to the enforced Anglican order was shown by the passage in the provincial General Assembly, six years after the Ministry Act, of a bill granting to every town power to call and settle a Protestant minister by majority vote of the people, which was not approved by the governor and council.[22]

The churches on western Long Island and in Westchester County whose beginnings have been described were severely affected by the events just mentioned.

The Hempstead church being vacant in 1705, as has been said, an Anglican minister, John Thomas, a missionary of the SPG, was arbitrarily inducted by Cornbury and placed in possession of the church building and parsonage. Evicted from their property and taxed for Anglican support, the people could not have a minister, but they kept up worship, served by occasional supplies. At length in 1721 they built a meetinghouse, where the church preserved its life.

In Jamaica during an absence of the minister, John Hubbard, his pulpit was sometimes occupied, under arrangement of Cornbury, by John Bartow, a missionary of the SPG, who was minister in Westchester. The vestry and churchwardens of Jamaica had recently called Hubbard, already their minister, thus confirming his title. One Sunday afternoon just after his return in 1703, Hubbard, going to the church, found Bartow holding service, whereupon he preached in an orchard hard

[22] Journal of . . . the General Assembly . . . of New York (New York, H. Gaine, 1764–1766), I, 101, and Eccles. Records, II, 1299, 1331.

by, pews being carried out of the church for his hearers. After a disorderly scene Cornbury forbade him ever to preach in the church. The Presbyterians, who were almost all of the people of Jamaica, held services in a building in the town, where Hubbard ministered. On the arrival of William Urquhart, another SPG missionary, intruded into the church by Cornbury, Hubbard in 1704 was ejected from the parsonage and glebe in favor of Urquhart. Thus the Presbyterians found themselves ousted from the church and property, and also taxed for Urquhart's salary. Collection of the tax was enforced by fines on the vestry and churchwardens.

But in 1708 the removal of Cornbury because of popular protest and the passing of authority in the province into the hands of men of different character changed the situation of the Presbyterians. After Urquhart's death in 1709 they regained permanently the parsonage and glebe. They seized the stone church, and during their brief occupancy the vestry and churchwardens, all Presbyterians, called to be minister George McNish, Moderator of the Presbytery of Philadelphia, a man of much leadership and determination. Before he came to Jamaica, the governor, Robert Hunter, caused Thomas Poyer, another SPG missionary, to be inducted into the church. Then ensued an extraordinary situation. McNish in 1711 was settled in the Presbyterian church, where he ministered influentially. He was put in possession of the parsonage and glebe and preached in a building erected by the Presbyterians. Poyer, as incumbent, conducted Anglican service for a small group in the stone church and had a melancholy experience. His salary raised by tax was not paid for five years and then only after lawsuits continuing until his retirement in 1731, and costly to the Presbyterians. The contest for the stone church ended in 1728, when a court decision confirmed to the town the title, and the Presbyterian congregation occupied the building.

Newtown, as has been said, had William Urquhart, incumbent of Jamaica, thrust upon it in 1704. Its pulpit was occupied by him once a month and was otherwise vacant, except when the services of dissenting ministers were obtained. Cornbury soon prohibited them from preaching without his special license. In 1708, the year of his removal, Samuel Pumroy of Northampton, Massachusetts, who had been called to be minister by a large number of the people, arrived in Newtown. Next year, at the request of the eight members in full communion and the rest of the congregation, he was ordained pastor of the Newtown church by a Congregational council in Northampton. It may be noted that a census of 1711 showed a population in the town of 1,003 souls, of whom 164 were Negro slaves. The church at Pumroy's coming was Congregational, and a town church. But in 1715, probably under the influence of McNish of Jamaica, Pumroy joined the Presbytery of Philadelphia. That the church was becoming Presbyterian appears from a deed of 1715 to trustees for "the Dissenting Presbyterian congregation of Newtown" of land for a new building.[23] Elders were chosen in 1724.

In Westchester County a special force for the Anglican cause was Caleb Heathcote, before referred to. A wealthy man, he came from England to Mamaroneck in 1692, and acquired large lands, part of which were the "manor of Scarsdale." He was commissioned by the governor colonel and judge of the county. Convinced that the Church of England was established in New York, he was indefatigable in efforts to extend it in Westchester County, about which he wrote in 1692 that there were "scarce six in the whole county who so much as inclined to the church."[24] He was largely instrumental in bringing from England into the county missionaries of the SPG after its foundation in 1701.

John Bartow, an SPG missionary inducted in 1702, remained in the town of Westchester until his death in 1726. He appears to have been a man of zeal and goodwill, though a stiff Anglican. His reports told of progress in his work but lack of enthusiasm in the people, because almost all had been "edu-

[23] J. Riker, op. cit., p. 151.   [24] W. J. Cumming, op. cit., p. 24.

cated Dissenters." [25] Nevertheless, there was in time acquiescence in the new order, and the church became Anglican.

In Eastchester, Bartow, intruded in 1702, held possession. Many of the people acquiesced, as in Westchester, and the Eastchester church also became Anglican. But a part of the original church maintained its life. For two years they had the service of Joseph Morgan, their minister who had been supplanted by Bartow. After this they held together, and for eighteen months in 1718–1720 they had as minister William Tennent, later a famous Presbyterian leader, who had just come from Ireland and had become a member of the Synod of Philadelphia.

In Rye, Thomas Pritchard, inducted by Cornbury in 1704, was speedily succeeded by George Muirson, a good and energetic minister. Under his leadership and that of Colonel Heathcote, a warden of the parish, a church building was begun by the town and covered by 1706. During the ministries of Muirson and of Christopher Bridge, 1710–1719, both men of winning spirit, some forty of the people conformed to the Church of England and more attended its services, there being no dissenting minister. But about two thirds, over four hundred, " continued to avow themselves Presbyterians." [26] For two years from 1720 they maintained a separate worship under the ministry of Stephen Buckingham, of Norwalk, Connecticut. About 1723 they obtained as minister John Walton, a member of the Presbytery of Philadelphia, a forceful man and able preacher. When Robert Jenney came as Anglican rector in 1722 he collected by legal process the arrears of salary since 1719 and used the money to finish the church. This embittered the Presbyterians, increased their number, and brought support to Walton's proposal of the building of a church of their own, which was finished about 1728.

Thomas Pritchard, intruded by Cornbury into the church at Bedford in 1704 during the ministry of John Jones, met resistance from the people, led by Zechariah Roberts, justice of the peace, and Jones, whose action caused them to be called to account before the governor and council. When George Muirson was Anglican rector at Rye he preached every fourth Sunday at Bedford, which was in the same parish, and reported there "a very wilful, stubborn people." [27] From 1705 to 1720 there was no resident minister in Bedford. The people, who at this time are always called Presbyterians, could not maintain a ministry of their own, because they were taxed, very unwillingly, for the support of the Anglican incumbent in Rye, but they retained their house of worship. In 1720, there being a vacancy in Rye, the Presbyterians called William Tennent from Eastchester. He served a devoted people until 1726.

In New Rochelle the people who continued the Reformed Church maintained worship, mostly in the house of Alexander Allaire. From 1718 they had the sacraments from J. J. B. de Moulinars, a minister of the older French church in New York. In 1726 he removed to New Rochelle, and served the Huguenot congregation to 1741. A church had been built in 1723.

New York City and the Makemie Trial. The company of Puritans in New Amsterdam to which Francis Doughty and Richard Denton ministered must have included a good number of Presbyterians, else they would not have been served by two clergymen of decided Presbyterian views. Among them were also Independents or Congregationalists, said by some to have been more numerous, by others fewer. These Puritans had no church organization and no building. They worshiped in "the church in the fort," used also by the Dutch and French congregations. Their growth is shown by the fact that in 1695 the vestry of New York, chosen under the Ministry Act, voted that "a Dissenting minister be called to officiate and have the care of Souls for this city." [28]

[27] R. Bolton, *op. cit.*, p. 166, cited by C. W. Baird, *History of Bedford Church*, p. 38.
[28] *Eccles. Records,* II, 1114-1115.

Accordingly, the vestry in 1696 chose William Vesey to be their minister. He was a Massachusetts and Harvard man, sent to New York by Increase Mather to strengthen the Puritan interest. He had preached in Hempstead and New York, which was the reason for his call. But in 1696 also, the Anglicans of New York formed a church and called Vesey, on condition of his taking orders in the Church of England. This he did, and became rector of Trinity Church.

Presbyterianism gained fame in New York through legal proceedings against two Presbyterian ministers. One of these was Francis Makemie, Moderator of the Presbytery of Philadelphia. He had come in 1683 from the north of Ireland to Maryland to minister among Scotch-Irish refugees. He had traveled and preached along the shores of Maryland, Virginia, and the Carolinas, becoming acquainted with Puritan settlers and beginning a lifelong friendship with their people. He had resided in Virginia and Barbados, preaching and trading, and according to strong tradition had founded churches in Maryland. He had twice visited England and won the sympathy of the United Brethren of London, Presbyterians and Congregationalists, for the American church life in which he was a leader. Thus it was natural that he should be the first moderator of the Presbytery, formed in 1706. In 1707 he arrived in New York, probably en route to Boston to consult with the Puritan ministers there. With him was John Hampton, another member of the Presbytery. At the request of the Presbyterians of the city, Makemie preached to a few people in a private house on January 20, 1707. On the same day Hampton preached in Newtown, Long Island. On the following Tuesday the two went to Newtown to preach the next day. But they were arrested on a warrant from Cornbury for preaching without a license. Taken to New York, they were imprisoned until March 1, when they were brought into court on a writ of habeas corpus. The charge against Hampton was dropped, but Makemie was required to give bail for appearance at trial in June.

At his trial he maintained his right as a dissenting preacher under the Toleration Act of 1689, showing his license granted in Barbados, recognized in Virginia and valid in the queen's dominions. He was defended by three able lawyers and acquitted. But Cornbury in revenge caused him to be loaded with all the costs of the trial. The issue of this Presbyterian minister's courage was a strengthening of religious liberty in New York and a good opinion of Presbyterianism among the dissenters of the colonies. Moreover, Cornbury's tyranny in Makemie's case was chief among the offences that caused his removal in 1708.

The Presbyterians to whom Makemie had preached held together after his trial, worshiping in private houses without a minister. In 1716, "Dr. John Nicoll, Patrick McKnight, Gilbert Livingstone . . . and Thomas Smith with a few others . . . entered upon the design of settling a congregation according to the method of the Presbyterian churches." [29] This congregation consisted of people from England, New England, Scotland, and Ulster. Thus began the First Presbyterian Church of New York. James Anderson, a Scot who was serving a church in New Castle, Delaware, was called to be the minister and began his work in 1717. After worshiping in the city hall the congregation in 1719 built a church in Wall Street, having help from the Connecticut churches and through the Synod of Philadelphia from Scotland.

3. THE FIRST PRESBYTERIES AND SYNOD

The Presbytery of Philadelphia was formed in 1706 by seven ministers, three New Englanders, three from the north of Ireland, and one Scot. Their churches were in Philadelphia and the neighboring parts of Delaware and Maryland. The congregations were largely composed of people from England and New England, with a good number from Scotland and Ulster, and some Welsh, Dutch, and Huguenots, thus prophetic of the

[29] *Minutes of the General Assembly of the Church of Scotland,* May 30, 1766, cited by Charles A. Briggs, *American Presbyterianism* (New York, Charles Scribner's Sons, 1885), p. 178.

mixed character of American Presbyterianism. The chief motive in the formation of the presbytery was desire to draw together in the presence of the rising power and ambitions of the Church of England in the middle colonies, shown in the activities of the missionaries of the SPG and of some English officers of government. The Presbytery had close sympathies with the Puritan churches of New England, which were troubled for the same reason. The Anglican purpose was to bring about a wider establishment of the Church of England, already considerably established in the south.

The Puritan congregations of Long Island, which were Presbyterianly inclined or Presbyterian, were naturally attracted to the Presbytery. Jamaica, as has been seen, called its moderator, George McNish, in 1710, and Samuel Pumroy, of Newtown, joined it in 1715. In 1716, Southampton called Samuel Gelston, a member of the Presbytery, and promised subjection to its authority. In its first decade several congregations in New Jersey, founded in the seventeenth century by Puritans, but later of mixed membership, came into the Presbytery. Some of these, such as Newark and Elizabeth, were important additions. The Presbytery gained strength also in Delaware and Maryland.

The Synod of Philadelphia. By 1716 the Presbytery had twenty-five ministers, eight Scots, seven from Ulster, seven New Englanders, three Welshmen. Since these men were pastors, the number of churches was probably at least as large. The Presbytery had so increased that in 1716 it was decided to form a synod. Three presbyteries were to compose it: Philadelphia, New Castle (in Delaware), Snow Hill (in Maryland) — but this third was never organized. It was decided also to ask McNish and Pumroy to secure other ministers to join them in forming a presbytery on Long Island.

The Presbytery of Long Island. The Synod met in Philadelphia in September, 1717. It was reported that the Presbytery of Long Island had been formed, and that Samuel Gelston had been ordained at Southampton by McNish, Pumroy, and George Phillips, minister at Setauket. Evidently Phillips had joined the other two to form the Presbytery of Long Island, and this was its first meeting.

II : *Growth and Controversy from 1717 to the First Synod of New York, 1745*

1. GROWTH OF PRESBYTERIANISM IN NEW YORK

In the years after the organization of the Presbytery of Long Island in 1717 the province of New York saw some rise of Presbyterian churches, some growth of churches which, though not Presbyterian in form, ultimately became such, and an important strengthening of general Presbyterian organization.

The Presbytery of Long Island. The Presbytery of Long Island at its beginning in 1717 was, as has been seen, almost as small as possible, consisting of two churches at the western end of the island, Jamaica and Newtown, and two at the eastern end, Southampton and Setauket. Since the records of the presbytery are lost, it is impossible to make exact statements about its later membership. But because the name of Joseph Lamb, minister in Mattituck, occurs in the records of the Synod for 1718 and following years, it would appear that this church was connected with the presbytery from this time. In the eastern part of the island there were Puritan churches, four already mentioned, which were later to become Presbyterian, but were not, so far as is known, of the presbytery, though representing

30

the same type of religious life: East Hampton, Bridgehampton, Southold, Huntington, Aquebogue, Babylon, Cutchogue, Smithtown.

One of the churches of the presbytery, Jamaica, was long troubled under the civil law. Until the Revolution there were both a Presbyterian pastor and an Anglican rector, the latter supported by tax, though the Presbyterian congregation was much the larger. In 1724 the rector brought suit of ejectment in order to get possession of the parsonage and glebe, which had been used by the pastor, George McNish, but the action went against him. In 1728 the town went to court to recover the stone church, which had been in Anglican possession since 1704, and thenceforth it was occupied by the Presbyterian congregation, according to the original intention.

In Jamaica church life was vigorous. McNish was followed by another highly regarded minister, Robert Cross, later active as an Old Side leader in Philadelphia. After him began in 1738 the short but gifted ministry of Walter Wilmot. In his time the Great Awakening touched Jamaica; both Whitefield and Gilbert Tennent preached there in 1740, with their usual reviving results. In Newtown nearby, Samuel Pumroy's strong service was carried on until his death in 1744. In the churches of the eastern end of the island there were long ministries, those of George Phillips at Setauket, Lamb at Mattituck, and Sylvanus White at Southampton, and there were good conditions, especially at Southampton.

The church of New York, according to entries in the records of the Synod from 1720 to 1728, was in those years under the jurisdiction of the Presbytery of Long Island. James Anderson continued as minister for most of that time. In 1722, after disagreement with him arose, a group separated and held its own services. They had for their minister Jonathan Edwards, barely nineteen, who had just finished graduate study at Yale. He has left records of happy associations in New York and of a celebrated incident in his own spiritual experience there. After only nine months he returned to Connecticut, and his congregation returned to the original church. In 1727, Ebenezer Pemberton, of Boston and Harvard, began his long and distinguished pastorate in the New York church. Early in his time, the church, finding incorporation denied through Anglican influence, in order to guard its property deeded it to the General Assembly of the Church of Scotland in trust.[1] In his first preaching tour in America, in 1739, Whitefield came to New York and found Pemberton's the only church open to him. For four days he preached there and outdoors. In a town that was a stranger to general religious concern he made a profound impression by his evangelical earnestness and pathos, and won a large following. At his farewell sermon there was a great popular demonstration. The Presbyterian church experienced a lasting revival.

The Presbytery of New York. The churches of Long Island Presbytery in east and west were far distant, and travel was difficult. By 1738 changes had been such that the Synod found that the presbytery was " reduced so that a quorum cannot meet statedly about business," and united it with the Presbytery of East Jersey under the name of the Presbytery of New York. East Jersey had been formed out of Philadelphia in 1733. It was composed chiefly of the churches founded in the preceding century by New Englanders in central and eastern New Jersey, now well established, and was influential in the Synod.

The Presbytery of New York included also, from East Jersey, churches in New York west of the Hudson. Here, in Orange and Ulster counties, a good part of the large Scotch-Irish immigration of 1714–1720 had found homes. There was also a considerable English and New England settlement. The church at Goshen was founded by English and Scotch-Irish people in 1720. Since it had a Scotch Presbyterian minister from 1721 to 1733, and had relations with the Synod in those years, it may

[1] Samuel Miller, *Sketch of the Early History of the First Presbyterian Church.* Reprint, 1937, pp. 10–11.

justly be called the oldest Presbyterian church in New York west of the Hudson. The Scotch-Irish churches of Goodwill (Walkill) and Bethlehem (Salisbury Mills), dating from about 1729, also had relations with the Synod before the formation of the Presbytery of New York, and were of this presbytery at its beginning.

The Presbytery of New York, thus formed, was one of the most important bodies of colonial Presbyterianism, as will appear in the history about to be narrated. The people of its churches were largely of New England descent, but in most parts contained many of other kinds, English, Scotch, Scotch-Irish, Welsh, Dutch, Huguenot. They had a good degree of religious training and some general education. The ministers were almost all New Englanders and all college-bred. Of the sixteen in 1738, twelve were graduates of Yale, three of Harvard, and one of an Irish institution. Among them was the ablest and most influential member of the Synod, Jonathan Dickinson, of Elizabeth, a strong and beloved pastor for thirty-nine years in that important town, a theologian of repute on both sides of the ocean, a foremost evangelist of the Great Awakening. Two other men of high distinction were Aaron Burr, of Newark, and Pemberton, of New York.

A frontier outpost of New York Presbyterianism, not at first of the Presbytery of New York, was Cherry Valley. This was founded in 1741, by a Scotch-Irish colony from Londonderry, New Hampshire, led by the Rev. Samuel Dunlop. They settled on land granted to John Lindesay, who had induced Dunlop to come. Cherry Valley adhered at first to the Presbytery of Boston, but joined the Presbytery of Dutchess County in 1765, then that of New York, and in 1790 that of Albany.

What was done by the Presbytery of New York for missions is memorable in missionary history. In 1740, Dickinson, Burr, and Pemberton urged the Society in Scotland for Propagating Christian Knowledge to send missionaries to the Indians in New Jersey, Long Island, and Pennsylvania. In those days missionary efforts for non-Christians were few among Protestants, so that these men were among the pioneers. The Society appointed the three its Correspondents and authorized them to employ missionaries. Hence, Azariah Horton, of Southold, a graduate of Yale, ordained by the Presbytery of New York in 1741, went to the Indians on the southern shore of Long Island, being the first Presbyterian missionary. He worked over a hundred miles of the shore, living in the wigwams of the Indians, eating their food, preaching to them, teaching them to read. There were only about four hundred of them, the remnants of a numerous population. Horton met many discouragements, and after eleven years went to the church at Madison, New Jersey; but he left Indian churches, two of which were living a hundred years after.

The Correspondents found another missionary in a brilliant Yale student, David Brainerd. They appointed him to service in 1742 and sent him for an apprenticeship to Indians near New Lebanon, New York. There he worked through an interpreter from John Sergeant's Indian school at Stockbridge, not far distant, and with advice from Sergeant. These Indians moving away, the Correspondents directed Brainerd to go to "the forks of the Delaware," near Easton. During his work with the Indians there, he traveled to Newark to attend a meeting of the Presbytery of New York, by which he was ordained in June, 1744. In this time also he rode through the wilderness to tribes on the Susquehanna, a journey later twice repeated. Then he settled among Indians whom he had gathered at Crosswicks, near Bordentown, New Jersey, and whom he moved to lands of their own near Cranbury. There he established a community called Bethel. Celebrated for the Christian character of its members, this was carried on after Brainerd's death by his brother John. David Brainerd had been burdened by illness during much of his work, and in 1747 he died, at the house in Northampton, Massachusetts, of Jonathan Edwards, to whose daughter he was engaged to be married. Dying in his thirtieth year, he left an undying legacy in his diary and journal, published first by Edwards and then

many times in America and Britain. They have been a strong
source of missionary spirit in the English-speaking world because through the old-fashioned language and some morbidity
of religious experience inevitable in a sick man there burns
such a flame of love for the souls of men in Christ and such un-
conquerable zeal.

Churches in Westchester and Putnam Counties. The Presbyterians of Rye, after the Anglican incumbent, Bridges, left the
town in 1719, maintained their own worship for two years under the ministry of Stephen Buckingham, of Norwalk. About
1723 they obtained as minister John Walton, a member of the
Presbytery of Philadelphia. Though under censure, Walton
was a forceful but erratic man and an able preacher, who built
up the congregation. He proposed two churches, one at Rye
and the other at "the White Plains," six miles away, where
there was a settlement dating from about 1721, and there evidently were Presbyterians. The Presbyterians of both places
spoke of themselves in 1727 as "but one society." [2] With the
support of the trustees of Yale College, they asked the General
Court of Connecticut to desire the churches of the province to
give aid toward the building, and it was given largely. In White
Plains the church was built about 1727 and that in Rye in 1729.

For thirteen years after 1729, Rye and White Plains had
only occasional supplies. The religious decline in many parts of
the colonies in the 1730's appeared in these villages. But this
ended soon after the Great Awakening made itself generally
felt, when in 1742 John Smith, the friend of Jonathan Edwards,
was ordained by the Fairfield East Consociation and began his
long and influential ministry in the two churches. He was a
memorable preacher and pastor, and under him the churches
prospered. In 1752 he became a member of the Presbytery of
New York, and thus Rye and White Plains came into its connection.

In Bedford the Presbyterians, relieved of tax because there

[2] Charles W. Baird, *History of Rye, 1660–1870*, p. 325.

was no rector in Rye, called from Eastchester in 1720 William Tennent, a member, as has been said, of the Presbytery of Philadelphia. He served a devoted people, preaching powerfully in the village and the country round about. Several tracts of land were given him by the people. During his time a bench of elders was formed in Bedford. There he had with him his four sons, all to be notable Presbyterian ministers, and it is said that there the eldest, Gilbert, began to preach. Gilbert received the degree of M.A. from Yale in 1725. After six years in Bedford, the father went to Neshaminy, northeast of Philadelphia, where later he established his renowned " Log College." He was followed by Henry Baldwin and Robert Sturgeon, of whom not much is known. During Tennent's later years and afterward, the tax for the salary of the rector was reimposed in Bedford and collected by legal process.

In 1743, Bedford came into connection with the Presbytery of New Brunswick, formed in 1738 out of the Presbytery of Philadelphia and New York, and containing the leaders of the revival in the Presbyterian Church. In 1742 this presbytery, in accordance with its spirit, sent one of its members, Samuel Sackett, as a missionary to Crompond, in northern Westchester County, and in the next year he was installed over that church and Bedford. He served ten years in Bedford, with great evangelistic zeal, " one of the most enthusiastic Methodists." [3]

Crompond, also called Hanover, Cortland Manor, and in modern times, Yorktown, was settled about 1730 by people of Puritan descent from Connecticut, southern Westchester, and Long Island. A church had been built in 1738, but Sackett was the first minister and the only minister for many years. He and William Tennent may be called the first Presbyterian ministers in Westchester County.

At the place in Putnam County where the church long called Southeast grew up, and the First Church of Phillipse Precinct,

[3] R. Bolton, *History of the Protestant Episcopal Church* . . . , *1693–1853* (New York, Stanford and Swords, 1855), p. 621; cited, Charles W. Baird, *History of Bedford Church*, p. 59.

now Brewster, a settlement was made about 1730 by Connecticut people. A log church is said to have been built in 1735. The first minister, Elisha Kent, began in 1740 the remarkable service as pastor, preacher, and religious leader that caused the region to be known as "Kent's parish." The church originally was decidedly Congregational, but became connected with a presbytery, Dutchess County, as will be seen.

Another church in Putnam County, which was called Philippi Second or Fredericksburg and latterly was known as Patterson, probably originated in 1745. The early settlers were largely of Scottish descent, coming principally from New England, and somewhat from Westchester County and New York City. Here also a log church was built. The church had no minister until 1758. Then came Joseph Peck, who was one of those who organized the Presbytery of Dutchess County.

In New Rochelle the Reformed people who had continued to worship with Calvin's liturgy had the sacraments from 1718 from a minister of the French Church in New York, J. J. B. de Moulinars. In 1726 he removed to New Rochelle and served the Huguenot church till his death in 1741. After 1741 there seem to have been occasional supplies from New York until Jean Carle came as minister in both places in 1754, serving till 1764.

2. THE ADOPTING ACT, THE GREAT AWAKENING, AND THE SCHISM OF 1741

The Adopting Act. Certain events in the Synod in these years were vital to the history of New York Presbyterianism. One of these was the difference over the adoption of the Westminster Confession of Faith and Catechisms. A controversy began in 1722 between a Scotch-Irish group who insisted on subscription by ministers to the Westminster symbols and a New England group, led by Jonathan Dickinson, who held that the Bible only was a sufficient doctrinal standard. These men opposed subscription, not because of theological dissent, but for the sake of evangelical liberty. "I have no worse opinion of

the Assemblies Confession," Dickinson wrote, "for the second
article in the XXth chapter: *God alone is Lord of the conscience,* etc. . . . and I must tell you that to subscribe this article, and *impose* the rest, appears to me the most glorious con-
tradiction." [4] But so determined were the "subscribers" that
there was danger of division until, through Dickinson's wisdom and love of unity, agreement was reached. In 1729 the
Synod enacted the famous Adopting Act.[5]

According to this, candidates and entering ministers were to
assent to the Confession and Catechisms "as being in all the
essential and necessary articles good forms of sound words
and systems of doctrine." But any person objecting to anything
in them might state "any scruple," and the Synod or the presbytery, if it judged the scruple "to be only about articles not
essential or necessary," should still admit him; thus the principle of liberty was declared. On the same day the members of
the Synod expressed their assent to the Confession and Catechisms, except for certain portions relating to church and state,
and in 1730 this was voted to be the standard attitude. But
differences as to the meaning of the subscription between the
stricter party and the liberals remained. Interpretation of subscription in the freedom of the gospel was maintained by the
men who were to dominate the Presbytery of New York.

The Great Awakening in New Jersey. The 1720's and 1730's
were a time of widespread coldness and deadness in the religious life of America, as also in Britain. Describing the later
1720's, Archibald Alexander, father of Princeton Seminary,
wrote, "The state of vital piety was very low in the Presbyterian church of America." [6] That extraordinary man, William
Tennent, whom we saw at Eastchester and Bedford, New York,
was, we must say, raised up by God to be a powerful instru-

---

[4] *Remarks Upon A Discourse Entitled An Overture,* p. 29; cited,
Charles A. Briggs, *American Presbyterianism,* p. 213.
[5] *Records of the Presbyterian Church,* 1904, p. 94.
[6] *Biographical Sketches of the Founder . . . of the Log College*
(Philadelphia, Presbyterian Board of Publication, 1851), p. 22.

ment of regeneration. Settling at Neshaminy, northeast of Philadelphia, in 1726 or 1727, and seeing the need of ministers who would promote " vital piety," he set about to train up such. First in his own house, and then in a log schoolhouse, the illustrious Log College, he taught altogether his sons and some sixteen other young men. He gave them a good classical education, and much more important, a knowledge of the gospel as the power of salvation, and inspiration to be such fervent evangelists as they all became.

The power of the Great Awakening first appeared in the Presbyterian Church in the preaching of Gilbert Tennent, William's oldest son, at New Brunswick, New Jersey, a preaching bringing to indifferent or complacent church people a revolutionary conception of the gospel and its effect. By 1729 his congregation in New Brunswick and preaching stations as far as Staten Island were showing new religious life. Then there settled in Presbyterian churches in central New Jersey ministers of his spirit, students of William Tennent. Revival came in many places under their " awakening " preaching. As was natural when religion had been lifeless and sleepy, there were emotional manifestations, outcries, prostrations. But this was superficial; there were in good measure real strengthening of vital Christianity and real moral renewal. The Great Awakening had come. By 1735 it was growing and widely known. Gilbert Tennent had preached in New York and published his sermons there and in Boston.

But opposition to the revival appeared in the Synod. By 1738 — an important date for this history — the Presbyterian Church had grown largely by immigration to Pennsylvania of people from the north of Ireland. The ministers who came with them were largely strangers to the kind of Christianity that had been spreading in the New Brunswick region, although Tennent himself had come from Ulster. Their Old World training had given them little understanding of this high-wrought religion — this deep conviction of sin, crying sense of the need of salvation, rapture of faith, joyful assurance of being born again, passion for goodness. Their conception of religion was static and formal. That people should be instructed according to the Westminster Confession was their chief concern. The important qualification for ministers, they held, was not that they should have Christian experience, but that they should be educated and orthodox and regularly ordained. Such men were in control of the Synod. In 1738 they brought about two acts of the Synod designed to check the revival, one restricting preaching away from ministers' churches and the other prescribing educational tests for ministers, designed to exclude the Log College men. It looked like defeat for the revival men in the church. They secured in this year the formation of the celebrated Presbytery of New Brunswick, containing Gilbert and William Tennent, the younger, and Samuel Blair, a Log College man and a powerful preacher of the revival. But the future did not look bright for their cause.

Whitefield Saving the Revival. The whole religious situation in the Presbyterian Church and the colonies was changed by George Whitefield. Preceded by reports of his astonishing preaching in England, he arrived in Philadelphia in November, 1739, and in nine days preached to thousands. Traveling to New York he met Gilbert Tennent at New Brunswick, finding in him at once a kindred spirit. In New York he preached outdoors and in Ebenezer Pemberton's Presbyterian church, with his usual effect. " In four days he had won a great popular following." Tennent also preached in the church, and Whitefield "never before heard such a searching sermon." [7] On his return journey to Philadelphia he strengthened the revival in the places where the Log College men had aroused it, and spread it in other towns. Preaching for five days in Philadelphia before he went south, he had his largest audiences yet. By early in the following spring, the Awakening was appearing in several distant places. A great revival that had sprung

[7] C. H. Maxson, *The Great Awakening in the Middle Colonies* (Chicago, University of Chicago Press, 1920), pp. 49–50.

up in 1739 in Aaron Burr's congregation in Newark was continuing. Another came in Orange County, New York, under the preaching of Silar Leonard, Presbyterian minister of Goshen. In eastern Long Island, James Davenport, minister of Southold, who was to be one of the most notable preachers of the Awakening, called out religious life as a power in East Hampton, not yet showing much of the fantastic methods that later marked him.

The year 1740 saw the Great Awakening at high tide. Whitefield made two evangelistic tours in the middle colonies, stirring people profoundly everywhere. A large church, his " tabernacle," was built in Philadelphia for his preaching. The men of New Brunswick Presbytery, now strengthened by Log College alumni, itinerated zealously in New Jersey, reaching to Cape May with the revival message of the new birth, and into Delaware and Maryland. A campaign of evangelistic meetings in Whitefield's tabernacle, where Gilbert and William Tennent, Samuel Blair, and Davenport preached for several days to " throngs from Philadelphia and nearby towns," showed the hold of the revival on the people. The newspapers in all parts of the colonies " carried glowing accounts of Whitefield's evangelistic preaching and its wonderful results." [8] One of his effects was to bind together in support of the revival New Brunswick Presbytery and the New England men of the Presbytery of New York, led by Dickinson, Burr, and Pemberton.

The Schism of 1741. But hostility to the revival grew in the Synod, centering in Pennsylvania. Against Whitefield and his work there was a campaign of pamphlets, sermons, letters to newspapers, mostly from Presbyterian sources. Opposition was stronger against the men of New Brunswick Presbytery and their sympathizers. It was said that some of the revival preachers overemphasized the terrors of the law and threw people into despair, which others of them admitted. The physical demonstrations at the preaching — the weeping, shouts, faintings —

---

[8] L. J. Trinterud, *The Forming of An American Tradition,* pp. 96, 87.

were objected to; and for this there was some ground, as Jonathan Dickinson, for example, thought. It was charged that the evangelists "intruded" into other men's parishes and divided churches. There were cases of this but many fewer than were alleged; the significant fact here was the spread of vital religion among the people and their hunger for preaching that would feed it.

Above all was the accusation that was made against the Awakening everywhere and that fills so large a place in its literature, "censoriousness." Ministers and people who criticized the revival or did not support it were charged, it was copiously said, with being unconverted and no Christians. The "Protestation" against the revivalists submitted to the Synod in 1741 [9] speaks of "their rash judging and condemning all who do not fall in with their measures, both ministers and people, as carnal, graceless, and enemies to the work of God." For a judgment on this, the situation must be viewed. Certainly there were in the Presbyterian Church ministers without Christian experience and unconverted people, dead Christians. Into such conditions came fervent evangelists, preaching with all their hearts the gospel of salvation, and meeting indifference or active opposition. It is not strange that they were tempted to be "censorious." In March, 1740, Gilbert Tennent had preached his famous sermon on "The Danger of an Unconverted Ministry." This really terrible denunciation of conditions in the church was understood by the opponents of the revival to be directed against them. Printed and circulated, it increased hostility, and was a principal cause of the division that was to come.

By 1741 the lines were drawn between friends and foes of the revival, New Side and Old Side. In the Synod of that year came the crisis. In their "Protestation" twelve Pennsylvania ministers led by Robert Cross, formerly of Jamaica, denounced the men of New Brunswick Presbytery and their supporters. They repeated in substance the criticisms of the revival that have been noticed, and added other accusations. In a revealing sentence they found fault with these men for their teaching that inner conviction, rather than regular ordination, constituted a call of God to the ministry, and that the preaching of ministers without Christian experience "can be of no saving benefit to souls." They deplored "their unwearied, unscriptural, anti-presbyterial, uncharitable, divisive practices." The signers declared that those against whom they protested had no right to be in the Synod and that further union with them was impossible. The men of the Presbytery of New York, who might have moderated the conflict, were absent. The outcome was "a disorderly rupture." [10] No regular action was taken. The New Brunswick men and their sympathizers, finding themselves slightly in the minority and ejected, withdrew from the meeting. The next day they met, asserted their rights as members of the Synod, and formed themselves into two presbyteries, the Conjunct Presbyteries. They at once began to carry out extensive plans for evangelism and for providing for churches that asked them for ministers. They sent Sackett, for example, to perform a missionary work in Westchester.

The Synod of New York. In the Synod the men of the Presbytery of New York, led by Dickinson and Burr and Pemberton, strove to heal the breach. They protested against the illegal exclusion of the New Brunswick party and said that they could not continue to sit in the Synod if these men were not restored. They protested also against the constant criticism of the revival. They sought to bring about reconciliation and fellowship in the work of the church. But from the Old Side they met only obstinacy and more hostility to the revival. Finally, in 1743, the Presbytery of New York proposed that a new synod should be erected, the two to act in concert and kindness. New York Presbytery began to act with the Conjunct Presbyteries in matters of the revival.

[10] C. Hodge, *Constitutional History of the Presbyterian Church* (Philadelphia, Presbyterian Board of Publication, 1851), II, 158.

Hence the Synod of New York was organized at Elizabeth on September 19, 1745, with Dickinson as moderator.[11] It contained the Presbyteries of New York, New Brunswick, and New Castle, this last being a new formation in the southern region. The Presbytery of New York covered Long Island, the rest of southern New York, and northern and eastern New Jersey. Most of the New Brunswick party, numbering thirteen ministers, went with the new synod, and New York brought in nine. The synod at this first meeting bore testimony to the revival, "the work of God's grace among us." It adopted the Westminster Standards as they were adopted in 1729, which meant that the subscribers were not bound to verbal assent. In order to settle the vexed question of ecclesiastical authority, which had underlain some of the troubles in the Synod of Philadelphia, it was agreed that in matters of discipline those who could not conscientiously submit to the decision of the majority should peaceably withdraw. To avoid affairs like the "Protestation" of 1741, it was agreed that charges against ministers should be only by regular disciplinary process. The synod declared that all ministers competent in knowledge, orthodox in doctrine, exemplary in life, and "diligent . . . to promote the important designs of vital godliness" should be admitted to fellowship. To guard against divisions in churches, it promised friendly relations and correspondence with the Synod of Philadelphia, as the older synod from this time was called. Thus the Synod of New York stood for the evangelism of the revival, for liberty in the gospel, for reasonable authority, for an open door to Christians, for peace and unity in the church. It was a new day in American Presbyterianism when the Synod of New York with this spirit was founded.

[11] *Records of the Presbyterian Church,* pp. 233–234.

III : *The First Synod of New York and the Shaping of American Presbyterianism, 1745–1789*

1. EXPANSION AND ORGANIZATION

Long Island. The reason for the merging of Long Island Presbytery and East Jersey in 1738, making New York Presbytery, was the weakness of Long Island. But in the eastern part of the island there was a body of churches of considerable strength, of Presbyterian inclinations, at least two of them definitely Presbyterian. Among them the Great Awakening had worked. Therefore on April 8, 1747, the ministers of Aquebogue, Bridgehampton, Cutchogue, East Hampton, Huntington, and Southampton met at Southampton and "on account of the disorders in churches which are due to the want of some stated rules of ecclesiastical government," decided to adopt Presbyterian order and approved of the Westminster Confession of Faith and Catechism. They determined to form a presbytery named Suffolk, and to propose to their churches the adoption of the Presbyterian form of government and of the Directory of the Church of Scotland "as the rule of our procedure in order and discipline." They voted that as soon as the churches had concurred they would send delegates to the

45

Synod of New York. Five elders and delegates of churches were present and concurred with the ministers. The body agreed "to bring the churches and the people of God within our county and bounds that are in an unsettled state and without pastors to compliance with the Presbyterian form of government and to subjection to our inspection, care and government as a presbytery."[1] The presbytery joined the Synod of New York in 1748.

The churches and ministers at the east end of the island, a flourishing region of growing population, came almost unanimously and rather quickly into the presbytery. Two old churches at the western end, Hempstead and Jamaica, eventually joined it. Two churches in Westchester County came into its connection, Bedford when Samuel Sackett, the minister, became a member in 1751, and Crompond (Hanover, Yorktown) when two years later he was installed there by the presbytery. By 1775, when its life was interrupted by the War of Independence, seventeen ministers had joined it and twelve churches had been added.

The strength of the presbytery was the churches at the east end. These consisted of New Englanders and people of New England descent, and the ministers were almost all from New England, chiefly graduates of Yale. In the churches the Congregational inheritance was strong, and while they belonged to the presbytery, they were slow in getting Presbyterian organization and several did not in the eighteenth century have elders, though elders were always present in presbytery meetings. The churches had close relations to those of New England, especially of Connecticut. Churches falling vacant would often seek "candidates" in Connecticut. There were cases of action by mixed councils, of Presbyterian and other ministers, such as the installation of William Throop at Southold in 1748. There were also in some churches strict Congregationalists, who produced divisions in them and formation of "separate" churches.

[1] MS. Minutes, Presbytery of Suffolk (1747–1789), pp. 2–4.

Though ministers were added to the presbytery, they were not enough. From about 1767 there were constant appeals to the presbytery from vacant churches for supplies and for " candidates." The need for ministers was due largely to a great revival beginning in East Hampton in 1764 under the preaching of Samuel Buell and spreading in the east end of the island, doubling some churches in two years and producing new Christian groups. In this year Whitefield preached at East Hampton, Southampton, Southold, and Shelter Island.

Suffolk Presbytery had strong ministers, Ebenezer Prime, for fifty years from 1722 in Huntington, Benjamin Goldsmith, of Aquebogue, famous as a peacemaker, and Samuel Buell, one of the most useful Presbyterian ministers of the eighteenth century. He began his ministry by preaching for Jonathan Edwards at Northampton for a few weeks, with an effect on the town that Edwards has recorded. He was installed in East Hampton in 1745, and served until 1798. He was remarkable as a preacher, a pastor, and a scholar, and was the reverenced leader of the community. It was under his preaching that the powerful revival of 1764 began.

New York City. In the church of New York the ministry of Ebenezer Pemberton continued in this period with power. The revival conditions resulting from Whitefield's preaching in 1739 persisted. The decade 1740-1750 saw rapid increase in the church and the accession of influential families. This growth was stimulated by an eight-day visit of Whitefield in 1747. Enlargement of the church building, completed in 1749, was needed. In that year the trustees recorded that " the bell was rung from a Presbyterian steeple for the first time in the city." [2] Alexander Cummings was ordained in 1750 as colleague to Pemberton.

But dissension arose in the congregation. There was dissatisfaction of a minority with the ministers. But the chief trouble

[2] Samuel Miller, *Sketch of the Early History of the First Presbyterian Church* (1937 reprint), p. 12.*

was over the introduction of Watts's *Psalms* instead of Rouse's or the old Scots version. The outcome was Pemberton's resignation, against the wishes of a majority of the congregation. His successor in 1756 was David Bostwick, of Jamaica, who accepted the call to New York by advice of the Synod, over the opposition of his congregation. Shortly a group of Scotch people, still dissatisfied over Watts's *Psalms* and minor causes, withdrew and formed a separate congregation, which in 1757 joined the Associate Presbyterian or Seceder communion of Scottish origin. From this as a beginning, through many changes, came the present Second Presbyterian Church of New York. "This secession," says a historian of First Church, "restored peace to the congregation,"[3] and it grew under Bostwick's gifted ministry until his early death in 1763. A third attempt to secure incorporation had been defeated by Anglican opposition.

A new chapter in the church's history opened in 1765 with the coming of John Rodgers, already eminent for his pastorate at St. George's, Delaware. Soon the congregation so increased that it was necessary to erect a second building on what is now Beekman Street. This, afterward called the Brick Church, was dedicated in 1768. There was not another church; the one church had two places of worship and centers of life in a collegiate relation. This Dutch Reformed pattern had its advantages when incorporation was denied to Presbyterians. Rodgers and Joseph Treat, who had come as colleague to Bostwick, ministered to both groups. The people who remained in the Wall Street church were mostly Scottish and Scotch-Irish; those who went to the "New Church" were mostly New Englanders and of New England descent. John Rodgers had a long and famous ministry in New York. His character, devotedly Christian and in all things exemplary, held the confidence and affection of his people. He excelled in every part of his ministry steadfastly for many years. He built up the church greatly and was a foremost leader in the presbytery and the synod. He

[3] *Ibid.*, p. 23.

took a chief part in the organization of the General Assembly and was chosen its first Moderator in 1789. Active in good works in the city, he was a commanding figure in its life. His conspicuous services in the War of Independence will be described in their place.

Westchester, Putnam, Dutchess Counties. The churches of Rye and White Plains, which had been revived at the coming of John Smith in 1742, flourished under his ministry. He was a memorable preacher and pastor, and influential in the country round about his churches. In 1763 he took the charge also of a Presbyterian congregation that had just been formed in Sing Sing. He joined the Presbytery of New York in 1752. This brought him into the Synod of New York, where he became prominent. In 1768 he asked for a colleague, and served with him until his death in 1771.

The Bedford church under Samuel Sackett's ministry from 1743 in the spirit of the Great Awakening had seasons of revival, but the congregation on the whole was conservative and wedded to old ways, and after ten years he was dismissed and went to Crompond. He had served there jointly with Bedford and for four years from 1749 at Bedford only. At Crompond he remained with a short interruption till his death in 1784, through the War of Independence. He was followed in Bedford by Eliphalet Ball, a man of like religious temper, and of remarkable enterprise and energy. Various contentions led to his resignation from Bedford in 1768. His founding of the church and town of Ballston will be described in connection with the Albany region.

Down to the war, settlement advanced rather rapidly in the lower Hudson Valley east of the river and back from it. The people came largely from Connecticut, and somewhat from Long Island, of New England descent. By 1770 there had sprung up in the three counties twelve churches with which we are concerned, in addition to those already mentioned, Rye, White Plains, Bedford, Crompond. These twelve were not decidedly marked denominationally, but all except two union churches were of Presbyterian or Congregational character. Some were connected with the Fairfield East Consociation; but in 1763 that body ruled out churches not in Connecticut.

In 1762, three ministers, Elisha Kent, of Southeast, Joseph Peck, of Philippi Second, and Solomon Mead, of Salem, met in Kent's parsonage, and thinking that it was "for the Interest of Religion to be regularly constituted a Presbytery," determined to apply to the Synod of New York and Philadelphia for such constitution.[4] The synod in 1763 "agreed to grant this request," on condition that the presbytery "adopt our Westminster Confession of Faith and Catechisms, and engage to observe the Directory as their Plan of Worship and Government," which the presbytery immediately did. The synod gave the presbytery the name of Dutchess County, and added to it John Smith and Chauncey Graham of the Presbytery of New York, and Samuel Sackett and Eliphalet Ball of the Presbytery of Suffolk.[5]

At 1775 the churches east of the Hudson, which were under the jurisdiction of the Presbytery of Dutchess County or in connection with it, in addition to the older churches already described of Bedford, Rye, White Plains, Crompond, Southeast, may be listed as follows. Patterson (Philippi II — Fredericksburg) was established, probably in 1745, by Scottish people from New England. The people of the Rumbout (Fishkill) church were gathered by Elisha Kent "before 1747," and Chauncey Graham became pastor in 1748 or 1749. He was pastor also from 1750 to 1752 of the church at Poughkeepsie, which was formed in 1749. Salem (South Salem) was organized in 1752 as Congregational, and became one of the first churches of the presbytery. Gilead (Carmel) had as its first pastor, from 1756 to 1759, Ebenezer Knibloe, and belonged to the Fairfield East Consociation until it became connected with the presbytery in 1774. As early as 1763, John Smith, of Rye

---

[4] W. J. Cumming, *History of Westchester Presbytery*, p. 31.
[5] *Records of the Presbyterian Church*, 1904, pp. 330–331.

and White Plains, was preaching also at Sing Sing. Through his membership in the presbytery, probably, the church that had sprung up there came under its care. At Pittsburgh (Charlotte Precinct) a church was started in 1747, and Wheeler Case was ordained and installed in 1765 over Pittsburgh and also Poughkeepsie, which had fallen vacant. Pound Ridge, a settlement of people from Stamford, Connecticut, was connected with the presbytery in the sense of receiving from it supplies from 1770 throughout its life. In Pleasant Valley a church was organized by 1765 and a meetinghouse erected by 1770. In the latter year, Wheeler Case, released from Poughkeepsie, began to preach there, maintaining his pastoral relation with Pittsburgh. At Upper Salem a "Presbyterian meeting house" was built in 1764, but the church was Congregational. It had supplies from the presbytery in this time before the Revolutionary War.

The Amenia churches, in northern Dutchess County, were in existence when the presbytery was formed. Amenia began in 1748, Smithfield in 1742, South Amenia in 1759. Smithfield was Congregational, and the other two had a good deal of union character. They never joined the presbytery. In the early nineteenth century all became Presbyterian.

How many of the churches of the presbytery "had a bench of elders and conducted their internal affairs according to the usages of the Presbyterian Church we are unable to say," [6] wrote the historian of Westchester Presbytery. Some had elders, such as Bedford under William Tennent in 1720–1726, and Crompond in 1765; others, as Southeast and Upper Salem, were like the later "Presbygational" churches of central and western New York, Congregational internally but connected with the presbytery. Ultimately these became Presbyterian.

The Presbytery of Dutchess County was faithful in supplying vacancies in its churches, but otherwise did not display much activity. It did little to increase the ministry. "When

[6] W. J. Cumming, *op. cit.*, p. 37.

largest, it had but ten ministers," and about fifteen churches. "The attendance at the meetings was usually from four to six ministers and from two to four elders." [7]

West of the Hudson. On the west bank of the Hudson, settlement proceeded more slowly than across the river, partly because the land was largely held in great manors. After Goodwill and Bethlehem, the next Presbyterian churches were Florida and Warwick, south of Goshen and near together, founded about 1750. The people were English, from New England and Long Island, and Dutch. Warwick became a Reformed church in 1804, but Florida remained Presbyterian. It was of the Presbytery of New York until the erection of the Presbytery of Hudson in 1795.

At Bloomingrove, east of Goshen, a church was organized in 1759, composed chiefly of immigrants from Suffolk County. Though of Congregational leanings, they had Presbyterian ministers for many years, and twice were in relations with presbyteries. But in 1833 the church declared itself Congregational.

At Marlborough, north of Newburgh, land was given for a church in 1764 on condition that the minister should be a Presbyterian. There was a Presbyterian minister for several years from 1765. A church was organized in 1793, under the Associated Presbytery of Morris County. In 1810 it went into the Presbytery of Hudson.

Among Scotch-Irish people at Little Britain, near Newburgh, a Presbyterian church was formed in 1765. A Presbyterian church was in existence nearby, at Bethlehem. But these people were of the Scottish Associate or Seceder Church, and of the Anti-Burgher branch of that church. Robert Annan was their minister from 1768 to 1783. When the Associate Reformed Church of America was formed in 1782, by union of parts of the Associate Church and the Reformed Presbyterian Church, the Little Britain church became Associate Reformed.

[7] *Ibid.*, p. 39.

Far away on the western frontier, Cherry Valley, at first independent, joined the Presbytery of Dutchess County in 1765, and then was transferred to the Presbytery of New York, probably in 1775. The town and the church prospered and Samuel Dunlop remained minister until the terrible massacre of 1778. Immediately after the war some of the people returned to the place of desolation and rebuilt the town. The church was revived, and in 1788 applied to the presbytery for supplies.

Farther south in the upper Susquehanna Valley a large and later distinguished Scotch-Irish family named Harper from Cherry Valley began settlement in 1771. This was Harpersfield, and here a Presbyterian church that was to be well-known sprang up. Other Ulster people came into this region before the Revolutionary War, and were part of the material for later Presbyterian churches.

The Albany Region. Albany from its settlement as Fort Orange early in the seventeenth century remained "almost as thoroughly Dutch as Holland" until well after the New Netherlands became English in 1664.[8] From the first part of the next century people from England and the north of Ireland came. In 1760 the Synod of New York and Philadelphia received "a very pressing application from the English Presbyterian gentlemen of Albany" for supplies, and such were sent. The church was formed probably in 1762. It was received in 1765 into the Presbytery of Dutchess County along with William Hanna as minister, who served about two years. In 1767–1768, in response to requests for supplies for "many vacancies" north of Albany, the synod sent ministers for short periods, among them John Rodgers, of New York, and Andrew Bay, "a broad Scotsman." Bay was called to the Albany church and remained until about 1773. In his time a building was erected at a cost of £2831, and the church appealed to the synod, in vain, for help in a debt incurred. During the Revolutionary

[8] John M. Blayney, *History of the First Presbyterian Church of Albany, N.Y.* (Albany, Jenkins & Johnston, 1877), p. 11.

War the church had no minister, but maintained services for prayer. In 1785 its first pastor, John MacDonald, a licentiate of the Church of Scotland, was installed. The church had been transferred by the synod in 1775 to the Presbytery of New York.

At Cambridge, northeast of Albany, the first settlers, early in the 1760's, were of three religious kinds: Congregationalists and Presbyterians from Connecticut, and Scotch-Irish. There came to be an Associate, Scotch congregation, and a Congregational. Out of these at length in 1793 there was formed a Presbyterian church. Its first pastor was Gershom Williams, who had been a missionary of the Synod of New York and Philadelphia in this region.

Salem, also northeast of Albany, was settled in 1764 by people from western Massachusetts — Puritan and Scotch-Irish. Another company came from the north of Ireland. After attempts to unite with them, the New Englanders formed a Presbyterian church in 1769. Another missionary of the synod, John Warford, came in 1787 to be their minister.

Congregationalists of Canaan, Connecticut, moved in 1762 to Stillwater, north of Albany, on the Hudson, and built a church. The life of this congregation was disrupted by the Revolutionary War and revived in 1784. Meanwhile another group of mixed membership — Dutch, New Englanders, Scots, Scotch-Irish — had erected a church and held services. Aaron Condict, another missionary of the synod, in 1794 organized these people into a Presbyterian church.

In 1771, a hundred and ten years after the beginning of the town, a Presbyterian congregation in Schenectady engaged in building a church appealed to the synod for money, but in vain. The application was made by Alexander Miller, of the Presbytery of New York, who a year before had been ordained and had become minister of the church. He reported to the synod in 1776 that he had supplied places in the neighborhood of Schenectady. When he had served that church about eleven years, the scattering of the people because of the Revolutionary War ended his ministry. After the war the church remained weak, and could support a minister only in conjunction with two neighboring congregations.

In Johnstown, farther to the west of Albany, a church was built in 1763 by Sir William Johnson and a larger one in 1767. Sir William was one of the largest landholders in the province, a very successful trader with the Indians, appointed Superintendent of Indian Affairs. He was a north of Ireland man, an Anglican, and concerned for the churches and for missionaries to the Indians. Since there were among his tenants Presbyterians and Anglicans, he allowed services of both kinds in the church he had built. On his death in 1774 his estate passed to his son, Sir John, who in the war became a loyalist. His property was confiscated, and the state legislature gave the church to the Presbyterians, with use of a few Sundays in the year for Anglicans and Lutherans. In 1790 began the long ministry of Simon Hosack under the new Presbytery of Albany.

Ballston owed its foundation as town and church to Eliphalet Ball, who left the church at Bedford, Westchester County, in 1768. In the wilderness of Saratoga County he obtained a grant of land on condition of bringing settlers. He brought a company of his former Bedford people, and there arose what was named Ball's Town after him. In 1775 a church was organized with him as minister on the basis of the Standards of the Church of Scotland, and he served eight years. William Schenck, a missionary sent to the Albany country after the war, became pastor in Ballston.

The region northwest of Albany after the middle of the eighteenth century was chiefly inhabited by Scots. Galway was settled in 1774. Other Scottish towns were New Scotland and Breadalbane. Presbyterian congregations sprang up in these places, and in the 1790's had Presbyterian ministers.

2. THE FIRST SYNOD OF NEW YORK AND THE REUNION, 1748–1758

The Synod of New York, whose foundation has been narrated, in its thirteen years wrote a memorable history and permanently influenced American Presbyterianism and American Christianity. As has been said, the synod included much territory outside the province of New York. But of its history the history of New York Presbyterianism is an integral part, and its characteristic spirit descended into the Presbyterians of New York.

Formed by friends and supporters of the Great Awakening, the synod soon put into action its evangelistic, expansionist spirit, its purpose to build up the church. There was considerable evangelistic opportunity in the middle colonies, where the Synod's presbyteries of New York, New Brunswick, and New Castle extended. By the middle of the eighteenth century the American frontier was developing, with its characteristic problems. Population was growing: somewhat by immigration from Europe, more by moving about among the colonies. Here were many people without ministers or churches. By 1745 the Awakening had somewhat spent its force in the middle colonies. But there were thousands of people who had felt its power and who spread its spirit. Outbursts of new religious life still appeared. The whole situation meant need for establishing churches and supplying and strengthening them. In the minutes of the synod there are many appeals from people lacking religious care and many appointments of ministers to visit them. The presbyteries of the synod were active in supplying churches and bringing on young ministers. In Virginia a remarkable evangelistic work was done under the synod. Numbers of Presbyterians had settled in the upland region and the valley. The minutes of the synod contain repeated requests from these " destitute settlements," and also from North Carolina, and appointments of ministers to go so far south, far indeed in the conditions of travel in those days. The result of the work of the evangelists of the synod, the New Side, was an extensive enduring revival of Christian life. The outcome in organization was the formation in 1755 of the synod's Presbytery of Hanover, long a center of evangelism and Presbyterianism.

So strong was the evangelistic spirit of the synod that whereas in 1745 it had twenty-three ministers, in 1758 it had seventy-four, of whom practically all were pastors of churches, signifying very rapid growth. The Presbytery of New York grew in these years from nine ministers to twenty-two. Meanwhile the Synod of Philadelphia had decreased from twenty-seven to twenty-three.

Missions to the Indians. When David Brainerd died in 1747, his brother, John, also a member of the Presbytery of New York, was called by the Correspondents of the Scottish Society to succeed him in the care of his Indian community. He trained the Indians for eight years until they were robbed of their lands. Meanwhile the synod, inspired by these missionary examples, in 1751 appointed annual collections for missions to Indians in the churches and later gave the proceeds to Brainerd. He was the first missionary supported by the American Presbyterian Church. New lands being given to the Indians in southern New Jersey by the provincial government, John Brainerd cared for them, and for white people who had no ministers, for the rest of his life. His support was carried on after 1758 by the Synod of New York and Philadelphia, so that the Synod of New York bequeathed its missionary interest to the reunited church.

Most of the Congregational and Presbyterian missions to the Iroquois were based on the New England missionary schools at Stockbridge and Lebanon. Their labors were rendered difficult by the intermittent frontier wars — with the French, Pontiac's rising, and then the Revolution — as well as by resentment against unscrupulous traders and the encroachments of white settlements on Indian lands.

Samson Occum, a Mohegan Indian, was born in 1723 in an Indian village near Norwich, Connecticut. During the Great Awakening, in 1741, under the influence of neighboring ministers, he was converted. Inspired with desire to teach his people, he became the first of the Indians taught in his house by Eleazar Wheelock, of Lebanon, with whom he studied four years. For about ten years from 1748 he worked among Indians at Montauk, first teaching and then also preaching. Under his ministry a number of Montauks were converted. While preaching he maintained himself by working with his hands. In 1759 he was ordained by the Presbytery of Suffolk and directed to "pursue his ministry at Montauk and among other Indians until a door should be opened for his ministry elsewhere." [9]

He was sent by the Correspondents of the Scottish Society for Propagating Christian Knowledge on a mission to the Oneida Indians. In 1763 the synod, "having considered the importance of the mission among the Oneida Indians and the small sum of money allowed by the Society in Britain to Mr. Occam, their missionary, have thought proper to take that mission under their . . . care for the ensuing year, and order that he be allowed £65 for this year. It is also requested of the Commissioners in New York that they immediately ask the Society in Scotland to grant a larger sum for the support of this mission." [10] In 1776, Occum went to Great Britain with the Rev. Nathaniel Whitaker, of Norwich, to raise money for Wheelock's Indian school. He preached between three and four hundred times in England and Scotland, arousing great interest, and secured over £10,000. He carried on itinerant labors among Indians until 1786, when he gathered after the war remains of several tribes of New England and Long Island and settled them at Brotherton, Oneida County,

---

[9] " Records of Suffolk Presbytery," Vol. I(B), 1757–1764 (typescript), p. 145. Cf. H. Blodgett, *Samson Occom* (Hanover, N.H., Dartmouth College Publications, 1935).

[10] *Records of the Presbyterian Church*, 1904, p. 324.

New York. Among them he worked till his death in 1792. He had left Suffolk Presbytery for New York, and joined Albany Presbytery at its formation in 1790.

Another Lebanon student was Samuel Kirkland. After study at Princeton, Kirkland went two hundred miles on snowshoes in 1765 into the wilderness of the upper Mohawk Valley to work with the Oneidas. He devoted forty years to this service, receiving some support from the Scotch Society. During the Revolution he was a chaplain, and was given much credit for holding the Six Nations neutral. After the war he founded an academy on the Lebanon model, which was later to develop into Hamilton College.

The College of New Jersey. The Synod of New York gave inestimable service to education. Members of the synod, three of the alumni of the Log College, founded and maintained three classical academies in Pennsylvania that trained eminent leaders in the church and education. But the synod's greatest educational contribution was the creation of the College of New Jersey, now Princeton University. This began with the Presbytery of New York. In its part of the church most recruits for the ministry came from Yale and Harvard. But the ministers of the presbytery had come to distrust the New England colleges, where most of them had been graduated, because opposition to the Great Awakening had developed there. The college came into being in 1747 at Elizabeth, with Jonathan Dickinson as its first president. Dying soon, he was followed by Aaron Burr, of Newark, and the college moved thither, to stay for eight years. Then it moved again, to Princeton. Burr was followed by Jonathan Edwards, his father-in-law, who lived only a month, and then by Samuel Davies, Samuel Finley, and John Blair, until John Witherspoon came in 1768. Thus for its first twenty-one years the college was led by ministers of the Synod of New York. All these years it was sending men of the spirit of the revival into the ministry of the synod. It was natural that the synod in 1752 and later years urged its churches to take collections for the college, and that it sent Samuel Davies and Gilbert Tennent to Britain to raise money for the institution, a fruitful expedition.

Through the college there grew up close relations between the synod and the New England churches. Men from parts of New England where the revival had been strong went to the college and returned to study theology with ministers of this spirit; men from the synod took their undergraduate work at Yale and their theology with Presbyterian ministers. These reciprocal intellectual ties had important effect in years to come on Congregational-Presbyterian relations.

Reunion. During almost its whole life the synod was working for reunion with the Old Side. An effort by Jonathan Dickinson in the very year of the rupture came to nothing through his death in 1747 and the stiff refusal which the synod met. In 1749 the synod proposed "that all our former differences be buried in perpetual oblivion and that . . . both Synods be united into one." [11] From this time the record of the negotiations shows the synod striving for this, undiscouraged by rebuffs, standing its ground on matters of principle, patiently endeavoring to remove obstacles. Meanwhile moderation of feelings proceeded, and the Synod of Philadelphia was doubtless influenced by being outstripped by New York. The plan of reunion, adopted in 1758,[12] showed that New York prevailed on vital points. The "Protestation" of 1741, which had precipitated the rupture, was disavowed by Philadelphia. A main contention of New York, that candidates for the ministry give satisfaction as to "experimental acquaintance with religion" was granted. The united synod agreed on a description of the kind of religion that the Awakening had propagated and the changes that this had wrought in men and a declaration that all such things were "a gracious work of God." So the principles of the revival triumphed.

Of the Synod of New York it has been well said that it "was

[11] *Ibid.,* p. 238.   [12] *Ibid.,* pp. 286–288.

the strongest Church in the middle colonies, made up of many congregations scattered from the Hudson Valley to North Carolina, from Southampton on eastern Long Island to regions in the wilderness near Fort Pitt, Pennsylvania. It was possessed of a thriving college and numerous classical schools. . . . Its clergy were among the finest on the American Continent. The new order, a truly American Presbyterianism, was distinguished by its tone, discipline and spiritual vitality." [13]

The reunited church called itself the Synod of New York and Philadelphia. The order of the names is significant of the situation. Three quarters of the strength of the church came from the Synod of New York. Of the ninety-six ministers in 1758, seventy-three were of New York. Twenty-eight were graduates of Yale and twenty of the College of New Jersey. The Presbytery of New York was twice as large as any other Charles Hodge in his history of 1851 named seventeen ministers of the time of the reunion who, he said, " were some of the most distinguished men who have ever adorned our annals "; [14] thirteen came from New York. Despite discords that the men of the New Side sought to allay, the reunited colonial church bore in large part the character thus derived from the Synod of New York.

3. THE REVOLUTIONARY EPOCH

Opposition to an Anglican Episcopate and Establishment. The province of New York in its late years covered a good part of the Presbytery of New York, which included also the strong churches of northeastern New Jersey, and the presbyteries of Suffolk and Dutchess County. Besides the city, as has been seen, New York Presbytery embraced churches on both sides of the Hudson. On the east side it extended in 1766 to Dutchess County Presbytery, which included Albany, across the river. On the west side it included fewer churches, scat-

[13] L. J. Trinterud, *The Forming of an American Tradition*, p. 134.
[14] Part II, p. 282.

tered as far north as Schenectady.

We have seen in the early years of the century Anglican attempts through the missionaries of the Society for the Propagation of the Gospel and the civil authorities to gain ecclesiastical control in New York at the expense of Presbyterian churches. There was a constant striving to secure recognition of Anglican establishment in New York, as in the other middle colonies. By the middle of the century the Presbyterian constituency in New York City was strong, and included a number of able laymen. In 1751 steps were taken toward the establishment of a college supported by public money. This was to be King's College, now Columbia University. The Anglican party tried to bring it about that the college should have an Anglican character, in that the president should be a member of the Church of England and that Anglican liturgy should be used in the college's public worship. Strong opposition to this was offered by Presbyterian laymen, led by the "three Presbyterian lawyers," William Livingston, John Morin Scott, and William Smith. They advocated a nondenominational institution controlled by the provincial Assembly. An active controversy was waged in periodicals about the college. In this the Anglican Church's claim to be established in the New York colony was combated, and there was discussion of the church's aims in New York and other colonies. While the Anglicans won with regard to the college, the anti-Anglican agitation contributed to anti-British feeling before the War of Independence.

The Presbyterian lawyers kept before the public also for years another grievance. For over half a century the Anglican church leaders, both in New York and in England, succeeded through timely interventions in delaying and preventing every attempt of the New York Presbyterian Church to secure an act of incorporation. Some six attempts were made, the last two in 1766 and 1775, directly to the King in Council.

In May, 1766, a meeting of Anglican clergymen of New York, New Jersey, and Connecticut was held in New York, to plan for an intercolonial Anglican convention. The main object in view was the establishment of an episcopate in the colonies. Efforts for this had long been carried on among Anglicans in England and America, by the bishops of London and the SPG missionaries. Sharp opposition was offered from about the mid-eighteenth century by Presbyterians, especially in New York, and by New England Congregationalists. The "three Presbyterian lawyers" of New York who had fought the Anglicanizing of King's College were leaders in this contest. The vehemence of the antibishop polemic of Jonathan Mayhew in Massachusetts is surprising. In response to the Anglican convention of 1766 the Synod of New York and Philadelphia in the same month proposed to "the consociated churches in Connecticut" a correspondence. The outcome was a "General Convention" of both bodies at Elizabeth in November, 1766, whose "general design" was stated to be, among other things, "to unite our endeavors and counsels for spreading the Gospel and preserving the religious liberties of our Churches." [15] What "religious liberties" meant may be learned from the fact that, a week before, an Anglican convention had framed petitions to the king and the bishops asking for an episcopate for America.

The synod of 1767 received from the Elizabeth General Convention "a plan of union proposed between the Congregational, consociated and Presbyterian churches." This was the first use of the phrase "plan of union" which was to have an eventful history in Presbyterian-Congregational relations. The synod chose delegates to another General Convention, four New York ministers among them, to meet at New Haven, "complete the plan of union," and transact business connected therewith.[16] Both parties were now aligned in opposition. Controversy in pamphlets and periodicals was maintained from both sides. The New York Presbyterians spoke in *The American Whig*. Some Anglican propaganda showed that what was

[15] *Records of the Presbyterian Church*, 1904, Supplement, Minutes of the General Convention, p. 18.
[16] *Ibid.*, p. 374.

sought was a bishop or bishops with not merely spiritual powers, but also with civil powers like those of English bishops, constituting a general establishment of the Church of England. The meetings of the General Convention of Presbyterians and Congregationalists were continued until 1775, when even graver matters filled the public mind. The whole effect of the matter of the episcopate was to incline these bodies to believe that their religious liberties were threatened and that their only defense was political liberty. New York City Presbyterians in these years were specially moved in this direction by the failure in 1767 of their fourth attempt to get a charter for their church, through the intervention of the bishop of London. These years after the enactment of the Stamp Act in 1765 saw the growth in the colonies generally, and eminently in New York City, of the spirit of resistance to British aggression. The leaders in New York of this movement, the organizers of the Sons of Liberty, were Presbyterians: the "three Presbyterian lawyers" and the merchant Alexander McDougal.

The War of Independence. In 1775, after the Battle of Lexington, the Synod of New York and Philadelphia, in a remarkable "Pastoral Letter"[17] to its churches, said, "All the horrors of a *civil* war throughout this great Continent are to be apprehended." This language indicated a division among the people of the colonies that had grown since the troubles over the Stamp Act of 1765. There were thoroughgoing partisans of the British government, favoring its complete supremacy, who as the war came on, were called loyalists or Tories. There were conservatives, for the most part sympathetic with the American grievances, desiring for the colonies a measure of self-government within the British Empire. There were radicals, seeking outright independence, who in the colonies as a whole were in the majority. With the presence of the British troops enforcing imperial authority, there was the material of a civil war.

[17] *Ibid.,* pp. 466–469.

New York before the war contained many British sympathizers. As hostilities came, numbers of loyalists were reported by the patriot organizations in every county. But very few Presbyterians were among them. Presbyterians were conservatives or, more numerously, radicals. The Declaration of Independence and the British occupation of southern New York in 1776 sent the conservatives over to the American cause, and the Presbyterians became practically solid in support of the war. The patriots of New York were called " the Presbyterian party." The leading Presbyterian laymen of New York City, John Morin Scott and McDougal at their head, were leaders in the American cause, except William Smith, who became a decided loyalist.

This position of the New York Presbyterians was common to the Presbyterians of all the colonies. Older historical causes of antipathy to the British government were felt by the Puritan and Scotch-Irish elements among American Presbyterians generally, and there was the recent cause of the plan for an American episcopate. But besides these, there were reasons of religious thought that brought it about that the war was regarded as " a holy cause." Calvinistic thinkers long known in the colonies to Presbyterian and Congregational ministers had justified on Biblical grounds resistance to tyranny by the representatives of a people, and had also taught the necessity of a free compact between king and people and of a fundamental written law. The commanding influence of John Locke had given to American Presbyterians, and Congregationalists as well, a powerful application to their political situation of these religiously founded ideas. Hence, Presbyterian ministers were inspired to uphold the war in their preaching and prayers and conduct.

So in New York did John Rodgers, of the City; Samuel Sackett, of Crompond, Westchester County; Ebenezer Prime, of Huntington, Long Island; and many more, according to Charles Inglis, rector of Trinity Church. In a much-quoted letter of October, 1776, he said that he knew of no Presbyterian minister, and had not been able after careful inquiry to hear of any, "who did not, by preaching and every effort in their power, promote all the measures of the congress, however extravagant."[18] Mr. Burnet, of the Jamaica church, was perhaps the only loyalist minister overlooked by Inglis. John Rodgers and Nathan Ker, of Goshen, were among the Presbyterian ministers of New York who served in the war as chaplains.

The patriotic reputation of Presbyterians brought upon them and their churches the special hostility of the British soldiers and the loyalists, in New York as elsewhere. After Manhattan Island fell into British possession in the summer of 1776 the Wall Street Church was converted into barracks and the New or Brick Church used as a hospital for prisoners of war. Both were completely ruined within. The ministers Dr. Rodgers and Joseph Treat, and many of the people of the congregations, went into voluntary exile. The western end of Long Island was the scene of fighting and of Washington's skillful retreat across the East River in August, 1776, and the whole island came under British occupation. The steeple of the church of Newtown was sawed off, the building used for a while as a prison, and finally demolished and the lumber used for soldiers' huts. The churches at Babylon and Islip were torn down. The whole town of Huntington, an object of particular hatred because of " the old rebel," Ebenezer Prime, was devastated. The church was made a military storehouse, then pulled down and the material used for blockhouses; barracks were built in the graveyard; tombstones turned into fireplaces and ovens. The Presbytery of Suffolk did not meet from 1775 to 1784. " The Presbytery by reason of the calamity of a Civil War, the Island being under the controls of the enimy have been prevented meeting for a long time," so read the minutes in 1784. Westchester County was entered by the British forces in October, 1776, and on the twenty-eighth came the battle of White Plains, followed a month later by Washington's with-

[18] H. Hastings, *Ecclesiastical Records of the State of New York*, VI, p. 4293.

drawal to New Jersey. Some American troops remained east of the Hudson, and for several years the country between Spuyten Duyvil Creek and the Croton River was called the Neutral Ground, being in possession of neither side and subject to ruinous raids by both. Northern Westchester also suffered at the hands of the enemy. The Presbyterian churches of Rye, Bedford, Pound Ridge, and Crompond were burned by British soldiers, and at White Plains the church and several other buildings were fired by Americans contrary to orders. Samuel Sackett, of Crompond, an outspoken patriot, took refuge in Sharon, Connecticut. Several Presbyterian ministers were robbed of their possessions. The congregations were scattered, most of the people seeking safety in Dutchess County and Connecticut. At the end of the war few Presbyterians remained in the lower part of the county. The Presbytery of Dutchess County did not meet from 1778 to 1780.

The Time of the Confederation, 1774–1788. New York churches shared with other Presbyterian churches in a measure of depression after the war. Depletion of congregations by removal of members, ruin of church buildings, prevailing poverty, reaching its climax in the inflation of 1783–1786, weakened the organizations. To the same effect worked the marked decline in the number of students for the ministry, causing vacancies in churches. An exception to the enfeeblement of the churches was to be found in New York City. Increase of population and commercial prosperity soon after the war brought it about that the buildings of the two churches were restored, in 1784–1785, and the congregations filled up. Generally, two factors counteracted spiritual life. Controversy for the control of the new state government distracted minds from religious concerns. What was more dangerous, deism and other forms of infidelity, which had arisen before the war and had grown during it, increased after it until the revivals in the early years of the nineteenth century. It is accepted that about 1790 church members were no more than 5 percent of the total population; and in no state was unbelief stronger than in New York. The opposition offered to infidelity by Presbyterians consisted mostly of theological polemics, the fervor descending from the Great Awakening having mostly passed away, and the arguments issued in little religious vitality.

Two movements away from the synod occurred in this time, one of some significance, the other abortive. The first was the rise of the Associated Presbyteries. In 1779, Jacob Green, a distinguished member of the Presbytery of New York who had been for thirty years pastor at Hanover, New Jersey, withdrew from the presbytery, principally because of objection to the authoritarian methods of the synod, " ordering, appointing and requiring, instead of recommending and desiring." [19] He would have the presbyteries enjoy a far greater measure of autonomy. Three like-minded men of the same presbytery, two of New Jersey and one of New York, in 1780 joined Green in forming what came to be called the Associated Presbytery of Morris County. Its constitution provided for no authoritative jurisdiction over the churches connected with it, but for advice and assistance on request. In other words, this was a mixture of Presbyterian and Congregational organization. As will be seen, the idea spread, and there was more organization on this plan.

The second tendency away from the synod was occasioned in 1787 by the movement for the reorganization of the church that resulted in the formation of the General Assembly. The Presbytery of Suffolk unanimously requested dismissal from the synod because of the distance of eastern Long Island, and because the proposed form of government involved too great authority over the churches, in which there remained a strong element of New England Congregationalism. The synod was alarmed because the withdrawal of Suffolk Presbytery, with the growth of the associated presbytery movement, might mean the loss of Long Island and parts of northern New Jersey and of the Hudson Valley. Two of the ablest men of the

[19] W. J. Cumming, *op. cit.*, p. 58.

synod, John Rodgers and Alexander McWhorter of Newark, were sent to confer with Suffolk and they prevailed upon it to withdraw its request.

The General Assembly. By the early 1780's it was evident that some form of organization other than the colonial synod must be adopted. The church was governed by a presbytery of the whole, in theory attended by all the ministers from Long Island to South Carolina and an elder from each church. In practice, in 1784 and 1785 the attendance was only thirty ministers and six elders in each year. The synod of 1785 began an effort at a reconstruction of the church. This was finally completed in 1788, in the adoption of " the Constitution of the Presbyterian Church in America," consisting of the Form of Government, Discipline, Confession of Faith, Catechisms, and Directory for Worship. At the same time the church was divided into four synods, those of New York and New Jersey, Philadelphia, Virginia, and the Carolinas. In the four synods sixteen presbyteries, the same number as before, were distributed, with some rearrangement of boundaries. The General Assembly over all met first in 1789 in Philadelphia, with John Witherspoon preaching the opening sermon and John Rodgers of New York as moderator.

The Synod of New York and New Jersey contained the presbyteries of Suffolk, Dutchess County, New York, and New Brunswick. The Presbyterians of New York State consisted of the presbyteries of Suffolk and Dutchess and the Presbytery of New York east and west of the Hudson, except the churches in northern and eastern New Jersey.

IV : *Westward Movement and Union Organization,* 1785–1825

1. To the End of the War of 1812

The Great Migration and the Second Awakening. The history of New York Presbyterians was permanently molded by a great movement of people that began at the close of the Revolutionary War and rose high after 1795. New Englanders migrated steadily into the upper Hudson Valley as before, though far less numerously than in lands farther west. Into the western Champlain Valley and the adjacent St. Lawrence country people in considerable numbers crossed the lake from Vermont. An immigration that began before the war and continued during and after it, important in Presbyterian origins, was Scottish and Scotch-Irish, partly from previous settlement in New England, partly directly from Scotland and the north of Ireland. This, in the early years of the migration, went chiefly into the regions east of Troy and northwest of Albany, and the upper Susquehanna and Delaware Valleys. New York City and its environs grew fast in population through newcomers of all sorts, many from New England. Thence numbers of people of high character and ability came in the first decades of the nineteenth century to shape the city's life.

70

But by far the largest migration — the largest yet known in the United States — was into the central and western parts of the state, beyond the old colonial frontier, the Fort Stanwix line. In the late eighteenth century these lands were opened for habitation by the extinguishment of Indian titles and the grant and purchase of vast territories — the Military Tract and the Phelps and Gorham, Pulteney and Holland, Purchases. Into these "new settlements," as they were always called, people poured. The territory beginning on the east with St. Lawrence, Herkimer, Otsego, and Delaware Counties, or the western watersheds of the Adirondacks and the Catskills, and extending westward to Lake Erie and the Niagara River, grew in population from a few thousands in 1790 to 131,000 in 1800, and 357,000 in 1810. Onondaga County quadrupled in this second decade, and Oneida nearly trebled. In this whole movement of population, especially in its earlier phases, there was some mixture of origins. Settlers came from the older eastern New York and from northern New Jersey. Up the Susquehanna from Pennsylvania east of the mountains considerable numbers came into the south central New York counties, in advance of the predominant Yankee tide. In the country between Cayuga and Seneca Lakes, for example, among the firstcomers were Pennsylvania Germans. Welsh people, later to figure in Presbyterian history, in the late eighteenth century began to settle the townships near Utica. But a very much greater number were from New England. The movement across the Hudson, traced in detail by Louise K. Mathews in *The Expansion of New England,* was a veritable flood, so that considerable parts, and the best parts, of New York in a few years became such an expansion. It seemed to President Timothy Dwight, traveling there in 1799, that the people of the two regions were the same people, "with the same interests of every kind." [1] The immigrants came largely from Connecticut, and secondarily from western Massachusetts, which in church matters was more sympathetic to Connecticut. "In reading the

[1] T. Dwight, *Travels* (New Haven, T. Dwight, 1821-1822), IV, 527.

local histories of New York," Miss Mathews wrote, "one feels that Connecticut must have been beggared of inhabitants, so fast did hundreds of her families make their way into New York; many who came from western Massachusetts and Vermont had been in those states only a short time, and were Connecticut men by birth." [2] An importance of this origin for this history lies in the fact that, as has been seen, the Congregationalists of Connecticut, to whom most of these people belonged, had in their church life a strong Presbyterianism.

Coincident with this movement of population was a lasting powerful religious quickening in the regions whence it came, the Second Awakening. The prevalent irreligion and indifference and the weakness of the churches, which followed the war, were transformed by 1820 through a series of times of revival covering large stretches of the Atlantic seaboard. The five years from 1797 saw a widespread popular movement in Connecticut, western Massachusetts and Vermont. In Connecticut there followed in three decades five prolonged periods of heightened religious life, leading to the greatest of such times in 1830–1831. Western Massachusetts had a somewhat parallel history. Comparing the 1820's with 1795, the Congregational churches of New England showed a revolutionary change in vitality, enthusiasm, and outgoing activity. In the middle states the Presbyterian Church, the strongest there, shared in the Awakening. After earlier deploring of "formality and deadness," the General Assemblies of 1799 and 1800 recorded notable encouragement in the spirit of the churches and the spread of the gospel. In northern New Jersey, from which many people and ministers went to central and western New York, congregations in several important places were in vigorous condition during the early years of the new century. Soon after 1800 new religious life appeared in New York City, and along the eastern border of the state, from which again many went westward in New York, New England revival con-

---

[2] L. K. Mathews, *The Expansion of New England* (Boston and New York, Houghton Mifflin Company, 1909), p. 157.

ditions extended. The " narratives " in the minutes of the Synod of New York and New Jersey in almost every year from 1799 to 1822 report strengthening religious interest and repeated revivals. During a generation a signal opportunity was given to the Congregational and Presbyterian churches by the rapid growth of population in New York, and for it they were prepared by the enduring Second Awakening.

It was in " the new settlements " that events decisive for this history took place in the missionary work of these churches. To the revived churches central and western New York offered a double religious appeal. Many of the settlers, especially of the first arrivals, were irreligious and in morals typical frontiersmen, making a rude, wild society. It should be remembered that in 1790 only about 5 percent of the whole population of the United States were full church members, and church membership grew slowly. The early people of the New York frontier somewhat exemplified this general situation, though probably their degradation has been exaggerated. The urgent religious need here, reported in the East by travelers, awakened missionary vision in the churches there. But among the settlers there were increasingly substantial people of religious training, minded to have churches as parts of their new life and of the new society that they were establishing. Sometimes laymen acted in church ways without clerical leadership, as at Clinton, where eight New England families had regular religious services from their coming in 1787 until an ecclesiastical organization was formed four years later. Among these religiously inclined settlers the predominant groups were Presbyterians from eastern New York and the south and Congregationalists from New England, the latter much more numerous. Their friends and kinsfolk in the older parts were moved to provide religious privileges for them.

Even before the revival had stirred the churches, this double missionary appeal began to work in the early years of the settlement. Despite laments, the churches were not so lifeless as to be wholly indifferent to such a need. In 1788 the Synod of New York and New Jersey expressed concern over "the distressed condition of the Presbyterian denomination on the frontiers," and desired "that missionaries should be sent among them next summer." [3] On the recommendation of this synod the General Assembly of 1790 appointed Nathan Ker, of Goshen, and Joshua Hart, of Suffolk County, "missionaries on the frontier settlements of New York and Pennsylvania, to the west branch of the Susquehanna, for at least three months." [4] From 1791 to 1796 ten more appointments were made for short terms in the same country. One of these missionaries, Ira Condict, in 1793, guided Long Island settlers in East Palmyra, far to the westward, in organizing a Congregational church. Another, Benjamin Judd, in the same year formed a Congregational church at Windsor on the Susquehanna. Still another, Daniel Thatcher, formed a Presbyterian church at Newtown (Elmira) in 1795 and others in the same year at Lima and Geneseo in the Genesee Valley. In 1793 the Synod of New York and New Jersey received letters from "societies" in several places in central New York expressing thanks for missionaries sent to them and asking that others be sent, which shows the existence of groups of religious-minded people, though nothing is known of church organization at the places named at this early date. Next year the synod voted to establish a "standing and continuous mission on the frontiers of the state of New York." [5] It continued to recommend missionaries to the General Assembly for appointment, and designated some for its own service.

The Congregational churches of Connecticut showed like early response to the appeals of the frontier, where many more of their people than of Presbyterians had settled. In 1788 or 1789, Samuel Eells, under a commission from the General Association of Connecticut, traveled as a missionary as far as Rome. Within eight years eleven more ministers had been sent

---

[3] MS. Minutes, 1789–1823, I, 8.
[4] *Minutes of the General Assembly*, 1789–1820, p. 23.
[5] MS. Minutes, 1789–1823, I, 70.

by the same authority to "the new settlements" for short missions. In 1796, Seth Williston, licentiate of the North Hartford Association, went into the Chenango valley "on his own," thus beginning a long and fruitful service. Next year he organized the First Congregational Church of Lisle, which was to be well known. The Congregational churches established by this year in central and western New York number at least ten.

The year 1798 saw the churches under the power of the Awakening, and the tide of immigration flowing faster and creating more religious need. From 1790 to 1802 nineteen missionaries in all were sent by the General Assembly to work on the New York frontier. All had annual appointments for limited terms. Some had more than one appointment. Eight were sent on the recommendation of the Synod of New York and New Jersey. In 1800, Jedediah Chapman, of Orange, New Jersey, who had done distinguished pastoral work there and had been moderator of the Synod of New York and Philadelphia, the supreme judicatory of the church, was appointed by the Assembly to give four years' service, living someplace on the field and spending half his time in traveling and establishing churches and advising missionaries. He lived at Geneva, founding there in 1800 what became the important First Presbyterian Church of that place, and later establishing ten other churches.

A historic case of the effect of the Awakening on the Congregational churches was that in 1798 the General Association of Connecticut organized itself as the Connecticut Missionary Society, to "Christianize the heathen in North America, and to support and promote Christian knowledge in the new settlements within the United States." [6] The need of "the new settlements" in New York was the dominant motive. In the same year and the same spirit the Berkshire and Columbia Missionary Society was formed in western Massachusetts and eastern New York, the next year the Massachusetts Missionary Society,

[6] O. W. Elsbree, *Rise of the Missionary Spirit in America, 1790-1815* (Williamsport, Pennsylvania, 1928), p. 56.

and in 1802 the Hampshire Missionary Society of Hampshire County, Massachusetts. Within four years from 1798 not less than sixteen Congregational ministers had done missionary work in central and western New York, most of them under the Connecticut Society. Three of them had been ordained pastors of Congregational churches. Two notable men among the missionaries were Williston and Jedediah Bushnell. Williston, who had a Connecticut Society appointment from 1798, worked with power in "the Genesee country," "the Military Tract" and "the Chenango country," finally settling at Lisle and traveling in the southern counties until 1809.[7] At about the same time Bushnell, a Connecticut missionary, evangelized with great effect in "the Ontario country" and "the Military Tract."

Another source of missionaries was the Associated Presbyteries. The rise of organizations of this kind, in the Morris County Associated Presbytery of 1780, has been described. The moving idea, that of a compromise between Congregationalism and Presbyterianism, naturally spread in the churches of Dutchess County Presbytery, where Congregationalism was strong. In 1792 six members of this presbytery and delegates of two churches formed the Associated Westchester Presbytery. This body, an affiliation of ministers and churches without authoritative jurisdiction over them, spread in the churches of Westchester, Dutchess, and Putnam Counties, and later across the river into Ulster, Orange, and Schoharie, and into Connecticut and New York City. It was rather loosely organized, and the relation of churches to it depended largely on the relation of ministers. There were delegates of churches in meetings, but no elders. At various times the names of thirty-nine ministers were on the records of the presbytery, but few were pastors of churches, many having short services. As many as twenty-five churches were connected with it in one way or another at one time or another during its life, which lasted till

[7] J. Q. Adams, ed., "Diaries of Rev. Seth Williston, D.D., 1796–1800," *Journal of the Presbyterian Historical Society*, Vols. VII–X.

1830, but weakly in its last ten years. Despite these numbers the presbytery was actually small; at its largest meeting eight ministers and nine delegates appeared. Small though it was, it had a core that displayed vitality. It ordained nineteen ministers and appointed supplies in churches. It sent candidates and members as missionaries into the valleys of the Delaware and the Susquehanna, who founded churches, and also farther west in New York. Among them was the well-known and much-traveled David Harrower. The example of this presbytery was followed soon by the Northern Associated Presbytery, formed in 1794 in the Albany region, on the borders of Presbyterianism and New England Congregationalism. This also sent missionaries farther west into New York. A fourth body of this kind was the Saratoga Associated Presbytery, formed in 1807. The Northern and Saratoga organizations did not survive beyond 1818. Their ministers and churches went into Congregational associations and presbyteries, those of New York and Hudson.

Into the field where the Awakening had sent so many missionaries the movement inevitably spread. In the early accounts of religious conditions here 1799 is always called "the year of the Great Revival." There had been minor awakenings that reached a climax then. The Great Revival arose early in 1799 in Ontario county, near the Genesee, moved across the state in the counties north and south, and finally in the summer of 1800 was strong in Otsego and Delaware counties, retaining its power in the intervening time. As ministers itinerated in "the new settlements," preaching often to people who had had Christian training but had been deprived of church privileges or to nonchurchgoing people, religious life was revived or born anew. The few ministers who were settled in churches reached out in the surroundings with like effect. Religious efforts, preaching, and conference meetings met with remarkable response. Williston, a sober judge, wrote, "It has been difficult during the winter to get places large enough to accommodate or even contain the people who have come together to hear about Jesus and his salvation." [8] There was no excitement or extravagant utterance. "The awakening among us is very free from noise or wildness." [9] Aside from preaching, the revival spread spontaneously from town to town. The missionaries generally reported strong religious interest, earnest desire for ministers' services, large congregations, many conversions. The movement resulted in what proved to be many stable, enduring churches and in the setting of a pattern of revivals that influenced the religious life of New York until nearly the time of the Civil War. After a decline there came a lesser high point of revival in 1807–1808, followed by another decline during the War of 1812. But in all these years there were scattered awakenings.

Before the Plan of Union of 1801, a landmark in the early religious history of New York, the pioneer churches had been increased by revivals so that from the eastern lines of St. Lawrence, Herkimer, Otsego, and Delaware Counties westward there were thirty-four Congregational churches and thirteen Presbyterian, which shows the New England preponderance. The Presbyterian churches were Cherry Valley, Cooperstown, Geneva, Harpersfield, Holland Patent, Lakeville (at Geneseo), Lima, Little Falls, Newtown (Elmira), Oneonta, Ovid (not the present Ovid), Springfield, Whitesboro. General church organization also reflected the strength of religious life. In 1800 the Association of Ontario was formed in Bristol, near Canandaigua, by Congregational ministers and churches, and in the same year the Oneida Association was organized in the Utica region. In 1805 the Presbytery of Oneida originated, out of Albany, to cover the state west of the line mentioned.

The Plan of Union. From the work of the Congregational and Presbyterian churches on the same ground came the Plan of Union of 1801, determinative of the history of New York

[8] James H. Hotchkin, *History . . . of Western New York* (New York, M. W. Dodd, 1848), p. 37.
[9] Williston, *loc. cit.*

Presbyterianism. Behind this lay a long history of kinship and association. The presbyterianizing character of Connecticut Congregationalism drew together the two churches, at home in the east and in the new settlements where churches and their fellowship were growing up. To the same end worked the substantial doctrinal agreement between the Presbyterian Church and the Congregational churches of Connecticut and western Massachusetts. The strong element of New England and especially Connecticut antecedents in the Presbyterian Church, in ministry and laity, was a constant influence in both these relations. Jedediah Chapman, called the father of Presbyterianism in central New York, was born in Connecticut and was a graduate of Yale. Asa Hillyer, a missionary of the General Assembly in 1798, was born in Massachusetts and a graduate of Yale. When such men met Congregational missionaries from New England on the missionary field, the two polities would not feel far apart. In 1799 the General Assembly appointed Methuselah Baldwin, a New England man, to work in Onondaga county " in connection with the Rev. Mr. Williston, a missionary from the General Association of Connecticut." [10]

On this kinship had been built a continuous formal association of the churches. This began with the joint convention of the Synod of New York and Philadelphia and " the consociated churches of Connecticut," held annually from 1767 to 1776 under what was called " a plan of union," primarily to agitate against the establishment of an Anglican episcopate in the colonies. In 1790 the General Assembly, unanimously declaring that it was " particularly desirous to review and strengthen every bond of union between brethren so nearly agreed in doctrine and forms of worship as the members of the Congregational and Presbyterian churches evidently are," resolved " that the ministers of the Congregational churches of New England be invited to renew their annual convention with the clergy of the Presbyterian church." [11] This led in 1792 to

[10] *Minutes of the General Assembly,* 1789–1820, p. 185.
[11] *Ibid.,* p. 29.

an arrangement between the General Assembly and the General Association of Connecticut for the attendance in meetings of each of delegates from the other, to whom in 1794–1795 voting power was given. The same arrangement was made with the General Associations of Vermont (1809), New Hampshire (1810), and Massachusetts (1811).

Here were two bodies of Christian churchmen, the General Assembly and the General Association of Connecticut, which had been in fraternal relations and had been talking about union for thirty years. They were bound together by manifold personal ties. Both faced a missionary emergency in New York, where settlers, many of them their own people, were increasing month by month. The missionaries of both had been working, and working together, on this field for ten years, but they were too few to meet the need for ministry of which they constantly heard. Both bodies were under the power of the Awakening, moving them to attempt something new and larger for "the Kingdom of the Redeemer." Nothing could have been more natural than what took place. The General Assembly of 1801 received a communication from the Connecticut Association, giving information that a committee had been appointed to confer with a committee of the Assembly, "to consider the measures proper to be adopted both by this Association and the said Assembly, to prevent alienation, to promote harmony, and to establish, as far as possible, an uniform system of Church Government, between those inhabitants of the new settlements who are attached to the Presbyterian form of church government and those who are attached to the Congregational form."[12] The Assembly appointed a committee with Jonathan Edwards the younger as chairman "to consider and digest a plan of government for the churches in the new settlements agreeably to the proposal of the General Association of Connecticut."[13] This committee's report of "regulations" was approved by the Assembly on May 29, 1801, sub-

[12] *Ibid.*, p. 212.   [13] *Ibid.*, p. 221.

ject to the approval of the General Association, which was given on June 16.

So originated the Plan of Union. It had four articles.[14] On all missionaries it was "strictly enjoined" that they should "promote . . . a spirit of accommodation" between Presbyterians and Congregationalists. Second, a Congregational church in "the new settlements" might settle a Presbyterian minister and still "conduct their discipline according to Congregational principles"; difficulties among the people to be settled by themselves or by "a council mutually agreed upon"; difficulties between the church and the minister to be referred to his presbytery if this was agreed to; or if not, by a council of equal denominational membership. The third article was the converse of the second: a Presbyterian church might settle a Congregational minister, and still manage its affairs in the Presbyterian way, questions between church and minister to be referred to the minister's association, and so forth. Fourth, if a group was partly Congregational and partly Presbyterian, this should be no obstacle to their "uniting in one church and settling a minister." In this case the church should choose "a standing committee" to have disciplinary authority. Appeal from its decision was allowed for a Presbyterian to the presbytery, for a Congregationalist to "the body of male communicants." With the consent of the church, a Presbyterian might further appeal to the synod and the General Assembly, or a Congregationalist to "a mutual council." Evidently the "uniting in one church" here allowed contemplated that Congregationalists and Presbyterians, remaining such, should associate for worship. This article further provided — and this was important as a precedent — that if a standing committee should depute one of its members to attend the presbytery, "he may have the same right to sit and act in the Presbytery as a ruling elder of the Presbyterian Church"; that is, an unordained delegate might be equal in presbytery to an ordained elder.

[14] Ibid., pp. 224, 225.

The Plan was obviously an arrangement for joint missionary and church extension work, economizing organization and ministerial personnel, thus allowing provision for more religious needs than the denominations could meet separately. It was framed in a true spirit of union, for united service in the gospel. The points at which it transgressed strict denominational order are obvious now and were obvious to its authors, who put Christian union above ecclesiastical legalism. The Plan, it will be noted, contemplated the existence of association and presbytery on the same ground. Such, as has been said, was the fact.

As for its spirit, in 1801 the Plan was no novelty in " the new settlements." From the beginning of missionary work in this field the two denominations had acted as if in anticipation of such an agreement. Presbyterian missionaries had guided the formation of Congregational churches. Congregational ministers had strengthened Presbyterian churches. Ministers of both denominations had worked together. Presbyterians and Congregationalists had joined in councils for ordaining and installing ministers. The spirit of the people generally was that of unity.

The Plan of 1801 had large results, but not by being a pattern of organization. As a working method, it was soon superseded by the Accommodation Plan introduced in 1808. The Plan of 1801 is often quoted as if its words represent the form taken by Congregational-Presbyterian relations from its date and for years following. But this is not at all the fact. Very little was done under its provisions in the formation and conduct of churches. After 1801 church organization proceeded generally as before. Presbyterian and Congregational churches continued to be established. The Middle Association in Onondaga and Cayuga Counties was formed in 1804, and the Presbytery of Geneva in 1805, covering New York from the west lines of Oneida and Chenango Counties westward.

The results of the Plan came otherwise than in organization. As a declaration of the spirit which ought to govern missionary work and church extension it was a standard accepted in both denominations until 1835, and for seventeen years more between New School Presbyterians and Congregationalists. The Plan strengthened the cooperation of the members of the two denominations variously. More than before missionaries of both kinds served churches of both kinds. More than before Presbyterians and Congregationalists joined in councils for ordination and installation. More than before among the people denominational indifference prevailed. Too great emphasis cannot be laid on this, in explaining what occurred in church organization in these parts at that time and long afterward. The people, as a rule, though there were strong exceptions, did not care much whether they were Presbyterians or Congregationalists. These two were the churches commonly thought of. It is not to be forgotten that in the beginning people of other denominations, Baptists, Methodists, Quakers, and Dutch Reformed, were among the first settlers, and Christians and Universalists soon followed, and their missionary work and church organization grew beside those of the Congregationalists and Presbyterians. But unquestionably these latter were the commanding churches at this early time in members and in influence in the young towns. Between these two there was not often strong insistence. What the people wanted commonly was a Christian church and minister. It is significant that a frequent name for the incorporated body of a church was "Religious Society," or sometimes "Ecclesiastical Society," without denominational label. Some churches were incorporated with the name "Presbyterian-Congregational."

The Accommodation Plan. In 1808 was introduced a pattern of organization and form of denominational cooperation that was regarded by all concerned as expressive of the spirit of the Plan of Union of 1801, and which proved to be, as that was not, the basis of "an uniform system of Church Government." In 1807 the Synod of Albany, comprising the Presbyteries of Albany, Columbia, Oneida, and Geneva, then reaching to the

Genesee, received from the Middle Association an overture for
"some form of Union and correspondence." In response the
synod made a momentous proposal. Since this is not so well
known as the Plan of 1801 and was so much more influential
respecting organization, and so clearly expressed the prevailing spirit, some of its words deserve quotation.

"We most cordially invite you to become a constituent part
of our body, by assuming the characteristic and scriptural
name of presbytery, adopt our standards of doctrine and government, and sit and vote with us, in all the great and interesting concerns of the church. Deeming the name, however, far
less important than the thing, although of consequence to uniformity in the same body; yet, should you be solicitous to re-
tain yours, it will not be considered, on our part, a bar to such
a union. Nor do we confine our invitation to you as ministers,
but we extend it also to delegates from your churches, whom
we are willing to receive as substantially the same with our
ruling elders, to assist us in our public deliberations and business. Knowing the influence of education and habit, should the
churches under your care prefer transacting their internal
concerns in their present mode of Congregational government,
we assure them of our utmost cheerfulness in leaving them un-
disturbed in the administration of that government, unless they
shall choose to alter it themselves.

"Should you accede to this plan of union and correspondence, and should our General Assembly permit us to form it,
which we are disposed to believe they will, we anticipate the
auspicious period as just at hand, when the Presbyterian and
Congregational churches in this Northern region, will form one
great Phalanx against the common enemy, and combine their
exertions to advance the mediatorial Kingdom of our exalted
Lord." [15]

The synod's plan having been sanctioned by the General Assembly of 1808, in June of this year the Middle Association

[15] "Records of the Middle Association . . . 1806–1810," ed. by
J. Q. Adams, *JPHS*, XI, pp. 25–27.

"voted unanimously that this body do accede to the plan of union with the Presbyterian Church in the U.S., on the condition proposed by the Synod of Albany in their letter of October 9, 1807, we retaining our present name and mode of Congregational government."[16] In October the synod "resolved that the Middle Association on the Military Tract and its vicinity, be received as a constituent branch of this synod, retaining their own name and usages in the administration and government of their Church according to the terms stated in the plan; and they are hereby received accordingly."[17]

Thus an association of Congregational ministers and churches, or rather consociation, for the Middle Association exercised the authority associated with this name, entered the synod in the same relation to it as that of a presbytery, its ministers members of the synod and the delegates of its churches in the same status as ruling elders. In 1810 commissioners sent by the Association were enrolled in the General Assembly. In September, 1810, "it was agreed (14 to 2) that we drop the name Association and assume the name of Presbytery."[18] At the same time it was voted that the association should become two presbyteries, those of "Courtland or Onondaga" — the latter prevailed — and Cayuga. Next month the Synod of Albany established these presbyteries.

Here then were two presbyteries of the Presbyterian Church composed almost entirely of Congregational ministers and churches — almost, for each presbytery had one Presbyterian church and Onondaga had one Presbyterian minister. The ministers became members of presbytery by action of the Synod, approved by the General Assembly. The churches were guaranteed in their liberty to remain Congregational internally. But they were in the fellowship and under the jurisdiction and discipline of the presbyteries, which was no great change for Congregationalists mostly from Connecticut. This was the beginning of the "Presbygational" status, Congregational churches under Presbyterian authority. Later derided, as this

[16] *Ibid.*, pp. 21–22.   [17] *Ibid.*, p. 30.   [18] *Ibid.*, p. 68.

nickname shows, and always perplexing or offensive to denominational rigorists, it expressed the prevailing spirit of unity and set the pattern for a considerable part of the religious foundations of central and western New York. For the principles of the Accommodation Plan spread fast and widely. Within thirty years from 1808 more than a hundred and fifty Congregational churches entered presbyteries. But this is to anticipate.

Down to the War of 1812, which caused some retardation, population flowed ever more rapidly into central and western New York. Christian men and organizations strove ever more faithfully to meet the need. Between 1802 and 1812 the General Assembly appointed ten missionaries for service in New York, these being mostly still itinerants for short terms, several having repeated appointments. The formation in 1802 of the Assembly's Standing Committee on Missions strengthened this work. Appointments were made by the Assembly as before, but on the Committee's recommendation, and the missionaries had the Committee's supervision. Jedediah Chapman, from Geneva, had oversight of the missionary concerns of the Committee as far west as Buffalo. Congregational missionary societies — the Connecticut, by far the most important, the Massachusetts, the Hampshire, the Berkshire and Columbia, and the New Hampshire — sent about forty missionaries in these years, more of these than of the Presbyterians going to settled pastorates. In the whole land west of the Adirondacks and the Catskills from 1801 to 1812 twenty-one Presbyterian churches were founded, and forty-seven Congregational. This again shows the New England and Congregational preponderance in the population, but not fully. General organization advanced correspondingly. After Oneida Presbytery in 1802 came Geneva in 1805, as has been said, and Cayuga and Onondaga in 1810. After the Ontario Association in 1800 came the Oneida and the Susquehanna in 1803, the Middle in 1804, the Union in the Chenango Valley in 1808, and the St. Lawrence and the Black River in 1810. It is impossible to write separately the histories of two denominations that were so closely related. The people were congenial and brotherly, and the ministers worked hand in hand.

The Older Settlements of Eastern New York. While foundations were being laid in the newer parts of the state, growing population and strengthening religious life caused church increase in the older parts. The Synod of New York and New Jersey, after several years of encouraging conditions, reported in 1808 " in many churches extraordinary revivals," these being " most remarkable in the Presbytery of New York," where eleven hundred had been added to the city's three Presbyterian churches, the First, the Brick, and the Rutgers.[19] These were in a collegiate relation until 1809. Three more churches were established between 1808 and 1811 — the Cedar Street, which became the Fifth Avenue, the Canal Street or Irish, and the Spring Street. The patriarch of the Presbytery of New York, John Rodgers, lived until 1811. In 1810, Gardiner Spring began his pastorate of sixty-three years in the Brick Church. The year 1809 saw reorganization in the presbytery. The churches in northern New Jersey, which had been an important part of the presbytery, became the Presbytery of New Jersey. New York Presbytery was enlarged so that its boundaries included that part of Westchester County lying south of Bedford and Peekskill, and that part of Long Island lying west of Hempstead Plains. This brought into the presbytery the three ancient churches of Hempstead, Jamaica, and Newtown.

Suffolk Presbytery became Long Island in 1790. By this time the churches had largely recovered from the losses of the war, and some had done more. Revivals of great power had occurred in some, notably at East Hampton under Lyman Beecher, pastor from 1799 to 1810. Thus strengthened, the

[19] MS. Minutes, Synod of New York and New Jersey, 1789-1823, I, 244.

presbytery underwent no considerable change in the early years of the nineteenth century, except the transfer of the three churches to New York.

In the Hudson Valley, church organization proceeded after the War of Independence, though not as rapidly as in the rest of the state, because there was not such an increase of population. The Presbytery of Hudson was formed in 1795, composed of the churches of New York Presbytery west of the Hudson and between the middle of Orange County and Albany Presbytery, and the churches remaining in Dutchess Presbytery, east of the river. Hudson began with eight ministers and sixteen churches. By 1819 there were twenty-five ministers and forty-one churches. Some of these churches were new, to meet religious need. Some had come from the Associated Westchester Presbytery. The church in the important town of Newburgh was organized during 1796–1798, and the church in Scotchtown, near Middletown, in 1798.

Of the Presbytery of Albany, erected in 1790, most of the churches came from New York Presbytery, and most were old foundations, like Albany, Schenectady, Johnstown, and Cherry Valley. By 1801 it had twenty-four churches, including Hudson, Troy, Lansingburg, and Plattsburg. Out of Albany Presbytery there was formed in 1803 the Presbytery of Columbia, easterly and southerly of Albany, and as has been said, the Presbytery of Oneida, covering the whole of "the new settlements." By 1810 five new churches had been founded north of Albany, and in 1813 the Presbytery of Champlain was erected, chiefly because of immigration from Vermont across the lake. This was added to the Synod of Albany, which had been formed in 1803 out of Albany, Columbia, and Oneida. In 1809 the Presbytery of Londonderry (New Hampshire) came into connection with the General Assembly and was assigned to the Synod of Albany. This consisted of churches mostly of Scotch-Irish membership in Massachusetts and New Hampshire. Churches of this character, founded in the eighteenth century in these states and in Maine and Vermont, had produced the independent Synod of New England in 1774. Because of the war this was reduced in 1782 to one presbytery, which took the name of the Presbytery of Londonderry, formed in 1729.

2. FROM THE WAR TO THE ERIE CANAL, 1825

Toward the end of the War of 1812, immigration again began to flow into central and western New York. With the Peace of Ghent in 1815 came a flood larger than ever, mostly from New England. In the eastern part of the state also population increased, but by no means so rapidly; here, too, the New England influx was large. Presbyterian organization reflected this growth, as did that of other denominations. Churches and presbyteries were formed or enlarged in rapid succession. Under the Accommodation Plan many churches formed as Congregational joined presbyteries. In 1822 there were no general Congregational organizations in central and western New York. Beginning the Presbyterian account in the west, the Synod of Geneva was established in 1812, comprising the presbytery of that name and those of Cayuga and Onondaga. To it were added the Presbyteries of Niagara (erected in 1817), Ontario (1817), Bath (1817), Genesee (1819), Rochester (1819), Cortland (1825). The dates show the swiftness of the organization of churches. The Synod of Genesee, formed in 1821 out of the four westernmost presbyteries of Geneva, had added to it in 1823 the Presbytery of Buffalo.

To the Synod of Albany there were added from 1812 onward the Presbyteries of Champlain, erected in 1813, St. Lawrence (1816, named Watertown from 1829), Otsego (1819), Troy (1821), Ogdensburg (1822, named St. Lawrence from 1830), Oswego (1823), and Newburyport (Massachusetts) in 1826.

Chiefly out of the Synod of Albany there was formed in 1829 the Synod of Utica, comprising the Presbyteries of Oneida, Otsego, Oswego, Watertown (former St. Lawrence), St. Lawrence (former Ogdensburg). The three Synods of Geneva, Genesee, and Utica were linked in momentous history beginning in 1837.

The Synod of New York was formed in 1823 by a division of the Synod of New York and New Jersey, and consisted of presbyteries in New York State, those of New York, New York Second, Long Island, Hudson, North River. New York Presbytery had grown rapidly from 1812, chiefly by a large increase of churches in New York City, composed mostly of New Englanders. New York Second was a presbytery of the Associate Reformed Church, part of which, including the presbytery, joined the Presbyterian Church in 1822. The Associate Reformed Church had been formed in 1782, by partial union of two American branches of churches of Scottish origin, the Associate, or Seceder, and the Reformed Presbyterian, or Covenanter. In other parts of New York State, Associate Reformed churches later joined presbyteries of the Presbyterian Church. Long Island Presbytery, which was quiescent in the eighteenth century, began a rapid growth with the founding of the First Presbyterian Church of Brooklyn in 1822. North River Presbytery was formed in 1819 out of churches of Hudson mostly east of the river, because new churches were established and older ones grew.

Revivals. Besides immigration, the principal cause of Presbyterian growth during these years was revivals. These occurred mostly in the central and western parts of the state, but also in the east, in New York City, the Albany region, and the northeast. After the War of 1812, during which revivals generally ceased, there came in the central and western parts religious upheavals far surpassing those of the first decade of the century, the Great Revival and its sequels. The years 1815 to 1817 saw widespread and powerful awakenings. The historian James H. Hotchkin records in 1816 and 1817 fifty-four towns from Norwich in the Chenango Valley to Buffalo in which Presbyterian and Congregational churches were visited by revivals.[20] In 1815 the Presbytery of Utica reported nearly as many conversions " as in the Finney revival a decade later." [21] A generally low period was reached during 1819 and 1820, though awakenings occurred. In the early 1820's came a fresh wave of revivalism. The awakenings of 1822 to 1824, though not equal to those of 1815 to 1817, were numerous, widespread, and powerful, and produced a lasting condition of religious awareness. Speaking of this time, 1815 to 1825, Whitney R. Cross says, "Western New York was more extensively engaged in revivalism than were other portions of the Northeast." [22] In it all other denominations, especially the Baptists and Methodists, were vigorously active. The Congregationalists worked in close fellowship with the Presbyterians.

The central and western parts of New York, referred to as the special scene of revivals, consisted of the region west of the Catskills and the Adirondacks, or west of the Counties of St. Lawrence, Herkimer, Otsego, and Delaware. This country had a distinctive character, resulting from the New England origin of the dominant element of its people. Their inheritance gave many of them a spiritual concern and intensity that made them prone to religious and moral enthusiasms. Many of them had experienced in New England the power of the Second Great Awakening. Furthermore, many had come from those parts of New England in which there was a strong inclination to new ideas and actions. All this was manifested in the "new settlements" in the Great Revival of 1799 and 1800, followed, as has been seen, by repeated revivals. From the fervor and excitement of successive awakenings came the expression "Burned-over District." Used with reference to particular localities, this came to be applied to the whole region above described. Then later the epithet gained significance from successive movements of moral and social reform and religious

---

[20] Hotchkin, op. cit., pp. 126, 131.

[21] Whitney R. Cross, The Burned-over District (Ithaca, Cornell University Press, 1950), p. 11.

[22] Ibid.

innovation, characterized by revivalistic high temperatures, in the second quarter of the nineteenth century.

Missionary Organizations. Besides revivals, another cause of church growth in these years down to 1825 was continued missionary work from without. The Standing Committee of the Presbyterian General Assembly still sent missionaries into western New York. In 1816, the missionary work of the church having grown beyond the power of the Committee, there was formed the "Board of Missions acting under the authority of the General Assembly of the Presbyterian Church in the United States," the predecessor of the Board of National Missions. Under the Board, missionaries in greater numbers went into New York. In 1824 "nearly half the Presbyterian clergymen in the country were laboring in this one state." [23] Even stronger was the missionary force from the New England Congregational societies. In 1814 the Connecticut and Massachusetts societies together maintained sixty-four ministers in New York, mostly in the western parts, and continued such support until about the time of the rise of the American Home Missionary Society in 1826. Three other New England societies in lesser degrees carried on work in New York these years. The brightest example of the achievements of these missionaries was given by John Spencer, "Father Spencer," who in 1809 came into Chautauqua County and worked under the Connecticut Society. His epitaph says: "He was the first gospel minister, who traversed the wilderness then called the Holland Purchase, and was the instrument under God in forming most of the Congregational and Presbyterian churches which existed in this region when he rested from his labors – 1826." [24]

A sign of the religious enthusiasm created by the revivals was the establishment of numerous indigenous missionary societies. As early as 1796, before the revivals, there had been formed in New York City the New York Missionary Society, composed largely of Presbyterian ministers and laymen, but

[23] *Ibid.*, p. 25.   [24] Hotchkin, *op. cit.*, p. 93.

also of Associate Reformed, Dutch Reformed, and Baptists. This devoted itself to the Indians, following much example of American Christians. In 1800 it employed a missionary to the Senecas and Tuscaroras near Buffalo, and maintained the mission, with the help of a strong auxiliary in the city, till 1821. Then it transferred this work to the United Foreign Missionary Society, which had been formed in 1817 by Presbyterians, Associate Reformed, and Dutch Reformed. Missions to the Indians were then called "foreign." The United Society in 1822 established a mission in Cattaraugus County for the Senecas. In 1797 the Northern Missionary Society had been formed, with membership similar to that of the New York Society, in the towns of the Albany region. It worked among the Oneidas and the Tuscaroras. In 1823 it also transferred its missions to the United Foreign Missionary Society. Next year the United Society joined with the American Board of Commissioners for Foreign Missions. This was older and stronger; it had a number of Presbyterians in its membership and at that time received about a third of its funds from New York Presbyterians. Thus these Presbyterians were involved in foreign missionary organization.

In close connection with the revivals there came on their ground numerous missionary societies, designed to strengthen new churches that had been created and as well those of older origin, and also to bring into being churches in " destitute regions." The Genesee Missionary Society was organized in 1810, consisting finally of the Presbyterian and Congregational ministers of the " Genesee country," that is, of the lower Genesee Valley and the adjacent region, and lay representatives of their churches. The mixed membership shows how the two denominations worked together. In its life, to 1818, the society sent about twenty missionaries to feeble churches and needy fields. Its funds were increased considerably by contributions from women's societies in churches, " female cent societies," as many were called.

The Young People's Missionary Society of Western New

York was formed in Utica about 1814, by young men and women, mostly Presbyterians. It first sent two Presbyterian missionaries to explore "the more unsettled portions . . . in western New York"[25] and form auxiliary missionary societies in the principal towns. Many such societies were formed, and other missionaries sent out over several years. The Female Missionary Society of the Western District was formed in 1819 by women of Utica. It organized many auxiliaries in the surrounding towns and sent missionaries to places needing the gospel, one of whom in 1824 was Charles Finney, just beginning his preaching in Jefferson County, north of Utica.

In 1815 there was formed in New York City the Young Men's Missionary Society, an outgrowth of the New York Society of 1796, and in the next year because of a theological difference the New York Evangelical Missionary Society. These were composed largely of Presbyterians, along with Dutch Reformed and Associate Reformed members. They sent out twenty missionaries, mostly in New York, east and west.

Out of these and other like societies in the state the United Domestic Missionary Society was formed in New York City in 1822 in order to obviate the weaknesses resulting from the presence of several local organizations for the same purpose. Its membership and support, as would be expected, were mainly Presbyterian, though the Dutch Reformed and Associate Reformed Churches were represented. The society was a success from the beginning. In 1826 it had one hundred missionaries in New York, and some others in other states. They were not itinerants, as previous missionaries in the state had been, but were appointed as ministers of churches, the society paying parts of their salaries.

The United Society, at a large meeting in New York in 1826, became the celebrated American Home Missionary Society. This was a national organization, with members in several states, and interdenominational, but largely Presbyterian and Congregational, most of its support at the beginning coming

[25] *Ibid.*, p. 195.

from New York Presbyterians. Its great work among Presbyterian churches and also Congregational churches in New York will be later described.

Education. Education must bulk large in the story of the Presbyterians. As early as 1794, after a vain start, Union College was founded at Schenectady. It was so named because men of several religious denominations were concerned with its beginning. But Presbyterians and Dutch Reformed were the leaders. The college's first president, John Blair Smith, was a Virginia Presbyterian. Many of its graduates became Presbyterian ministers. In 1812 Hamilton College at Clinton was chartered, an outgrowth of the academy established by Samuel Kirkland, for many years a missionary among the Oneida Indians, which began its work in 1797. The college was strongly Presbyterian by affiliation, and from the first sent its graduates largely into Presbyterian and also Congregational churches.

The Presbyterian churches early gave direct attention to education for the ministry. In 1806 the General Assembly recommended that the presbyteries look out for suitable young men and secure money for their training. In the years following 1814 some funds were collected for this purpose by presbyteries in western New York. In the east the Synod of New York raised money in its churches in 1820-1822 for the endowment of a professorship in Princeton Seminary. In 1819 the Western Education Society was organized in Utica to aid young men in their training for the ministry. Its field of activity was not only in the western part of the state, but also in the central and northern parts, and it did much to provide the churches with ministers. It was nonsectarian in its policy, benefiting students of several denominations, but its principal support came from Presbyterians. The Western Society in 1822 enlarged its work by becoming auxiliary to the Presbyterian Education Society, formed in New York City in 1818. Another educational organization of the same time was the Presbyterian Board of Education, formed in New York in 1819.

Princeton Seminary, however, and Andover, were remote from the enormously expanding settlements of central and western New York. There seemed to be a better prospect of securing pastors for the region and of interesting the churches in ministerial education with an upstate seminary. When the General Assembly of 1818 declined to express an opinion on the project, the young Synod of Geneva undertook it. The seminary was founded in 1818 at Auburn, the largest village west of Utica. New England-trained men predominated in its leadership. D. C. Lansing was the chief promoter and became professor of practical theology. James Richards left the Newark church, second largest in the denomination, to become professor of theology.[26] Within a decade the student body was about two thirds that of Princeton.

[26] R. B. Welch, "James Richards and His Theology," *Presbyterian Review*, V (1884), 193 ff., 401 ff.

V : *Growth and Disruption,*

1825–1838

In the 1820's, New York State was growing and developing more rapidly than any other part of the nation. The Erie Canal was completed in 1825 and thereafter the rate of immigration moved even faster, especially into the western portions and into New York City. Five counties around the western end of the canal doubled their population in a decade. The pioneering stage was past by 1825, and the saturation point in farmland was reached shortly thereafter in most of western New York. The countryside was well occupied and flourishing, and the further growth was to come in the towns and cities where diversified industry and lively commerce were already established. The cultural tone was set by the New England tradition, which was the strongest element in the new population. Public schools were widespread, and the level of education was higher than any other portion of the nation save New England. Practically every village had at least one newssheet, and the publication and circulation of newspapers was probably the highest of any region in the nation.

1. Church Life and Organization

In this New York society the organization of religion was very similar to that of New England, save that the place of

97

Congregationalism in the latter was here taken by Presbyterianism. It is probable that the more popular Methodist and Baptist churches already outstripped the Presbyterians in numbers, but the social and cultural predominance of the latter was unquestioned. Religious life in New York City at this time was also dominated by the Presbyterians. Here it was also the strongest numerically. Presbyterianism was relatively more influential in New York State in this generation than in any later period. Similarly, New York State Presbyterianism constituted a more considerable portion of the national church, about one third, than would later be the case.

The basic outline of synodical structure had been laid down before 1825, and in the following period up to the schism of 1838 the great gains chiefly put flesh on this skeleton. There were in 1825 four synods on state territory, New York, Genesee, Geneva, and Albany. Albany Synod was divided in 1829 when the new Synod of Utica emerged.

In the period under consideration ten new presbyteries were created, chiefly in the western area and around New York City. Utica Synod did not change, Albany and Genesee each added one, but New York Synod increased from five to eight and Geneva from four to nine. Six new presbyteries were erected in central and western New York, all originally in Geneva Synod, but Angelica was transferred to Genesee in 1834. New York Synod, meanwhile, was enlarged by New York Third Presbytery (1830), Long Island Second (1833), and Bedford (1829). Another New England presbytery, that of Newburyport, was added to the roll of Albany Synod. In the Utica Synod there was a confusing change of names when St. Lawrence became Watertown in 1828 and Ogdensburg was rechristened St. Lawrence two years later.

It is necessary also to keep in mind the developments in Congregationalism, which was so inextricably involved with Presbyterianism in New York. By 1825, as we have seen, all the major district associations in the state had been assimilated into presbyteries. In the late twenties, however, district associations or consociations began to form again. In 1833 the revived Oneida Association, whose leading spirit had been William R. Weeks, called a meeting to organize a state Congregational Association. The General Association of New York came into being at Clinton the next year, although in 1835 it still engaged only seven representatives from three district associations. In the following years, consequently, when violent attacks were being made against the Congregational elements in New York Presbyterianism, there was in existence, if only barely in existence, an alternative Congregational organization to which churches disaffected by Presbyterian views on new measures, new divinity, or abolition might retire. The leaders of this association appealed to the "Presbygational" churches, of whom they calculated over a hundred at that time, to join them.

Revivalism: New Measures. If we seek to characterize the religion of the New York Presbyterian churches of this period, perhaps the best beginning is to say that this was preeminently revivalist Calvinism. The church life of the region was brought into being and shaped by revivalism, and the whole conception of piety, theology, and church methods presupposed revivals. No other section of the Presbyterian Church, at least in the North, was so characterized by revivalism.

In the history of revivalism 1825 marks an epoch. The revivals of the preceding generation in New York, especially in 1800–1801, 1807–1808, 1816–1817, and 1819–1820, had been of a piece with the Second Great Awakening in New England. That is to say, they were, with some exceptions, conducted chiefly by settled pastors within the structure of parish activities, were accompanied by careful doctrinal instruction, and were generally restrained and orderly in manner. Such revivalism continued after 1825, and very effectively, but it was for a time overshadowed before the public by a new type of revivalism introduced and popularized in Presbyterian and Congregational circles by Charles G. Finney.

Finney was to prove himself one of the most powerful personal influences in American religious history. He was converted in the revival of 1821 as a young lawyer. He offered himself as a home missionary and for two years worked in Jefferson and St. Lawrence Counties, being licensed by Oneida in 1824. The area, he found, had been "burned over" by sensational Methodist preaching, and nothing less exciting could win attention. Such methods had hitherto been repudiated by Presbyterians and Congregationalists. But in 1825, as Finney returned to take part in an awakening spreading in the Mohawk Valley, he brought these practices with him. Some five hundred conversions were recorded at Rome, of whom over half were received in the Presbyterian Church. A comparable number were converted in Utica early in 1826 and in the following summer over six hundred new members were added in Cayuga Presbytery, especially at Auburn. The Utica movement continued for three years, producing some three thousand conversions in all. Many congregations leaped in a matter of weeks to new levels of enduring strength, and Finney and his methods gained nationwide attention.

Finney's "new measures" were opposed by many. Oneida Presbytery was not happy, but their hands were tied by the great apparent success. Dr. Richards was critical of the revival at Auburn. William R. Weeks, the strict predestinarian follower of Emmons, was generally credited with the authorship of a *Pastoral Letter* of the revived Oneida Association,[1] which furnished ammunition for other opponents of Finney. New England Congregationalists also took alarm, and N. S. S. Beman of Troy, in whose church Finney preached over the winter of 1826–1827, arranged with Lyman Beecher a conference of leaders from each side. It was held at New Lebanon in 1827.[2] Perhaps the most shocking innovation to the New Eng-

---

[1] *Pastoral Letter of the . . . Oneida Association . . . on . . . Revivals of Religion*, Utica, 1827.

[2] C. C. Cole, "The New Lebanon Convention," *New York History*, October, 1950, pp. 385–397.

landers was permitting women to exhort and pray in public meetings. Finney himself apparently was not particularly responsible for this practice, but it was observed rather widely in central New York revivals. The denunciation of more staid ministers as " cold " and the invasion of their parishes without their consent was another abuse of which Finney had been guilty. Some of the methods of prayer were also criticized, especially what were called " particularity," and the " prayer of faith." The revivals generally grew out of prayer meetings, more often than not composed of women, or out of Sabbath schools, and they frequently resorted to the practice of praying for the conversion of particular individuals, sometimes without their knowledge. Watertown Presbytery had deprecated this practice.[3] It was also rather widely taught that if complete unanimity in prayer were achieved, it would infallibly be granted as asked. This was the " prayer of faith," which was disowned or criticized by several theologians and judicatories. There were also various devices for singling out and publicly committing those troubled in conscience: having them rise in their places or come forward or — this generally only after 1830 — sit together on an " anxious bench." The hasty admission of the " converts " of these revivals to church membership was also criticized.

The apparent outcome of the New Lebanon conference was a stalemate, as the New Yorkers declined to acknowledge the authority of the New England clergy. But Finney himself, if not his followers, restrained himself increasingly in the following years. No doubt he also learned from the social customs of large cities like Philadelphia and New York, where he preached in 1827 and 1829. He grew less denunciatory, less sensational, and his language became less coarse and irreverent. His greatest triumph came in Rochester in 1830 and 1831. This revival was remarkable for its dignity and restrained power and appeal, particularly to the leading business and professional

---

[3] Philemon H. Fowler, *Presbyterianism in Central New York* (Utica, New York, Curtiss & Childs, 1877), p. 269.

classes. The three Presbyterian churches, First, Brick, and Third Church were strengthened by the addition of some six hundred members in the first year, and the tone and character of the whole city, then numbering about ten thousand, were enduringly affected.

From Rochester the Awakening spread widely, continuing in 1831. In the latter year the Synod of Geneva reported revivals in almost every church, with many congregations admitting more than one hundred new members. The churches of the synod probably added four or five thousand new members in all. Genesee Synod reported gains of the same dimensions. The following illustrated what the movement in 1831 meant to individual congregations: Ithaca added 220; Geneva, 270; Penn Yan, 123; Watertown, 100; Clyde, 100; Seneca Falls, 127; Troy Second Church, 156; Salem, 212; Clinton, 134; Auburn, 235; Rochester First Church, 150; and Rochester Third, 635. Such phenomenal gains marked an epoch in the church life of the state, and indeed the revival was felt over much of the nation.

In the great revivals of the years following 1830 the predominant pattern was that of "protracted meetings" conducted by itinerant revivalists. The protracted meetings, lasting from a week to a month, were an adaptation of the camp meeting. The itinerants were generally laymen who had discovered the gift of "getting up" a revival, but were often religiously shallow and intellectually incompetent. None approached Finney in ability. The presbyteries had a good deal of trouble with some of them. The laymen often supported them against discipline, and for a time in some areas settled pastorates were fewer and terms of service shorter while itinerants circulated about the region.

Jeremiah Burchard, for example, conducted sensational revivals over much of the state for twenty years. He lost the respect of many ministers and eventually retired to secular activities. Luther Myrick preached over the central part of the state from 1830 to 1834, but was suspended for doctrinal error by Oneida Presbytery in 1833. Cayuga and Onondaga Presbyteries warned their congregations against him. Some thirty churches were disturbed by his perfectionist teachings. James Boyle, another Oneida Presbytery evangelist, held revivals in the Genesee country in 1830 and 1831. But he, too, developed perfectionist views, and became associated with J. H. Noyes in New England. Boyle was suspended in 1835, then deposed and excommunicated. He left the church. In Angelica Presbytery a vulgar enthusiast named Littlejohn was able to establish himself against the opposition of the older ministers and the repeated warnings of the synod until finally, in 1841, he was convicted of five cases of attempted or successful seduction. Finney himself, of course, left the state in 1835, and moved thereafter to theological perfectionism at Oberlin.

There were thus signficant irregularities in the revivalist excitement, both practical and doctrinal, and there was some ground for the reputation of western New York as a whole as a " burned-over district." But most of the disorders were due to itinerants, while the great body of Presbyterian churches and ministers deplored them, and the judicatories of the church labored, often at some cost, to regulate them. There were some defections, to be sure, but the mainstay of the churches of the region for the next generation was that great company who had become members after a revivalist conversion.

Evangelistic and Reform Societies. Connected with the revivals was a whole new pattern of congregational activity that emerged at this time. The average congregation was now organized into a large variety of groups, mostly evangelistic in character, which were related to similar groups in other congregations in voluntary societies, regional or national in scope. Missionary societies, especially " female " missionary societies, had been among the earliest. Prayer circles, Bible classes, Sabbath schools, Bible- and tract-distributing societies, temperance and moral reform societies of various types, were now found in every strong church. These gatherings of the more earnest were usually the nurseries of the revival in a congregation, and in turn the chief beneficiaries of the fresh energies of the converted.[4]

In a survey of these evangelistic programs and societies, missions should come first. Time and again the newly established churches of western New York are found sending missionary sons to the Pacific or India or Africa within a decade of their founding. This stream of missionary personnel, with the financial contributions and the general interest that made it possible, is one of the best keys to the intensely evangelistic spirit of these churches. New York Presbyterians were deeply involved in the ABCFM from the beginning. They furnished hundreds of "honorary members" for the board and had no less than six auxiliary agencies gathering for the cause within their bounds. The *Panoplist* was widely read in the churches, and most Presbyterian congregations observed the "monthly concert of prayer" for the conversion of the world and the inauguration of the millennium.

Tract and Bible societies were also missionary agencies, which, like the ABCFM, were organized on nominally undenominational principles. But Presbyterians dominated them in New York. Every county in the state had at least one Bible society, and beginning with Monroe in 1824, every county had a campaign to supply a copy to every family in its territory lacking a Bible. In 1829 the American Bible Society had one hundred subsidiaries in New York State. In twenty years New Yorkers bought over twice as many Bibles as New England, and gave more to this cause than Massachusetts and Connecticut.[5]

The American Tract Society was organized in New York City in 1825. In ten years some thirty million tracts had been published, of which probably three fourths circulated in New York.[6] There were scores of auxiliary societies in the state, in

---

[4] James H. Hotchkin, *History of . . . Western New York,* p. 161.
[5] Whitney R. Cross, *The Burned-over District,* p. 25.
[6] *Ibid.*

which Presbyterians and Congregationalists supplied most of the funds and labor. Tracts were distributed systematically in cities, towns, and villages, often by the colporteur system of house-to-house selling. Such distribution was especially successful in communities stirred by revivals.[7]

Sabbath schools, originally undenominational and for the children of the poor, had by 1825 become part of the normal congregational pattern of New York Presbyterian churches. By 1829 New York had two thousand five hundred schools and seventy-five thousand scholars, more than all New England, and probably more than all the rest of the United States.[8] Presbyterians were prominent in the American Sabbath School Union and in the local subsidiaries to such a degree that the society was accused of Presbyterian sectarianism. The societies sought to raise funds, to organize schools, to establish repositories from which books could be supplied. Synodical narratives from about 1830 lament that Sabbath schools were apparently driving out the old system of catechizing by the pastor, and for a few years special efforts were vainly made to maintain the earlier system.

A second set of activities and societies would come under the modern category of church extension. We have earlier seen how the United Domestic Missionary Society, a merger of several earlier local agencies, was reorganized in 1826 as the American Home Missionary Society. Although in accordance with its title this society undertook work on a national basis, in fact it gave New York State the bulk of its attention. Of the 169 missionaries subsidized in the first year (1826–1827), no less than 120 worked in New York. These men were not itinerants, but regular settled pastors in one or two congregations. The 1835 report stated that in nine years the AHMS had strengthened more than 200 Presbyterian (and Congregational) churches in seventeen western counties alone. Such was the general sympathy with the whole program that contributions from the area exceeded the expenditures there, a fact that goes

[7] Hotchkin, *op. cit.*, p. 165. [8] Cross, *op. cit.*, p. 128.

far to explain the concentration of AHMS activity in the state. The national office was in New York City, where the corresponding secretary, Dr. Absalom Peters, probably accomplished more for church extension than any other man in America from 1826 to 1837. Under his leadership the income of the AHMS tripled and the number of its missionaries quadrupled. He wrote the first twelve annual reports and edited *The Home Missionary and Pastor's Journal.*

Closely related to the AHMS program of subsidizing ministers' salaries was the subsidization of the education of ministerial candidates carried on by the American Education Society. There had been local societies in New York State devoted to this cause from the time of the War of 1812. The Presbyterian Education Society, which absorbed many of them, was itself affiliated to the AES in 1827 as an auxiliary. But the Presbyterian tail was soon wagging the dog, and in 1830 the AES moved its office and executive, Elias Cornelius, from Boston to New York City. From 1827 the resources of the AES expanded explosively. In its first decade the AES had spent ten thousand to fifteen thousand dollars annually in support of one or two hundred students. But the budget doubled in 1827 and reached fifty thousand dollars in 1834 and eighty thousand dollars in 1835. The number of beneficiaries increased proportionately from two hundred to one thousand in 1835. Although the AES, like the AHMS, was nominally undenominational, the bulk of its beneficiaries were Presbyterian and Congregational. Almost half, four hundred fifty out of one thousand, were in 1835 handled by the Presbyterian Educational Society auxiliary alone. Dr. William Patton was its executive. There was much overlapping of officers of the AHMS and AES, and the two organizations worked closely together, both of them concentrating the bulk of their activity in New York State and its Presbyterianism.

Some of the new societies and congregational activities were evangelistic, some served church extension, but some rather aimed at moral and social reform. In this respect they carried on in a new form the traditional Calvinist theocratic impulse. But the moral reform efforts of New York Presbyterians were to reach greater dimensions than those of New England Congregationalism, and to have more influence on the nation generally. Three crusades in particular preoccupied the Presbyterian churches of New York, those for Sabbath observance, temperance, and the abolition of slavery. There were others, such as anti-Masonry, the peace movement, McDowell's efforts for "females who had deviated from the paths of virtue," but none approached the three first named in extent of participation or in public effect.

The building of the canal proved the occasion for the most debated reformist campaign of the 1820's, the effort to enforce Sabbath observance. As early as 1824 the Synod of Albany commended petitions to the legislature to bar canal traffic on Sunday and urged Christians to patronize only such stage and boat lines as observed the Sabbath.[9] A campaign to persuade Congress to bar Sunday mails raised fear of Presbyterian clericalism. The political efforts all failed, but in the revival years from 1830 to 1834 considerable local improvement in Sabbath observance was noted in New York state.

The temperance cause spread from New England, where Lyman Beecher had been an early advocate. The movement coagulated into another national society in 1826, called the American Temperance Society, with Justin Edwards as secretary. There were scores of local societies in New York and in 1830 a state society was organized. By 1833 this society had half of all the temperance auxiliaries in the nation. Presbyterian ministers were leaders in this campaign, and many or most of the locals were in congregations. Half a dozen presbyteries passed resolutions that abstinence from distilled liquors was to be considered a normal obligation of church membership. At the suggestion of several Presbyterian synods, the state legislature itself adjourned for three days to honor a "temperance fast" in 1829, and several localities went dry, ei-

[9] MS. Minutes of the Synod of Albany, 1824, p. 243.

ther by ordinance or social pressure. Universalists again raised the cry of " Priestcraft! Church and state! " [10]

A distinctive aspect of the temperance movement in this period came from its alliance with revivalist religion. In Finney's Rochester campaign of 1830 the temperance pledge became a revivalist " new measure," symbolizing the new life of obedience that was consecrated in the revival. Thereafter the revivalist typically singled out drink as his greatest enemy, and the last barrier to the coming millennium. Intemperate or even temperate consumption of alcohol became sin per se, and the taint extended to the manufacture or sale of intoxicating beverages. Wine for the sacrament proved but a temporary difficulty. Presbyterians were persuaded to overrule Scripture in the interest of the abstinence crusade.[11] And they were ready to support the political form of the temperance movement, which succeeded the revivalist phase after the depression of 1837.

In connection with the evangelistic and reform societies, it is important to notice the character and location of their ruling bodies. Several of them had been founded in New England, but by 1825, New York City had replaced Boston as the nation's chief center of religious organizations. The societies were nominally national and interdenominational, and they usually picked directors to be representative in both respects. But the actual executive bodies were composed chiefly of Presbyterian ministers and elders of New York City. The interlocking directorates justify the term " the benevolent empire," which was applied especially to the " great eight ": [12] ABCFM; AHMS; American Bible Society; AES; American Tract Society; American Sabbath School Union; Seaman's

[10] Cross, op. cit., p. 131.

[11] Cf. MS. Minutes of the Synod of New York, OS, 1842: " Tremblingly alive to the rashness of those who would lay profane hands on the significant and immutable symbols of the body and blood of their adorable Lord."

[12] Cf. Gilbert H. Barnes, The Antislavery Impulse, 1830–1844 (New York, London, D. Appleton-Century Company, Inc., 1933), pp. 17–28; and Charles I. Foster, An Errand of Mercy (Chapel Hill, University of North Carolina Press, 1960), Part II.

Friend Society; American Temperance Society.

Among the directors the Tappan brothers were most conspicuous, especially Arthur and Lewis. From about 1828, indeed, Arthur Tappan made the benevolent empire his chief occupation, while Lewis ran most of their importing and merchandising business. In 1834 the annual income of the empire totaled nine million dollars.

The societies held their "Anniversaries" in May in New York City. There, mass meetings listened to addresses and reports, and elected officers. From 1832 they were held in the Chatham Street Chapel, a former theater leased for the "First Free Presbyterian Church" of New York City. (The "free" aspect was the absence of pew rents, which barred Presbyterian churches to many people of limited means at that time. The Tappans led the movement in their concern to evangelize the unchurched of New York City. They had opened a hall in 1830 and brought a revivalist from upstate as pastor. In 1832 they installed Finney at the Chatham Chapel.) Then the Broadway Tabernacle, the largest Protestant church in the country, was built for him and for the use of the Anniversaries. Finney was thus preacher at the cathedral church of the empire, symbolizing the union of revivalism with humanitarian activity. Half a dozen more "free churches" were opened in the next few years, the ministers all coming from the revivalist area upstate. The empire acquired a newspaper, the *New York Evangelist*, to serve its interests. Upstate, the *Western Recorder*, of Utica, and the Rochester *Observer* represented the same outlook.

While from their own perspective the national societies were unsectarian and liberal, they did not appear so to all denominations. They represented what was historically the orthodoxy of New England and New York, the Reformed and Calvinist tradition. And implicit in their claim to be "American" societies was the assumption that this was of right the dominant faith of the nation. Presbyterians, Congregationalists, Dutch Reformed, and minor Scottish bodies could readily unite on this pan-Reformed national platform. But Episcopalians, Methodists, and to some extent Baptists, resented the claim and the assumption. "These great national societies" wrote a Methodist editor, "should assume their proper denomination, and be declared Presbyterian, as they really are in effect." [13]

Doctrine and Polity. The theological orientation of New York State Presbyterians requires some examination, especially since it was to occasion so much controversy. As the bulk of them were of New England origin, so was their theology. It was imbibed in part at Andover, the Congregational seminary, which sent nearly half its graduates into the Presbyterian Church, and even more at the colleges from which so many graduates went to New York — Amherst, Williams, Dartmouth, Middlebury, Yale. Union and Hamilton, the two chief colleges for Presbyterians upstate, both stood in this New England tradition and derived most of their faculties thence.

These various institutions taught, on the whole, one or another variety of the revivalist Calvinist tradition begun by Jonathan Edwards in the Great Awakening. This tradition generically was often loosely labeled the "New England theology" or "Hopkinsianism" from the author of its first systematics. All were predestinarian Calvinists, but the Hopkinsians differed from the formulations of the Confession on a number of special points. They rejected the legal metaphors explaining the solidarity of sinners with Adam — the "covenant head" or legal "representative" — whose guilt was "imputed" to his descendants, in favor of Edwards' theory. They made a distinction between the moral and physical inability of fallen man to obey God, holding that depravity was a matter of the will, and that the sinner had the physical capacity to do good if only he could will to do so. They denied that the scope of Christ's atoning work was limited to the elect in intention. Rather, he died for the world, although, to be sure, only the elect were effectively benefited. Many New York

[13] Barnes, *op. cit.,* p. 19.

Presbyterians also followed Dwight and the younger Edwards in preferring the "governmental" theory of the atonement to that of penal substitution. Hopkinsian views on these four heads, at least, were very widespread, probably predominant, in New York Presbyterianism. Several of these distinctive views were especially suited to preaching revivals, which all regarded as desirable. The conversion of the world was a constant subject of preaching and prayer, and the exaltation of the recurrent revivals seemed a foretaste of the promised triumph of the millennium.

These Edwardean or Hopkinsian peculiarities were understood in New York as minor variations within the general Calvinist system of the Westminster Standards, and thus as compatible with a sincere subscription to the latter. Ever since the Adopting Act, New York Presbyterians were accustomed to subcribe to the "system" of the Confession in such a manner as to suppose that some of its formulations might be secondary, nonessential, and nonobligatory in the judgment of the presbytery. In the long run this conception of subscription was to be their most important and controversial theological position.

There had been sharp controversy over Hopkinsianism in New York City and northern New Jersey just after the War of 1812.[14] The Young Men's Missionary Society of New York had split in two over the issue. The Presbytery of Hudson had refused to permit the settlement of a Hopkinsian minister, had been overruled by the Synod of New York and New Jersey, and then sustained, on appeal in 1817, by the General Assembly. The Synod of Philadelphia warned in 1816 against "Arian, Socinian, Arminian, and Hopkinsian heresies." And the Synods of New York and Philadelphia were unable to unite in supporting the African School because of this issue. Philadelphia wanted to insist on the Princeton type of subscription to the Standards, which was as exclusive as words could make it. The

[14] Samuel J. Baird, *History of the New School* (Philadelphia, Claxton, Remsen & Haffelfinger, 1868), pp. 235–256.

New York Hopkinsians on the Board declined to accept this "new test" and insisted on more liberal terms of subscription. A sharp divergence was thus apparent at this date between Pennsylvania Presbyterians, insisting on subscription *ipsissimis verbis,* and most New York Presbyterians, defending a form of subscription that permitted Hopkinsian readings of the Standards. By 1825 the debate had died down, and there were a number of Hopkinsians to be found south of New York and New Jersey.

After 1825, however, Presbyterians were to become aware of a new and even more disturbing theological tendency, the "New Haven theology" of Nathaniel Taylor and the new Yale Divinity School. Taylor was a vigorous revivalist, pastor of Center Church, in New Haven. He was concerned to find a place for "real" freedom and responsibility, and to remove the grounds for the Unitarian charges that Calvinism taught fatalism and in effect made God the author of sin. Taylor insisted that all men were without exception sinners and guilty before God, but he denied the conventional explanation of this fact by "original sin." Sin properly applied, he held, only to deliberate acts of the will. One could not be guilty of Adam's sin or anyone else's save one's own, and an infant was not a sinner until his first moral act. Whatever it was in human nature that made it a certainty that every man would develop into a sinner, it was not itself "sin" or deserving of punishment. Yet while holding such views, Taylor had subscribed the Saybrook Platform, which affirmed Westminster doctrines on these points.

Hopkinsians were as scandalized as covenant theologians. A Hartford group and some at Andover struck an alliance with the covenant theologians at Princeton to fight the "New Divinity." For the decade from 1828 to the split in the Presbyterian Church, Taylor was the archheretic and "Taylorism" was the accusation leveled against many and sometimes all Presbyterians of New England antecedents. In fact, the number of Presbyterian disciples of Taylor seems to have been small. The dominant tendency in New York throughout was, rather, Hop-kinsian.

On the popular level, however, it seems likely that there was a distinct theological tendency involved in Finneyite revivalism. One obvious danger of the Finneyite tendency was its moralism. Man was asked to dedicate himself, to convert himself by an act of will. And various practical goals were set for him — evangelistic missionary work in numerous agencies needed help and funds, there was the abstinence pledge, the Sabbath to observe, slavery to be renounced. But however good and useful these various activities taken as ends in themselves or as moral issues, they were something other than forgiveness and the new life of communion with God through Christ. There was a steady leakage both of revivalists and of their disciples to merely humanitarian reform. The large inroads of perfectionism betrayed the fact that religion was understood by many in terms of moral absolutes. We have seen how many of the revivalists moved into perfectionism and then to secularism. Of the abolitionists also, Beriah Green, T. D. Weld, Gerrit Smith, eventually left evangelical Christianity and the church.

As we have noted earlier, the Plan of Union and Accommodation Plans occasioned some distinctive features in polity in parts of New York State. The Congregational churches that entered into arrangements with Presbyterians did so deliberately. They considered that in a new area and without the support of a church establishment they needed some structure like a presbytery for joint action and to maintain order and unity. But some of them did not wish the Presbyterian judicial apparatus of appeals to synod or General Assembly. In some cases accommodation plans provided that such appeals should not be taken, and synods recognized that they had no jurisdiction with such churches. Lyman Beecher illustrates this view. "A Presbytery," he said, "made up of New England men, raised Congregationalists, is the nearest the Bible of anything there is. But if you go to sticking it up, Scotch fashion, with appeals, etc., I wouldn't put myself into the hands of such a power all over the United States." [15]

A second, and more frequently noted, peculiarity had to do with the eldership. Congregationalists were accustomed to government of the congregation by the male communicants rather than by a session. And under accommodation plans churches often kept such government internally. In the presbytery they would be represented by elected lay delegates in place of ruling elders. When such delegates were sent to the General Assembly, objections were increasingly raised from strict Presbyterian sections of the church.

Another Congregational practice widespread in New York Presbyterianism was the custom of having every member adopt a congregational " covenant." These covenants usually included a doctrinal statement, and there was some variation among them. New York Presbyterians were thus accustomed to attempts to restate the faith, in comparison to churches that never used anything but the Westminster Standards.

There were also some practices that differed from classical Presbyterianism but probably owed as much to revivalism as to Congregationalism. Church membership was now based on an experience of regeneration rather than on baptism. Those who were baptized in infancy were not seen as church members in the full sense, but only those who were converted. And children were not baptized unless at least one parent was a " visible saint." The communicant members listed in the church statistics were thus a small minority of the regular attendants upon public worship. It has been estimated that the membership figures would have to be multiplied by as much as eight to reach the latter figure.[16] This stress on the conversion experience was associated with a loss of meaning of both the sacraments. Similar individualistic and nonsacramental tenden-

[15] L. Beecher, *Autobiography* (Cambridge, Belknap Press of Harvard University Press, 1961), Cross ed., I, 80.
[16] Cross, *op. cit.*, p. 41.

cies, however, were observable also in the Scotch-Irish sections of the church with no Congregational sympathies.

2. OLD SCHOOL — NEW SCHOOL AND ABOLITIONIST CONTROVERSY

Such were the prevailing tendencies in the church life and organization and theology of New York Presbyterianism in this period. Their very vitality and success proved their undoing. By 1830 the three western Synods of Utica, Geneva, and Genesee numbered more than the whole Presbyterian Church of thirty years before, which had authorized the cooperation with Congregationalists in the area. From being a device to husband desperately inadequate resources of church extension in new territory, the Plan of Union and related plans had become a pattern of modified Presbyterianism that threatened to dominate the whole church. Jealousy and fear awakened elsewhere, particularly in the Philadelphia area, which was accustomed to lead the church.

This jealousy was heightened by the confessional revival which swept across much of Europe and America in the 1820's and 1830's. A more rigorous and authoritarian enforcement of both doctrine and church order was demanded, and such compromises and variants as were practiced in New York "Presbygationalism" were attacked. Presbyterian church order was insisted upon as *iure divino* by some, and a virtually Roman Catholic position on the authority of the confessional tradition. This type of theological traditionalism was illustrated by the pledge required of Princeton Seminary professors, each of whom promised he would not "inculcate, teach, or insinuate anything which shall appear to me to contradict or contravene, either directly or impliedly, anything taught in the said Confession of Faith or Catechisms." [17] The Princeton professors themselves did not try to impose such shackles on all

[17] *Charter and Plan,* rev. to February, 1927, p. 27.

ministers. But for the militants (many of them ex-Seceders) the Princeton oath described their conception of every minister's obligation. It would never have occurred to them that Calvin, Knox, and the Westminster fathers would probably have refused that pledge.

Old School and New School Parties. By 1829 or 1830 two distinct parties were emerging, especially in the two chief cities of New York and Philadelphia. They were first separated organizationally in New York by the application of what came to be called "elective affinity" to demarcate the bounds of judicatories. At the request of eight churches of the New England party, a new presbytery was separated off from New York First by the Synod of New York in 1830. It was called New York Third Presbytery, since the small group that had joined from the Seceder Church in 1822 was known as New York Second. The Third Presbytery included the bulk of the key directors of the benevolent empire and grew rapidly with the revival of 1831 and the following years, soon equaling in numbers the First and Second Presbyteries together. This principle of constituting more than one presbytery in the same geographical area on grounds of "elective affinity" was then extended by the Assembly to Philadelphia in the attempt to moderate the controversies displayed there in the Barnes case. In Philadelphia, where the New England wing was in a minority, the principle was resisted, and long and complicated struggles ensued.

In 1831 the General Assembly itself was divided into what had come to be called Old School and New School parties. For the following six years the Assemblies were increasingly partisan until the rupture of 1837. As Finney put it in 1835, "Their contentions and janglings are so ridiculous, so wicked, so outrageous that no doubt there is a jubilee in hell every year about the time of the meeting of the General Assembly." [18]

[18] C. G. Finney, *Lectures on Revivals*, McLoughlin ed. (Cambridge, Belknap Press of Harvard University Press, 1960), p. 291.

To a considerable degree the schools were identified with the New England churches of New York State and the Scotch-Irish of Pennsylvania. The South remained uncommitted.

The parties in the church formed first of all on the question of the proper means of church extension and the attitude to be taken toward the AHMS and the AES. These organizations were so eminently successful in developing new churches and ministers that they threatened to be able to control the whole church. Such an outcome would mean the triumph of the New England wing, with its "new measures" revivalism, its Congregational traits in polity, its alternatives to the theology of the Confessions. The new confessionalist party consequently labored desperately to breath life into the ineffective denominational Boards of Missions and Education, arguing that church extension should be carried on only under ecclesiastical control and under strict application of confessional Standards.

When the overture to reorganize and reanimate the Board of Missions was first presented in 1828, it was rejected by a large majority. But the minority were so concerned about the matter that by way of concession the action was reversed. The new Board started from 31 home missionaries in 1827, and raised these to 101 in 1829 and 198 in 1830, which last figure was still only half the size of the AHMS staff. The inevitable outcome was that the agents and missionaries of the two organizations were forced into competition, especially in the Mississippi Valley. Theological debate became a weapon of institutional rivalry and often descended to misrepresentation and bigotry. When the number of ministers supported ran into the hundreds on both sides, they became nucleating organizations for parties on the floor of the Assembly. No less than forty men in the Assembly of 1831 were agents of the two Boards. New York churches, as we have seen, were generally committed to the AHMS. Here they first looked for help when they needed it, and here they sent their benevolences. The

Board of Missions was unable to carry on much of a program within the state. In Pennsylvania, on the other hand, several presbyteries condemned the operations of the AHMS in Presbyterian bounds. And in the west there was strenuous rivalry after 1831.

The General Assembly of 1831 marked an epoch. Despite the advance preparations of the OS, they lost control of the Assembly for the first time. Revivalist New York was growing faster and supplied the first NS moderator, N. S. S. Beman, of Troy. The election of directors for the Board of Missions produced the greatest excitement. Hitherto that Board had been controlled by the OS party of the Philadelphia area. Now the OS was shocked and frightened to realize that this control could be lost by a vote of the Assembly. At a motion to add some NS men to that Board such a tumult was raised as the Assembly had never seen before, and the meetings had to be recessed. With commendable moderation the NS withdrew the proposal and permitted the Board to continue as a party organ of what was now the minority. They also permitted the election of an OS Board for Princeton Seminary. But the group in Philadelphia Presbytery, who had hitherto run the two Boards and Princeton, was shaken. Their control of the institutions of the church hung by a hair. Some OS men began discussing a possible division of the church.

Some of the complaints about irregularities were closely related to the struggle for control of the Assembly. There was the issue of recognition of "committee-men" from "Presbygational" churches as commissioners to the General Assembly. A "committee-man" from Western Reserve was voted in by the NS majority in 1831, it being noted that under accommodation plans presbyteries had been given to understand that they had a right to such representation. But at the end of the Assembly, when early departures had given the OS a majority, the Assembly resolved that the practice was of questionable constitutionality and ought not to be continued.

Under the close association of the preceding generation,

delegates from New England bodies had similarly been given full rights to sit in major committees and to vote in the Assembly. Negotiations were undertaken in the late 1820's with the New England bodies to withdraw voting privileges from corresponding delegates, and by 1830 the change had been made. Step by step the near merger of Congregationalism and Presbyterianism was being undone.

Another troublesome problem was that of the divergent requirements for licensure and ordination. While many Pennsylvania presbyteries exacted unqualified subscription to the Standards, New England and Western Reserve generally did not do so. The subscription in Connecticut and New York was generally in the looser form of the Adopting Act. An issue that was bitterly argued, consequently, was whether a presbytery might or must examine licentiates or ministers transferring from other presbyteries or from Congregational bodies and require them to subscribe the Confession of Faith.

While the party struggles continued for control of the Assemblies and on behalf of the rival systems of church extension, the doctrinal issues were aired in a series of heresy trials. Few of these were heard before New York judicatories, although two of the indicted ministers, Albert Barnes and Lyman Beecher, had previously lived in the state. Albert Barnes came from Rome and was converted while a senior at Hamilton College. He went on to Princeton Seminary. When he was called to Old First Church in Philadelphia in 1830, *The Philadelphia Presbyterian*, the most influential militant OS paper, accused him of New Haven heresy. The case at length came before the General Assembly in 1831. At the motion of Professor Miller, of Princeton, a compromise solution was reached whereby the assembly objected to some of Barnes's expressions but ordered no further proceedings.

In the next four years there were further trials, of Duffield, of three Yale men in Illinois, of Lyman Beecher in Cincinnati. And in 1836 a second case against Albert Barnes became the climax of the series, focusing the doctrinal issues and revealing the distribution of opinion in the church.[19]

Before the great Barnes trial of 1836, however, the OS had adopted another tactic, of drafting manifestos and soliciting signatures as a way of influencing the Assembly. The "Western Memorial" of 1833 complained particularly of the AHMS, urging that all Presbyterian home and foreign missionary work be controlled by the General Assembly, that the Plan of Union be ended, that candidates be ordained only by the presbytery where they were to serve (not by some Eastern presbytery such as New York Third, from which AHMS missionaries might be sent to the West), and that action be taken against doctrinal errors. Some nine errors were specified, with references to writings of Beman, Barnes, Beecher and Duffield. It was also urged that a convention of those sympathetic to these proposals should meet before the Assembly of 1834.

The Assembly of 1834, however, declined to follow any of these recommendations or to condemn the errors specified, which, as Charles Hodge observed, were incompetently drafted. The militants of the OS minority met during this Assembly and adopted a more careful list of heresies, the "Act and Testimony." It was circulated for signatures as a new league and covenant and a test of orthodoxy. The whole procedure threatened revolutionary action and schism, and in fact the "Act and Testimony" was the first definite step toward the division of the church.

The conductors of the *Princeton Review* reacted with restraint and good sense to the "Act and Testimony." Hodge was not convinced "that one-tenth of the ministers of the Presbyterian church would deliberately countenance and sustain the errors specified," with the possible exception of one on imputation that might involve many Hopkinsians.[20] There was, no doubt, disorder, error, and lax discipline in the church, but

[19] A. J. Stansbury, *Trial of the Rev. Albert Barnes* (New York, Van Nostrand & Dwight, 1836).

[20] "The Act and Testimony," *Biblical Repertory and Princeton Review*, VI (1834), 511.

not such as to justify schism. The indications were rather that revivalistic "new measures" were already dead and that the New Divinity was on the decline. While the reference was not always made explicit, what was under discussion here primarily was the condition of Presbyterianism in New York State.

The supporters of the "Act and Testimony" met in Pittsburgh in May, 1835, representing 36 presbyteries and 13 minorities of presbyteries. Of the thirty-some presbyteries in New York State only three had sent delegates. A "Memorial" was drafted to guide the Assembly. Again it was urged that the AHMS and AES be barred from Presbyterian bounds, and that the Plan of Union be abrogated and correspondence with Congregational bodies be ended. New School theology was described as "another Gospel . . . entirely and essentially different" from that of the Bible and Westminster Confession.[21]

At the Pittsburgh Assembly the Old School finally broke through the NS majority that had controlled the Assemblies from 1831. As Moderator they elected the most conspicuous OS militant in New York State, the former Seceder W. W. Phillips, now pastor of the Wall Street Church. The Assembly was thus able to take the Pittsburgh "Memorial" for its agenda, although it did not carry it all through. They did not discountenance the interdenominational societies, although it was declared that the church's first duty was to her own Boards, but they did resolve that the Plan of Union should be discontinued. The Assembly also recorded its testimony that the doctrinal errors specified in the memorial did exist, were in substance Pelagian or Arminian and incompatible with Presbyterian Standards.

The reaction against interdenominational societies was car-

---

[21] Texts of "Western Memorial," "Act and Testimony," Memorial of 1835 in Samuel J. Baird, *Collections of the Acts . . . of the Presbyterian Church* (Philadelphia, Presbyterian Board of Publication, 1855), pp. 659–684.

ried by this Assembly into another area, that of foreign missions. Hitherto the Presbyterians had carried on their foreign missions through the American Board. But as suspicion and hostility increased toward Congregationalists in the controversy over the AHMS and New Divinity, the proposal developed of a denominational Board of Foreign Missions under the General Assembly. When the General Assembly's Committee had advised in 1832 against the erection of a denominational board in the face of the ABCFM, there was already in the field a synodical board. Philadelphia Synod joined Pittsburgh in its support, and by the spring of 1835, Pennsylvania Presbyterians were maintaining twenty missionaries through the Western Foreign Mission Society. (The American Board, to which the great bulk of New York Presbyterians were committed, had fifteen times as many men in the field.) Now on the very last afternoon of the 1835 Assembly, when two thirds of the commissioners had already left, a committee was assigned to negotiate with the Pittsburgh Synod about the transfer of the WFMS to the General Assembly's control.

Abolition. Another major topic portentous with future controversy emerged at the Pittsburgh Assembly of 1835 — abolitionism. The rising tide of abolition sentiment that year forced the Assembly to face an issue that it had evaded for more than a decade, and led to a significant realignment of parties in the church. This, it will be recalled, was the third and most important of the chief moral reform programs that were influential in New York Presbyterianism in this period.

There had been antislavery agitation among Presbyterians since the late eighteenth century, and in 1818 the General Assembly had gone on record in condemnation of the institution. Thereafter the touchy issue was avoided by the Assembly until the mid-thirties. The debates in the British Parliament in 1830 over the proposal to abolish West Indian slavery, which were very widely discussed in America, had opened a new phase. The Tappans took it up as a humanitarian cause and wished to add another voluntary society to the benevolent empire in this interest. Public hostility delayed its organization until 1833. Then the New York City Anti-Slavery Society was founded in the Chatham Street Chapel while a mob rioted outside. Its program was "immediate emancipation," by which was meant, after the fashion of Lewis Carroll's Red Queen, "gradual emancipation immediately undertaken." The New York abolitionists went on in December to organize their proposed national society with the same program. They permitted Garrison's already notorious name to be identified with the new venture, and the press and churches were almost unanimously opposed. Lewis Tappan's home was wrecked, and that of Dr. Cox, of the Laight Street Presbyterian Church. The clerks in the Tappan stores were armed to repel threatened attack. The society and program seemed to have little future before it until, like the temperance movement, it was geared into the Finney revival movement in central and western New York.

The most important figure in this assimilation of abolitionism to revival religion was Theodore Dwight Weld, who had been "converted" by Finney while a student at Hamilton. Weld became the center of a group of young converts of the revival who were headed for the ministry. Finney's former pastor, Gale, developed an Oneida Institute on the "manual labor plan," to provide a cheap training for such men. Oneida Presbytery supported it, as did Arthur Tappan, and the project prospered. A theological seminary on the same manual labor basis was proposed. Outside Cincinnati they found land and a charter already designated for a theological seminary by the gift of the Lanes. Weld collected students for the largest seminary class in the United States, many or most of them converts from the New York revivals, from Utica, Auburn, Rochester, a score from Oneida Institute. Tappan secured Lyman Beecher as president, and Lane Seminary was launched.

Weld had become, under the influence of his patron, Stuart, a convinced abolitionist, and he went to work to win over his fellow students. In the famous "Lane debates" of February, 1834, he did so. The news spread across the country, awakening reverberations in other seminaries and colleges. At the May Anniversaries in 1834 in New York a group of frightened educational leaders agreed to suppress such discussions. The Lane trustees expelled Weld, abolished the student antislavery society, and forbade the educational and religious projects among the free blacks of Cincinnati, which the students had begun. But the students, some fifty of them, refused to submit. They moved in a body to the proposed new college and seminary in the woods at Oberlin. Arthur Tappan supported this enterprise also, lent thousands of dollars, and persuaded Finney to leave the Broadway Tabernacle to become president. Thus in the spring of 1835, Finney was reunited with his New York converts in Oberlin and on a platform of abolition.

Weld, meanwhile, had become field agent of the American Anti-Slavery Society, and spent 1834–1835 conducting abolition revivals in Ohio. He used the protracted meeting technique, speaking two to five hours a night for a week or two or three. He usually began in a Presbyterian church but often had to find other accommodations. He was mobbed and stoned, even in the pulpit, but he regularly converted his opponents, ending his final address by having those stand who were ready to take the abolitionist pledge. Weld thus established some thirty local abolitionist centers in Ohio, the first time the abolitionist movement succeeded in rooting itself in local communities. It was done among church people and with the Finney technique. Weld drew in his former fellow students, so that eventually some thirty of them became AASS agents, the backbone of the effective staff of the society. Four synods in the old Northwest Territory declared against slavery as sin in 1835.

In New York State a state antislavery society was organized in October, 1835, in Utica. There were very few sympathizers in the city, and many protests. When the convention assembled in the Bleecker Street Presbyterian Church, a mob gathered outside and raised a great din with bells, gunfire, and hooting. Despite the uproar, a proposed constitution was adopted.

By the following spring the AASS was convinced that no other form of propaganda could be compared with Weld's type of campaign based on the conception that slaveholding was a sin to be denounced rather than an evil to be remedied. Weld was instructed to select a list of seventy missionaries and put them to work. And he himself campaigned in New York, beginning in the Utica church from which the first state convention had been driven in the spring. Weld won the city in sixteen nights. He went to Buffalo and Rochester and won them also. Troy, however, defeated him. Beaten and stoned for days, he was determined on martyrdom but was forced out of the city by the authorities. The whole campaign, however, consolidated in New York the strongest of the state antislavery societies, making the state the center of the abolitionist movement. After 1837 the revivalist type of abolition disintegrated. But it had left in New York and elsewhere a current of opinion that would play a major part in national history in the following three decades. The American Anti-Slavery Society as a whole was described by a Methodist as "an important link in the great chain of operations of the Presbyterian and Congregational churches." [22]

Weld had interrupted his work in the spring of 1835 to lobby at the General Assembly in Pittsburgh. At the end of the sessions he reported triumphantly that he had lined up forty-seven commissioners, nearly a quarter of the whole Assembly. Most of these were from New York, Ohio, and western Pennsylvania, and they were predominantly New School men. From some of the synods in these areas further antislavery resolutions were to come that fall, including the Synods of Utica, Genesee, and Western Reserve. And the Assembly itself had been driven to take the first action on the subject since 1818. A representative committee under the chairman-

[22] Barnes, *op. cit.*, p. 90.

ship of Professor Miller, of Princeton, was appointed to make a general inquiry into slaveholding in the Presbyterian Church and to report to the Assembly of 1836.

The response in the South was swift and radical. In the very years since 1830 when the abolitionist movement had been organizing in the North, the Southern justification for slavery had taken on new dimensions. The Nat Turner slave rising of 1831 had sent a tremor of panic through all slave territory. And from 1833, Southern clergy, led by the Presbyterians, developed vigorously a Biblical apologetic for slavery. Consequently, in the months after the Assembly of 1835, about a dozen Southern presbyteries adopted declarations that the Assembly had no authority to legislate on the subject assigned to the Miller committee, and they served notice that they would withdraw if it were even discussed by the Assembly.

A division of the church on slavery lines, however, was the last thing the Old School militants wanted, for it would leave the Northern church in the control of the New School. The Old School militants recognized that they could win their campaign only with Southern support and by going to meet Southern terms on slavery. With some local exceptions, the South was prevailingly Old School in theology, but not polemically so.

The General Assembly of 1836. Consequently, when the General Assembly met in 1836, it had to deal with two distinct, explosive controversies, each quite capable of splitting the church along its own peculiar fault lines. The doctrine and polity controversy would find its focus in the organization of mission boards and the Barnes heresy case. The slavery issue was to be posed by the report of the Miller committee.

At the opening of the Assembly the Old School were able to elect the Moderator, and their choice was significant — a Southerner and a slaveholder, John Witherspoon. The Miller committee had been unable to find middle ground in this matter and submitted majority and minority reports. For some days a schism on slavery lines hung in the balance until at length a substantial majority voted to postpone action. Some of the Southern commissioners walked out even so, as instructed. The intransigents on the other side who recorded " Protests " against such postponement were, however, all New School men. The Southern leaders were to demonstrate in the post-Assembly OS Convention that they had noticed this phenomenon. At that time the decisive antiabolitionist-Old School alliance was cemented. But we must also note how the actions of the Assembly on the Board controversy and the heresy trials developed.

The New School majority defeated the arrangements made with the Synod of Pittsburgh for the transfer of its Western Foreign Missionary Society to Assembly control, by 110 to 106. They remained satisfied in their traditional relation to the ABCFM, on which Board there were at that time a majority of Presbyterians. Thus the confessionalists were not permitted a board of their own for foreign missions as had been done for home missions in 1828. The Assembly held " whatever advantages or disadvantages may have resulted from the divisions of the church into numerous denominations, with conflicting opinions, it cannot be our duty, as Christians, to perpetuate and extend these divisions by incorporating them in our arrangements to spread the gospel in heathen lands." The Presbyterian Church would more effectively obey the missionary commission by uniting with other denominations in the work.[23]

In similar fashion the OS party found itself frustrated in its effort to discipline Albert Barnes for heresy. This was, of course, the second time Barnes was put in peril before the Assembly. The occasion was his continuing publications. Since 1832 he had been writing a series of popular exegetical volumes for the use of Sabbath school teachers, a series that was to sell eventually over a million copies. When the case finally came before the Assembly it occupied more time than any previous trial in Assembly history. And the votes on the case

[23] *Minutes of the General Assembly,* 1836, p. 292.

give some indication of theological opinion in various parts of the church.

In the trial it became apparent that a substantial section of the New School were not only ready to extend Barnes room within the permissible latitude of interpretation but actually agreed with him in many of his opinions. Thomas Skinner declared that this was the trial of a thousand ministers, or "perhaps a majority of this Assembly." [24] And Absalom Peters, whose representative character is indicated by the fact that he had been the NS candidate for Moderator, affirmed, "I not only adhere to the doctrines, but for the most part, to the very language of Mr. Barnes's book." [25] The vote of 134 to 96 indicates that the NS voted almost unanimously to sustain the appeal. There were seven New York Presbyteries which voted against Barnes's ideas: Albany, Londonderry, Bedford, Hudson, New York First, New York Second, and Long Island Second. The rest of New York, some twenty-four presbyteries, including the Synods of Genesee, Geneva, and Utica entire, and the larger part of Albany and New York Synods, supported Barnes in the three recorded votes. The New York State count was 60 to 15, a ratio of 4 to 1. And the New York NS votes were just about half of the total on that side.

Although several of the charges were shown to be based on false constructions, and although Barnes had modified his language on some points, it was quite clear that he taught views divergent from the Confessions in several particulars. He was not a strict confessionalist, but of the Hopkinsian or perhaps even New Haven school on original sin and imputation, and maintained the governmental conception of the atonement rather than that of penal substitution. The real question was, as Barnes himself had stated, whether such opinions could be held within the Westminster "system of doctrine."

The outraged OS minority continued in caucus after the ad-

---

[24] N.Y. Observer, September 10, 1836.
[25] [A. Peters], Plea for Voluntary Societies (New York, Taylor, 1837), p. 143.

journment of the Assembly of 1836. The exculpation of Barnes had seemed to demonstrate the impossibility of enforcing their Standards of confessional orthodoxy by disciplinary measures. The New School had refused to give them a denominational Board of Missions, and they suspected there were plans for a NS coup with the existing Boards of Missions and Education and the Directors of Princeton. The abolitionist contingent of the New School were certain to reopen their irreconcilable feud with the South. Trust and respect were gone, and the OS leaders could see no alternative to a rupture. Some were for immediate secession, but the majority preferred a last desperate effort to capture the next Assembly and thus be in a position to set the terms of the division.

The greatest embarrassment to the war party was the influential Princeton faculty with its obstinate refusal to approve revolutionary measures. At length a deputation called on the faculty privately in the fall and delivered an ultimatum. The committee was prepared to abandon Princeton and launch an uncompromisingly OS seminary, for which they had a site and directors chosen and the assurance of Lenox money. Thereafter the professors played their expected roles in the strategy of the militants.

The Princeton faculty may have been assisted in their reorientation by a consideration of the opening of the Union Theological Seminary in New York City. This was essentially the creation of the NS Third Presbytery, to which seven of the ten first clerical Directors belonged, including such conspicuous leaders as Thomas Skinner, Absalom Peters, and William Patton. The first classes assembled in December, 1836, and the seminary promised from the beginning to provide heavier competition for Princeton than Auburn had been able to give. If there were to be also a new strong OS seminary, Princeton might well suffer.

The General Assembly of 1837. In May, 1837, the OS convention met before the Assembly in Philadelphia to agree on ways and means of effecting the division. The South was strongly represented in accordance with the strategy developed since the last Assembly, and Professor Baxter, of Richmond, was made president of the convention. Two or three different proposals as to procedure were debated inconclusively, but the basis of common action with the South was definitely established. The only workable platform would be an agreement to prevent any Assembly action on the subject of slavery whatever, and on this formula the bargain was evidently closed. Breckenridge drafted a new "Testimony and Memorial," listing ten irregularities in church order, five disciplinary abuses, sixteen doctrinal errors, and calling for the discountenancing of the American Home Mission Society and the American Education Society, the abrogation of the Plan of Union, and the immediate citation, trial, and correction or separation of all individuals, churches, presbyteries, or synods guilty of error or disorder.[26]

When the Assembly was organized the convention learned with unspeakable relief that they held a comfortable majority. The "Testimony and Memorial," with its proposal for citation and trial of unsound members, was at once put before the Assembly. And the first resolution based on the memorial that came to the vote abrogated the Plan of Union as unconstitutional because it had never been submitted to the presbyteries. The Plan was declared to have "opened wide the floodgates of error and fanaticism." The churches formed under it had "always opposed the Boards of Education and of Missions, and the efforts toward reform, and the suppression of errors and of schismatical contentions." [27]

The proposal for the citation and trial was developed slowly, and concurrently with it negotiations for amicable separation were carried on. At this juncture Professor Baxter proposed to the convention a legal device that had occurred to him. He

[26] Samuel J. Baird, *Collection of the Acts . . . of the Presbyterian Church*, rev. ed., 1855, pp. 712–715.

[27] *Minutes of the General Assembly*, 1837, pp. 421, 458.

had observed that practically all the judicatories suspected of unsound doctrine (and tainted with abolition) were in Plan of Union territory. The Plan of Union had just been abrogated as unconstitutional from the beginning. What then was the status of ecclesiastical bodies erected on such a basis? Must they not be declared also outside the Constitution of the church?

So it was done. "By the operation of the abrogation of the Plan of Union" the Synods of Western Reserve, Utica, Geneva, and Genesee were resolved by the Assembly to be no longer parts of the Presbyterian Church. The urgency of the action was explained in part by "the gross disorders which are ascertained to have prevailed in those Synods." But because there were reported to be "several churches and ministers, if not one or two presbyteries" in the area "strictly Presbyterian in doctrine and order," the Assembly directed all such to apply for admission.[28] The resolutions had "exscinded" some six hundred churches and five hundred ministers, three fourths of them in New York State. The apparatus of citation and trial was thus rendered superfluous.

Breckenridge, who had been a lawyer, knew what he was doing. As he said in the course of the debate on the resolutions to cut off the four synods, "Moderator, I am aware the Constitution makes no provision for acts like these, but the fact is, we have the power in our hands now, and we must use it." [29] It was an ecclesiastical *coup d'état* rendered necessary, it was thought, by the desperate situation. It would also be necessary, of course, to defend elaborately the constitutionality of the action, and this was done for years.

The "Circular Letter" of the Assembly explained that "one of the most formidable evils of the present crisis is the wide spread and ever restless spirit of *radicalism,* manifest both in

[28] *Ibid.,* p. 445.
[29] [G. N. Judd], *History of the Division of the Presbyterian Church* (New York, M. W. Dodd, 1852), p. 153; cf. [A Member of the Presbytery of Newark] *The Other Side: No. II,* Newark, 1850, p. 7.

the church and in the state. Its leading principle everywhere seems to be to level all order to the dust." Without using the word "abolition," the letter continued: "It has, in succession, driven to extreme fanaticism the great causes of revivals of religion, of temperance, and of the rights of man. It has aimed to transmute our pure faith into destructive heresy, our scriptural order into confusion and misrule. It has crowded many of our churches with ignorant zealots and unholy members; driven our pastors from their flocks, and with strange fire consumed the heritage of the Lord, filling our churches with confusion and our judicatories with conflict; making our venerated name and beloved institutions, so far as its fearful influence extends, a hissing and a byword before the American people; and even threatening the dissolution of our national Union, as well as the dismemberment of the Presbyterian Church." [30]

The Assembly bore its testimony against the errors of doctrine, infractions of order, and practical abuses of the "Testimony and Memorial" with the implication that these were widely prevalent in the exscinded bodies. Five other largely NS synods, Albany, New Jersey, Michigan, Cincinnati, and Illinois, were directed to take special action on errors of doctrine or church order and to report in writing to the Assembly of 1838. The "elective affinity" Presbytery of Philadelphia was dissolved. The Board question was also settled decisively. The Western Foreign Missionary Society was taken over as the Assembly's Board of Foreign Missions, and the American Home Missionary Society and American Education Society were advised to cease operations in the Presbyterian Church. Against the whole series of actions no less than eight formal "Protests" were written into the record, including an important statement of NS theology. [31]

The excision of 1837 was predicated, as Beecher observed at the time, on the support of the South over the slavery issue.

[30] *Minutes of the General Assembly,* 1837, pp. 507–508.
[31] *Ibid.,* pp. 484–486.

Every one of the exscinded synods had defined slaveholding as sin, and these were the largest synods that had done so. These were undoubtedly the considerations that swung the South, hitherto divided over the "Act and Testimony" and over Barnes, to vote as a unit. It is probably too much to say that "had it not been for the developments concerning slavery in the Assemblies of 1835–1836 the break would never have occurred." [32] It would almost certainly have occurred over doctrinal and polity matters, but instead of an excision of New York Presbyterians, it would probably have come as a secession of Pennsylvania Presbyterians.

The Auburn Convention. How did the New York churches respond to this sudden blow? They were wholly taken aback. Many had expected trouble at the Assembly, but no one had foreseen anything like this court-martial. Now what should they do? The OS leaders generally expected and hoped that they would disintegrate as judicatories, some falling over to Congregationalism and a few Presbyterian remnants submitting to close scrutiny and readmission. And the new Congregational General Association of New York did issue an invitation to the injured churches. On the other side some few churches felt that they were obliged to submit to General Assembly rulings even when unjust and unwise.

Two months after the revolutionary Assembly a convention met in the heart of Geneva, the largest exscinded synod, in the First Presbyterian Church of Auburn. It included 178 delegates and members from the four exscinded synods, with other sympathizers from New York, Albany, Philadelphia, New Jersey, and other synods. Professor Richards, of Auburn Seminary, was elected chairman, and the Union and Lane faculty and directors were well represented. Here a course was set with gratifying unanimity.

The Auburn delegates refused to accept their exile from the

[32] C. B. Staiger, "Abolition and the Presbyterian Schism," *Mississippi Valley Historical Review*, December, 1949, pp. 392, 414.

Presbyterian Church. They protested against the Exscinding Acts as unconstitutional and of no effect. They urged their churches, consequently, to remain in present relations and to send representatives to the General Assembly of 1838. And they adopted several reports that set forth various aspects of their situation and views, expanding the arguments offered in the many "Protests" registered in the 1837 Assembly.

In a "Report on the Facts of the Formation of the Churches in the Exscinded Synods," it was shown that not a synod or presbytery had been formed on the basis of the Plan of Union. All the synods and presbyteries had been Constitutionally erected with no reference to the Plan of Union. And only a few individual churches had been formed on the Plan. The imperfectly Presbyterian churches of New York were patterned after the Accommodation Plan approved by the General Assembly in 1808, which was still in force. They were imperfect in that they lacked a session and elders, but instead conducted business and discipline by the male church members. Even these, however, were less than one third of all the churches in the attainted New York synods. Perhaps a handful of presbyteries were predominantly semi-Congregationalist, but no synods. And all the ministers were regular Presbyterians.

The bearing of the Plan of Union was thus shown to be highly dubious on the exscinded synods and presbyteries. In addition, it was argued that an abrogation of such an agreement as the Plan of Union could not in justice be made retroactive so as to affect rights and institutions created by it. These previously Congregational churches had been admitted by the presbyteries under instructions from the General Assembly, and the presbyteries themselves had been recognized as fully legitimate for years. The only Constitutional way of cutting off such sections would have been the procedure of citation and trial. The General Assembly had no power to complete such an action in one set of sittings without reference to presbyteries.

For our purposes the declarations on doctrine and conditions in the exscinded synods are at least as important as the

Constitutional questions. The reports did not deny that there had been disorders and doctrinal aberrations within the bounds of the four synods, largely associated with the revivals. But they declared, " Such errors and irregularities have never been sanctioned by these synods or presbyteries" and that when known such departures were subject to corrections. The " epidemic radicalism" charged against them, had " appeared, for the most part, in such forms as would have rendered the effort to repress them by immediate coercive discipline the sure means of their propagation and the division of the churches. They were not, however, tolerated, but prayerfully resisted from the pulpit and the press, and in Presbyteries by arguments, resolutions, and expostulations, and the result of this was the formation in our churches of a correct public sentiment, before which these ephemeral epidemics have passed and are passing away, as no coercive discipline could have driven them. These Synods have been exiled from the Church as delinquents, while in fact they have been occupied in a discreet and successful performance of their duty, in circumstances of great delicacy and difficulty." [33]

With regard to doctrine, the members of the convention declared the faith of their synods and presbyteries to be represented by a cordial adoption of the Westminster Confession under the terms of the Adopting Act of 1729, which provided for scrupling of items that were esteemed by the presbyteries to be not essential or necessary.

On material points the Auburn Convention adopted as the statement for their churches the list of " true doctrines" drawn up for the " Protest" against the Assembly's resolutions on doctrinal errors by Baxter Dickinson at the Assembly. This was to be in effect the doctrinal platform of the New School throughout its existence, and of its reconciliation with the Old, so that it constitutes the most important official or semiofficial doctrinal formulation of the Presbyterian Church since the

[33] *Minutes of the Auburn Convention,* pp. 28, 20–21.

Adopting Act itself.[34] It was in general an exposition of Hop-
kinsian doctrine on the sixteen points raised by Breckenridge.
In addition, the Report identified the most widely used theo-
logical authorities of the New School as Jonathan Edwards,
John Witherspoon, Timothy Dwight, Dr. Smalley, and Andrew
Fuller, and the Biblical commentators Henry Doddridge and
Thomas Scott.

Apparently the Old School also generally accepted the Auburn Declaration as fair and adequate, both in 1837 and 1838
when they condemned it, and in 1868–1870 when they accepted it. The New School, on the other hand, had never accepted as fair statements any of the Old School syllabi of errors, from the "Western Memorial" on to the "Testimony and
Memorial." All of them had been disfigured by misrepresenta-
tions.

The Two Assemblies, 1838. The last scene of the drama was
enacted in the spring of 1838 at the organization of the General Assembly. Both "schools" held caucuses shortly before
the opening date, and negotiations occurred as well as infor-
mal personal conferences. The NS caucus pursued the policy
laid down at Auburn of seeking a nullification of the Exscinding Acts as unconstitutional, and a return to the church. The
Old School was adamant; whatever doubts some among them
had about the constitutionality of the Exscinding Acts as such,
they were as a party vastly relieved at the division and had no
intention of reopening the issue.

What were the NS commissioners to do? If they submitted
to the Exscinding Acts, they must then petition for examination
and admission to whatever judicatories the Old School might
set up within the bounds, on some such extra-Constitutional
test as the "Testimony and Memorial" doctrinal statement.
They could be sure that a substantial portion of their churches
would be denied restoration if only to prevent the possibility

    [34] E. D. Morris, "The Auburn Declaration," *Presbyterian Quarterly
and Princeton Review,* V (1876), 5–40.

of any future NS majority. These churches would be cast loose to seek affiliation elsewhere. Thus synods, presbyteries, and sometimes individual congregations would be split, and at least two denominations would be left to contest the constituency of New York State Presbyterianism. The work of the church in the area would surely be crippled. For this they were not prepared to make themselves responsible. They must hold together, at least temporarily, as a denomination, while claiming their rightful place as part of the Presbyterian Church.

And they determined to appeal to the civil courts. Under advice of counsel, accordingly, they occasioned an irregular scene at the organization of the Assembly. After repeated vain efforts to force the officers of the Assembly to add the delegates of the exscinded synods to the roll, these men then went through the legal formalities of organizing an assembly while standing in the aisles, and voted to adjourn to the lecture room of Albert Barnes's First Church. Thus were constituted two General Assemblies meeting concurrently in Philadelphia. The NS church contained about four ninths of the ministers and members of the undivided church. Each Assembly set up some skeleton judicatories in territory dominated by the other, and each proceeded to elect Directors of the Boards and in general to carry on the whole business of the church. In such fashion was celebrated the fiftieth anniversary of the founding of the General Assembly!

VI : *The Separated Churches,*

1838–1870

The Exscinding Acts of 1837 bore primarily on New York State Presbyterianism. Over three fourths of the evicted ministers, congregations, and communicants were from this state. After the Auburn Convention and the formation of a New School General Assembly in 1838, further major sections of New York Presbyterianism attached themselves to the ejected synods. Ultimately about five out of six New York Presbyterians were related to the New School denomination, and for the following generation New York Presbyterian history is essentially New School history. This New York section constituted the strongest and most compact portion of the whole New School church, and slightly over half its total constituency in 1839.

Local Divisions. There were a few defections of individual churches and ministers in the bounds of the three expelled synods, both to the Old School church and to Congregationalism. The presbyteries of Rochester and Ontario, indeed, sat loose to the New School General Assembly for a dozen years or so, but they maintained their synodical relations and eventually participated again in the NS Assembly. Some five congregations and eight ministers, scattered over the Presbyteries of Bath, Genesee, Ontario, and Rochester, were collected into a

138

presbytery of "Caledonia," attached to the Synod of New Jersey in the OS statistics for 1839. In the northern part of Utica Synod, meanwhile, three ministers and churches left St. Lawrence Presbytery and were formed into an OS "Ogdensburg" Presbytery. These two nuclei in the bounds of Utica and Genesee Synods were to develop into a small OS synod in the following years.

Albany Synod had not been put out of the church in 1837, although it had been instructed to put its house in order. The bulk of its churches, however, were sympathetic to the three synods to the west. At the first meeting after the formation of the NS Assembly, the synod split. President Eliphalet Nott of Union College led a withdrawal of adherents to the OS Assembly, over a third of the total, to form a separate Synod of Albany (OS). The OS group had a majority in only one presbytery, that of Albany, and its only significant minority was in Troy Presbytery. Columbia and Champlain went New School entire, together with four fifths of the churches in Troy Presbytery. Most of Albany Synod thus adhered to the NS church, although there remained a group of some thirty Old School congregations in the Mohawk and Hudson Valleys, including some of the strongest churches in the cities of Albany, Troy, and Schenectady.

The remaining synod within the territory of the state, that of New York, similarly divided into two synods in the fall of 1838. An attempt at an amicable separation was made by having all delegates declare which assembly they recognized. Over half of the NS delegates, however, refused to do so on the ground that such an action would by implication recognize the legitimacy of the Exscinding Acts. In the end each school organized as a "Synod of New York," the Old School holding a bare majority of three votes. The rearrangement of presbyteries was complicated, since North River, Hudson, and New York Second were all split, the majority of the second and last going Old School, of the first, New School. Long Island First and New York Third went New School, whereas Bedford, Long

Island Second, and New York First adhered to the Old. The New School Synod erected a new Presbytery of Brooklyn, with four churches. There was also some relocation of individual congregations among these reorganized presbyteries.

There were also distressing divisions within individual congregations in various parts of the state. The First Church of Brooklyn, whose pastor was the fiery Samuel Cox (NS), was a conspicuous instance. In the end each Assembly listed a "First Church of Brooklyn."

1. THE NEW SCHOOL CHURCH IN NEW YORK

One of the most striking aspects of the history of the New School church is exhibited in its membership statistics. The figures rose from 100,000 in 1839 to 145,000 in 1846. Then there was a net loss, and the figure of 145,000 was not again attained for two decades. Only during the Civil War did the church again grow. But at a time when the population as a whole was rapidly increasing, the church membership was static, a phenomenon resembling that of the separate life of the eighteenth-century Old Side church.

One would not expect much change in the presbyterial structure of the New School church in these decades of little growth, and this was largely the case. The five original synods were increased to seven by subdivision, adding Susquehanna in 1853 (Otsego, Chenango, and Delaware presbyteries) and Onondaga in 1855 (Onondaga, Cayuga, Cortland, Tioga presbyteries), but none of these constituent presbyteries were new. New York Synod meanwhile became the Synod of New York and New Jersey. The only new presbyteries of the period were Brooklyn (1838), Ithaca (1839), Catskill (1852), and Lyons (1856). The contrast was thus very marked with the expansion of the generation before the schism.

There were, however, five or six changes of names. Utica Presbytery appeared in 1843 as a daughter of Oneida. Three years later the two were rejoined under the name of Utica, whereby the name of Oneida disappeared, "almost sacrilegiously." [1] The Synod of Geneva changed Bath to Steuben and Pennsylvania to Wellsborough in 1862. In 1858, Genesee changed Angelica to Genesee Valley, adding a few churches from Buffalo Presbytery. In 1845 the Synod of New York and New Jersey changed the name of the NS Second Presbytery of New York to the Fourth Presbytery of New York, and strengthened it by transferring some ministers and churches from the Third Presbytery.

Population Movements. One important cause of the lack of growth of the church was sociological. There was a rapid net growth of population in the state in these years, resulting in a total of nearly four millions, over one million of them in the metropolitan area, by 1861. But by that date nearly a million more had also left the state, especially to the Old Northwest. Of those who had come into the state to replace these losses, one million were foreign-born, chiefly Irish and German. The losses were chiefly in the villages and countryside, the gains in the industrial cities. Hundreds of townships actually lost population between 1830 and 1860. [2] The turnover of population is illustrated in the case of one city by the fact that nearly 70 percent of the names in the Rochester Directory for 1827 had moved on before 1834. [3] Those who left were, in general, of the New England background where the Presbyterian Church was strongest; those who replaced them were from European societies least congenial to Presbyterianism. The result was that in these decades the church did not maintain its strength relative to the growth of population, while by 1861 the Roman Catholic Church had gained from relative insignificance to become the largest single denomination in the state.

In the cities, of course, the church grew, but not enough to

---

[1] Philemon H. Fowler, *Presbyterianism in Central New York,* p. 9.

[2] David M. Ellis, *et al., Short History of New York State* (Ithaca, Cornell University Press, 1957), p. 281.

[3] *Ibid.,* p. 291.

make up its losses in the countryside. In 1861, in cities like New York, Buffalo, Rochester, the foreign-born constituted nearly half the total. New York was the largest Irish city after Dublin, and there were few churches less appealing to Irish Roman Catholics than the Presbyterian. The number of churches in New York City increased rapidly, but scarcely in proportion to the population, which almost quadrupled between 1825 and 1855,[4] while Brooklyn leaped from 10,000 to 205,000.

The synods and presbyteries were aware of the problem. The records of the Synods of Genesee, Geneva, Susquehanna, and Albany refer repeatedly to depletions by emigration through the forties and fifties. The losses were the more serious in that those who left were generally the younger and more enterprising members. Viewed from another perspective, of course, the type of Presbyterianism characteristic of New York was extending its influence nationally, especially in the states of the old Northwest Territory.

Revivals. Revivalism had been the means of the rapid expansion of churches at the peak of New England immigration. It was less successful during the turnover of population. Frequent revivals, it was noted, were needed merely to hold even, and they were not in fact so frequent. Amid all the controversy of 1837 and 1838, to be sure, revivals were relatively widespread within the bounds of the ejected synods. The churches were now more cautious about itinerants. Much was done by regular pastors, such as Orton, Wisner, and Avery, who took leave for revival campaigns. A general movement was perceptible again in 1842 and 1843, but thereafter followed a long dry spell. The narratives of religion of synods and presbyteries consistently lamented the low estate of vital religion for more than a decade after 1843, up to the Great Revival of 1857–1858. It may also be significant that Finney no longer seemed wel-

4 *Ibid.,* p. 280.

come in the 1850's. His theology, of course, was now in its "perfectionist" phase, and much more definitely heterodox than it had been in the 1830's. It may also be that his style of preaching was now passé. In any case Rome and Rochester would not invite him.

The Great Revival of 1857–1858 arose and spread at first without benefit of itinerants and professionals. It was distinguished by the leadership of laymen. The characteristic pattern was that of the interdenominational noonday prayer meeting. It had grown up around systematic visitation evangelism sponsored in New York City by the Sunday School Union. Some two thousand laymen were enlisted in this work in 1857, and out of their preparatory meetings the revival spread. The "testimony" of the lay workers was more characteristic than the sermon of the revivalist, and the lay temper was evident in the stress on practical service and the depreciation of denominational theology. The financial panic doubtless played a role in setting a psychological atmosphere. The peak of intensity was reached in the first six months of 1858. Virtually every denomination was affected, and the movement spread from the cities to the town and country churches. An embodiment of the genius of the revival of 1858 was the Young Men's Christian Association, a movement of laymen from all evangelical denominations, with a double concern for evangelism and for practical humanitarian service. The same spirit was to animate the United States Christian Commission after the war broke out, as an organization to minister to the spiritual and physical needs of the troops.

During the war, despite all its distractions, the New School church experienced many revivals and began to record net gains in membership. The tendency increased after the war, and the last half decade of the sixties was the period of greatest prosperity in the separate life of that church. In five years the church increased by almost as much as had been added in the previous quarter century. One of the most conspicuous revivalists of the period was William E. Boardman, wartime secretary of the U. S. Christian Commission, who became a full-time evangelist thereafter. A Lane graduate, Boardman's views were in fact close to those of Finney, both in his fusion of conversion and humanitarianism, and in his perfectionism.

Perfectionism remained, in fact, the chief theological threat in the early years of the New School church, as in the preceding decade. Congregationalists also were distressed by the developments at Oberlin, where Finney and Mahan propagated a new version of perfect sanctification quite incompatible with the Westminster Confession. There was a large contingent of New Yorkers at Oberlin, and the *Oberlin Evangelist* was widely read in the state. The Synods of Genesee, Geneva, New York and New Jersey, and presbyteries in Onondaga and Susquehanna Synods all warned against the Oberlin variety of perfectionism. A minister was disciplined in North River for preaching " entire perfection." On appeal, the Synod of New York and New Jersey decided unanimously that no Presbyterian minister could hold or teach such views.[5]

What is most striking about this story is the rather sudden reconciliation of the New School church, if not to Oberlinism, at least to Methodism. The Assembly of 1849 approved the exchange of delegates with Methodist bodies and the Synods of Geneva and New York and New Jersey were soon exchanging with the Oneida Conference of The Methodist Episcopal Church. Other Presbyterian bodies followed. Was this reversal a result of the influence of the Evangelical Alliance and the enthusiasm for church unity of the middle forties? In any case, it represented the bridging of a theological divergence hitherto viewed as serious.

The Voluntary Societies. A major theme of the history of the New School church is its changing relation to the voluntary societies. The benevolent empire, which was so conspicuous on the American religious scene in the twenties and thirties,

[5] MS. Minutes of the Synod of New York and New Jersey, 1843, p. 121.

suffered two mortal injuries in 1837. The effects of the Old School attack and the Presbyterian schism we must consider further. But the panic and depression of 1837, which were particularly ruinous in New York, crippled the empire financially. Banks failed; factories closed; construction was suspended on canals and railroads; something like one third of the whole labor force was unemployed. The interlocking directorate of New York philanthropists was decimated by bankruptcies such as that of Arthur and Lewis Tappan. Contributions fell off for all benevolent causes, including church boards and voluntary societies. Some of the societies collapsed altogether and even the strongest, such as the American Home Missionary Society, went on Spartan rations.

This weakening of the central organization of the benevolent empire in New York City did not, to be sure, seriously affect the pattern of congregational activities through societies. Many of the societies survived and continued to command the support of the churches. Their representatives were often heard in New School church judicatories. The older societies were even joined in the forties and fifties by newcomers, four of which may be noticed. The American Peace Society was most successful at the time of the Mexican War, which was widely deprecated in New York as a step in the expansion program of the slave empire. The Society for the Promotion of Collegiate and Theological Education at the West, or The College Society, was created to pool the askings of a group of Presbyterian-Congregational colleges and seminaries in the old Northwest. The American and Foreign Christian Union was a combination of three earlier organizations for missions to the "two hundred millions in the Romish corporation under the dominion of the Man of Sin." [6] New York synods repeatedly commended this work to their churches and also called attention in the 1850's and 1860's to the dangers to civil liberty from Roman Catholic expansion. They were chiefly disturbed by the attacks on the public school system and Bishop

[6] *Ibid.*, 1855, p. 501.

Hughes' campaign to secure public subsidy for Roman Catholic schools and other institutions.

New School Presbyterians were also conspicuous in the launching of the Evangelical Alliance, which might be described as the voluntary-society approach to " ecumenical evangelism." Of the nearly seventy Americans who went to London in 1846, Robert Baird, Samuel Cox, William Patton, and Lyman Beecher were perhaps the most active, and all were Presbyterian. Six men went from the Synod of New York and New Jersey alone. This synod, to be sure, was at the chief point of overseas contact and always had more of such relations than other parts of the church. But there was also a special congeniality here. The Evangelical Alliance represented much of the strongly evangelistic, denominationally inclusive and cooperative spirit of New School Presbyterianism. It was ironical that British abolitionism prevented full American participation, for almost all the Americans there were outspoken opponents of slavery. After the Civil War, as we shall see, New School Presbyterians were to lead again in the Evangelical Alliance movement.

But despite this continuation and even expansion of the system of voluntary nondenominational societies, their rationale had been severely damaged by the church struggle of the late thirties.[7] The benevolent system rested on an etherealized notion of an interdenominational but generically Calvinist national church, which was characteristic especially of New Englanders. It had been kept at a high emotional pitch of millennial optimism by the revivals. But the bitter attacks from the confessional exclusiveness of the Old School shredded the dream to tatters. Congregationalists and New School Presbyterians reluctantly accepted denominational and geographical definitions and status for societies they had habitually labeled " American."

The New School synods had on excision reaffirmed their

[7] Cf. E. A. Smith, " The Forming of a Modern American Denomination," *Church History*, March, 1962, pp. 74–99.

commitment on principle to the cooperative agencies, specifically the American Home Missionary Society and the American Education Society, so bitterly attacked by the Old School. The NS Assembly emphatically commended the voluntary societies in 1838 and in 1840 passed an extended resolution in favor of the American Home Missionary Society, American Bible Society, American Education Society, American Board of Commissioners for Foreign Missions, American Tract Society, and the American Sabbath School Union.[8] The New York State synods took similar action and reaffirmed it through the 1840's, and in some cases into the 1850's. But from the 1840's the operations of these societies were increasingly handicapped by the rise of denominationalism, both Congregational and Presbyterian. The New School had been expelled in part for its loyalty to the policy of cooperation with the Congregationalists, with the Plan of Union, the Accommodation Plans, the AHMS, the AES, the ABCFM. The irony of the situation was that just as they had been forced into separate denominational life on this basis, the ground for such cooperation was undermined. From this point of view New School history up to the Civil War is the story of the increasing estrangement of Presbyterians and Congregationalists, and the gradual dismantling of the organizations and agencies of their cooperation. The process was contrary to the traditions and feelings of the churches, who had been arguing for years against the policy of strictly denominational agencies. It took half a generation to push the NS church to equip itself hesitantly and regretfully with denominational boards and agencies. One suspects that some explanation of the lack of growth of membership is to be found here, both in relative lack of vigorous efficiency and in seepage to the renascent Congregationalists.

We may begin with the formal relations of Presbyterians and Congregationalists. The OS majority in the General Assembly had sought to abrogate the Plan of Union in 1835 and had de-

---

[8] *Minutes of the General Assembly,* NS, 1840, pp. 21–22.

clared it null and void in 1837. But the accommodation plans, which were the actual basis of most of the combination arrangements, remained in force in much of New York, and indeed the exscinded synods intended to maintain the Plan of Union also.

There were a number of churches, consequently, which retained Congregational government internally, while functioning as members of presbyteries. Some Congregational churches, on the other hand, remained independent as churches, while their pastors were members of presbytery. There were also instances of Congregational churches newly establishing such accommodation relations after 1837, others that became wholly Presbyterian, and also "Presbygational" churches that acquired sessions and became fully Presbyterian, a trend noted before the schism.

The new development in the situation thereafter was the movement in the opposite direction, back to Congregationalism. The district and state associations of Congregationalism expanded in this period, to a considerable degree, at the expense of Presbyterianism and "Presbygationalism." The proselyting pressure they exerted was a continual threat to the integrity of the New School presbyteries, in the 1840's and 1850's. The corresponding delegates no longer functioned effectively as ministers of reconciliation.[9] Fowler, writing in 1877, reported thirty-one churches in central New York that had left presbyteries for Congregational associations.[10] There were probably at least as many more in other parts of the state. Perhaps as important as the loss of whole congregations was the disaffection of families and individuals. And one can only speculate as to how many of the emigrants ended up in the Congregational rather than Presbyterian churches of the Midwest. Accurate statistics can no longer be compiled, but it seems more than likely that in the 1840's and 1850's New York Presbyterianism lost more to Congregationalism than it gained.

---

[9] *Ibid.*, 1851, pp. 36–38. [10] Fowler, *op. cit.*, p. 68.

In the case of both Presbyterians and Congregationalists, denominational pressure developed most strongly in the Midwest. Congregational State Associations developed in New York in 1834, in the Western Reserve in 1836, in Iowa in 1840. In the 1840's the rising sectarian feeling made it difficult for Congregationalists and Presbyterians to work or worship together effectively in joint bodies. The newly militant Midwestern Congregationalism held a convention at Michigan City in 1846 and declared itself opposed to the Plan of Union.

The year after this Congregational repudiation, the NS General Assembly heard an extended memorial on the need of aggressive Presbyterian work in home missions in the West. Three years later the report of a special committee, and the actions based on it by the Assembly of 1852, marked an epoch in the life of the NS church. The Assembly authorized standing committees on home missions and the support of ministerial education in all presbyteries and synods. These local organizations were to work with the central offices of the AHMS and the AES, and so far as possible to replace the regional interdenominational agencies. This was a hybrid pattern. In the field of doctrinal publications and church extension, where there were no voluntary societies already in the field, a denominational organization was set up on the national level as well as in the synods and presbyteries. Thus arose, in effect, the first "boards" of the NS denomination.[11] Men like Beman fought against this whole trend in vain.

Five months after the Presbyterian Assembly of 1852 had thus at last begun to organize its own boards, there convened in Albany the first denominationwide gathering of Congregationalists since the Cambridge Synod of 1648. Conspicuous on its roll were names that had been eminent in preceding decades in New York Presbyterianism — Dirck Lansing, William Patton, Lewis Tappan, Joshua Leavitt, R. B. Cheever. The Convention disavowed sectarian zeal, but displayed a vivid

---

11 *Minutes of the General Assembly*, NS, 1852, pp. 169–175.

sense of injury. It was alleged that the Plan of Union had cost Congregationalism two thousand churches (which was probably about four times the true figure). "They have milked our Congregational cows, but they have made nothing but Presbyterian butter and cheese."[12] The Convention requested a stop to cooperative work under the Plan of Union and urged "Presbygational" churches to insist on their full Congregational rights.

In church extension rivalry was sharp. The Albany Convention voted to raise $50,000 to build Congregational churches in the Midwest, and the next year the NS Assembly authorized a similar fund of $100,000 and a permanent committee. This was the first attempt at a board levy in the NS church, and it was generally approved by the New York synods and presbyteries. Similarly, the question of a permanent committee on ministerial education was hotly debated in the General Assemblies of 1853 and 1854 and then the step was taken. These permanent Assembly Committees of Church Extension and Ministerial Education were designed, it was said, to "supplement" the AHMS and AES. There were frequent assurances that they were not to prejudice cooperation with the Congregationalists. When, for example, the Synod of New York voted to support the new Committee on Church Extension in 1857, it was urged that contributions to the AHMS should not be allowed to suffer.[13] But they did suffer. Presbyterian contributions generally went down, to 32 percent in 1855, 23 percent in 1859, 19 percent in 1861. The AHMS forced the issue by refusing to distribute to Presbyterian causes more than came from Presbyterian sources, and in 1861 the General Assembly finally set up a Committee of Home Missions. The AHMS, nursing mother to upstate New York Presbyterianism, was thus cast off by her children and became a solely Congregational society. It had taken a quarter of a century to disentangle the most notable

12 *Proceedings of the General Convention . . . at Albany*, 1852, p. 71.
13 MS. Minutes of the Synod of New York and New Jersey, 1857, p. 58.

effort at interdenominational cooperation in American church history prior to the twentieth century, and to organize the NS church as a fully-equipped denomination.

From another perspective, however, this protracted and painful separation from Congregationalism removed the occasion for many of the OS objections to the New School. At the time of the excision the OS leaders probably expected the bulk of the NS churches to fall over into Congregationalism. Instead, they maintained their unity on the whole and had withdrawn from the Congregational alliance. There was in 1861 no widespread urge to reunion of Old School and New, but when it should come, it would be found that a large number of difficulties had disappeared with the rupture with Congregationalism.

Auburn and Union Seminaries. The NS church had three theological seminaries, Auburn, Lane, and Union, but none of them had even the precarious financial stability of Princeton. And at least in the early years they had few pretensions to theological scholarship. Through the forties Union had only two professors, and Auburn rarely had its full faculty complement. Salaries were inadequate and irregular. Union came very near closing altogether in 1840 and Auburn actually did so for the year of 1854–1855. But the seminaries did turn out hundreds of ministers and scores of missionaries. Auburn classes averaged from about fifteen to twenty, those of Union from forty to fifty. At the General Assembly of 1857, what was apparently the first Auburn reunion convened, and it was found that a third of the ministerial commissioners were Auburn men. By that time Union had probably about as many alumni as Auburn.

The two New York seminaries drew students chiefly from the upstate area and from New England. The three chief college feeders to Auburn were Hamilton, Union College, and Williams, all strongly evangelical at this time. The most eminent member of the Auburn faculty in these years was probably Dr. Laurens Hickok, who came from Western Reserve to succeed Dr. Richards in theology, and after some years at Auburn, went on to a distinguished career at Union College. Hickok and three other Auburn professors served as Moderators of the Assembly. Albert Barnes served as a Union director for years and once declined a call to an Auburn professorship.

Despite the size of its student body, which was surpassed only by Andover and Princeton Seminaries, Union had difficult sailing for some years. Located on the outskirts of the city (on University Place!), it was kept alive chiefly by good friends in the neighboring Mercer Street Church, where Thomas Skinner was pastor. One of its professors, Edward Robinson, was a philologist and archaeologist of distinction. He had studied in Germany and traveled in the Holy Land. He published lexicons and archaeological works, as well as editing the *Biblical Repository*.

In 1850, Union made a major acquisition in Henry B. Smith, the most effective teacher at Amherst and one of the most gifted theologians in New England. He, too, had studied in Germany and was in a position to bring new perspectives to bear on the rival schools of American Calvinism. Almost at once he became the chief power of the Union faculty and the leading theologian of the NS church, fully able to deal on equal terms with Hodge of Princeton and Park of Andover. In 1853 he was transferred to systematic theology. In 1859 he became editor of *The American Theological Review*. Three years later this was merged with the *Presbyterian Quarterly Review* as the *American Presbyterian and Theological Review*, with Smith as editor. This quarterly was the NS counterpart of Hodge's *Biblical Repertory and Princeton Review*, and through it Smith exercised more influence on the church at large than by his teaching.

Ecclesiastically, as well as theologically, Smith was a prophetic power. He was always prominent in the judicatories of the church, and his influence was for a deeper and more catholic understanding of the church. The sermon he preached as

Moderator in 1864 set the key for the following movement for the reunion of New School and Old, in which he was the most important single leader. He was also the leading American figure in developing an effective relationship with the Evangelical Alliance. He was chairman of the committee to report to the 1866 meeting of that organization and proposed the meeting in New York that eventually occurred in 1873. He probably contributed more than anyone else to bringing this assembly to pass, although he was by the time of its meeting on the verge of retirement due to ill health, and had passed on his role as ecumenical organizer to Philip Schaff.

Sabbatarianism and Temperance. The Presbyterians had no qualms in this generation about seeking legislation in support of their favorite social reforms, Sabbath rest, temperance, and, for some at least, the abolition of slavery. In the forties and fifties, indeed, all these movements turned definitely to political action. All three causes, on the other hand, were opposed by the immigrant and largely Roman Catholic population in the industrial cities, and the Presbyterian political ascendancy became increasingly less effective.

New School and Old School held common ground on the Puritan Sabbath. Ministers preached on Sabbath observance on stated days, and at the beginning of the period, sessions exercised close discipline, at least upstate. Stockholders in steamboat and railroad lines were held responsible for the enforcement of the Fourth Commandment. Even post-office officials were expected to maintain the Decalogue against government orders. In the mid-fifties a campaign of memorials to various railroad companies in the state was mounted. For a time the New York Central responded favorably, but resumed Sunday service in 1856. In New York City it had become apparent by the late forties that the larger community could not be controlled. The synods lamented the fact that even church members were becoming involved in Sunday travel and amusements. Employers, even Christians, it was said, recognized no responsibility for organizing work so that the Sabbath could be observed. The churches, one infers, had largely given up the attempt to enforce discipline in this area, although the clergy still continued to protest.

Abstinence, or temperance as it was still called, remained with Sabbatarianism the nearly universal social reform program of New York Presbyterianism, New School and Old School. The narratives of religion of the various presbyteries and synods almost always noted the relative prosperity of this cause. The judicatories commended the state temperance society repeatedly. Some censured hop-raising and vine-growing. Many churches made abstinence a condition of membership. A system of licensing amounting to local option was adopted in the mid-forties and most upstate towns went dry. There was a marked divergence on this point, however, between the cities and the countryside. The throngs of new immigrants, chiefly Germans and Irish, demanded their saloons, and Horace Greeley estimated seven thousand grogshops in New York City.

In the fifties the movement developed into a campaign for legal prohibition of the sale of intoxicating beverages. The New York State Temperance Society had made this its program, and the passage of such a law by the State of Maine in 1851 gave it great impetus. The Presbyterian synods and the Congregational Convention of 1852 declared for the principle and urged churchmen to vote for legislators who would work for prohibition in New York. Such a bill was passed in 1855 but declared unconstitutional by the Court of Appeals the following year. While still in effect the law was not enforced in the cities, where the authorities feared the political power of the saloonkeepers and the foreign-born vote. The cultural line was already sharp between the upstate, Protestant "dry" and the urban, largely Roman Catholic, and immigrant "wet."

The churches were evidently aware of what they were doing. The Synod of Geneva specifically defended the duty of the Christian citizen to take political action in this sphere.[14] The synod was also aware that enforcement would depend on public opinion, and that the churches must work as hard with the law as without it if anything was to be accomplished. A general decline in temperance, however, was observed after the court ruling against the law, especially during the Civil War.

Abolition. The most explosive of the social issues before the church was, of course, abolition. On this question there were sharp differences within the NS church as a whole, and within its New York sections. There were scarcely any defenders of the institution outright in New York, but there was sufficient divergence of opinion on how to deal with it for bitter controversy. In the 1840's and 1850's neither political parties nor churches in New York were able to enforce conformity to one policy on slavery, and the integrity and effectiveness of both were frequently threatened.

The methods of abolitionist agitation had changed. At the end of the thirties both the American Anti-Slavery Society in New York City and the state society in Utica were bankrupt and ceased to be the chief focuses of activity. The movement had become both more local and more political, concentrating on influencing the elections of state and national legislators and on petition campaigns to the Congress. And in the forties a group of abolitionist congressmen, several of them Presbyterian elders, took the effective leadership of the movement nationally.

The strength of New York State abolitionism lay largely west of Utica, although the national antislavery society had its headquarters in New York City and there were conspicuous leaders there. As we have seen, the exscinded synods had been marked down for expulsion partly because they had been the most vigorous in opposition to slavery before 1837, and they

14 MS. Minutes of the Synod of Geneva, 1854, p. 406.

grew, if anything, more militant in the following decades. The Synod of New York (NS) was badly split, with a majority usually able to vote down the actions urged by the abolitionist wing. Albany Synod (NS), on the other hand, avoided the subject as systematically as the Old School Synods of Albany and New York.

On the level of the local church the abolition controversy often became involved with the problem of defections to Congregationalism. The Congregationalists of New England were on the whole less sympathetic to abolitionism than the NS Presbyterians of New York, but in the latter state as in the old Northwest, those for whom Presbyterianism moved too slowly tended to hive off as Congregational bodies. In Syracuse, Rochester, Penn Yan, the first Congregational churches were formed by the withdrawal of abolitionist members from the Presbyterian churches. In Auburn and Elmira similar divisions took place, but the new churches remained Presbyterian. In Oneida Presbytery a whole Congregational association of seceding abolitionists was constituted. Here were three of the chief abolitionists of the state: Alvan Stewart, head of the State Anti-Slavery Society; Beriah Green, who had succeeded Gale as President of the Oneida Institute; and T. D. Weld. Gerrit Smith lived close at hand. Such ruptures usually left sore feelings in the congregations affected.

In the General Assembly, New York presbyteries pressed continually for action on slavery right up to the Civil War. The Assembly of 1839, for example, had among several overtures on the subject, a request from the Synod of Genesee to seek the extinction of slaveholding from the Presbyterian Church as soon as possible, on the ground that every Christian must at once cease all participation direct or indirect in this sin, and that the church dare not remain silent.[15] But this same General Assembly recorded on its roll a Southern contingent: 39 churches in Missouri, 20 in Mississippi, 14 in Virginia, 46 in Tennessee, and 8 in South Carolina and Georgia. This was not

[15] MS. Minutes of the Synod of Genesee, 1838, pp. 353–354; cf. 301.

a large body, but it was sufficiently substantial to provide significant opposition to the abolitionists for two decades. The Assemblies of 1839 and 1840 heard heated but inconclusive debates on the subject. It was pointed out that disciplinary action on such matters was the responsibility of the local judicatories rather than the Assembly. And the historian of the NS church suggested that the desire to avoid or reduce these unresolvable contentions on the floor of the Assembly may have been an operative consideration in the decision of 1840 to schedule Assemblies only once every three years.[16]

The triennial Assemblies of 1843, 1846, and 1849, however, found no more peace in this matter. Overtures continued to come in, especially from western New York presbyteries and synods, demanding action. In 1846, when memorials came up from twenty presbyteries and four synods, the Assembly took no less than eight days for this issue, every single commissioner delivering himself on it. So much of the agenda remained that an adjourned meeting had to be convened the following year to deal in particular with the urgent problems of home missions. The Assembly of 1849 received nineteen memorials on slavery, and the Assembly of 1850, the first back on the annual schedule, debated the topic for five of its twelve days of sessions. The outcome was always the same, a condemnation of slaveholding in general, but a recognition of excusable forms of collaboration with it. The militants of the western New York synods, on the other hand, wanted to bar slaveholders from the Communion Table and pulpit.[17]

The passage of the Fugitive Slave Law of 1850 embittered feeling further. Such political figures in New York as Weed and W. H. Seward, and Horace Greeley's *Tribune* denounced the law. Sentiment upstate was such that it was difficult to enforce the law. The Synod of New York and the General As-

[16] Edward D. Morris, *A Book of Remembrance. The Presbyterian Church New School, 1837–1869* (Columbus, Ohio, Champlin Press, 1905), p. 99.
[17] Fowler, *op. cit.*, p. 158.

sembly refused to take action on the morality of the law, as some of their members urged. But in 1851 a Negro was taken away from federal officers by leading citizens in Syracuse. And churchmen were active in the Underground Railroad. The houses, for example, of Josiah Tryon, an elder, at Lewiston, and of Pliny Sexton, of Palmyra, were stations on the Railroad. The session at Palmyra had petitioned the General Assembly in 1848 as to whether church members assisting fugitives were liable to discipline.[18] Judicatories and individual Christians wrestled with the question whether the law of the land should be broken in obedience to Seward's "higher law."

The controversy reached a new stage in the General Assembly of 1853, which had received eleven memorials calling for action. After prolonged debates it was recommended to the Southern presbyteries that they investigate and report on the extent of slaveholding and its character within their bounds. As might have been expected, no reports were submitted on slavery by Southern presbyteries at the synod of 1854.

In 1854 the Kansas-Nebraska bill marked a further advance of the slavery cause. Seward again was the leading spokesman against it. An Emigrant Aid Society went to work in New York to assist those desiring to enter Kansas. In 1855 actual civil war broke out in Kansas. Even the cautious Synod of New York at this time joined the Synods of Geneva, Onondaga, and Susquehanna in condemnation of the moves to extend the territory open to slavery.[19]

At the General Assembly of 1855 the effort was renewed to organize an inquiry into slaveholding in the Southern presbyteries. A committee appointed to study the matter reported that the General Assembly had no Constitutional power to discipline individual slaveholders. The Assembly of 1856, however, claimed the right to press inquiries of presbyteries, de-

[18] *Manual of the Presbyterian Church of Palmyra,* p. 6.
[19] MS. Minutes of the Synod of New York and New Jersey, 1856, pp. 36–37.

spite a minority report to the contrary. And in 1857 abolitionist pressure finally forced the issue. Over the warnings of the Southern presbyteries that this threatened to be another "excision act," a declaration was passed affirming the right of discipline.

The result was another rupture. The Southern NS presbyteries met at Richmond in the summer after the Assembly and organized themselves into a separate United Synod of the Presbyterian Church. The twenty years' battle over the question whether slaveholding was a sin requiring disciplinary action was now ended. Some 285 churches with sixteen thousand communicants organized in twenty-one presbyteries and six synods, had left the NS Assembly. The western New York synods had led in insistence on a decision.

2. THE OLD SCHOOL CHURCH IN NEW YORK

By the fifties the controversial attitude between the schools was visibly moderating. Ten years after the schism the Synod of Buffalo was still describing western New York as "missionary ground" that it was their duty and policy to occupy. They were a self-conscious army of Gideon, surrounded by "errorists" on every side and deaf to all specious appeals to peace and unity. But in the fifties they began to exchange delegates with NS synods and even Congregational bodies. Ogdensburg Presbytery (OS) suggested reunion to St. Lawrence (NS) in 1852, and these two were thenceforth to be its most persistent champions.

As we have already seen, the attitudes of the two schools on temperance and the Sabbath were so similar as to be most conveniently described together. And in such matters as revivals and abolition there were conspicuous exceptions to the obvious generalizations about contrasts. Lewis Cheeseman, of Rochester, wrote a work on the differences between the two schools in which he contended, amid fantastic charges about

NS theology, that there was no difference in attitudes toward revivalism.[20] And this was probably largely true in the upstate region, where the Old School had also some vigorous opponents of slavery, such as Dr. Lord, of Buffalo. On the other side, as we have seen, the New School Synod of Albany refused to discuss slavery, and the Synod of New York and New Jersey was not able to agree on a very advanced position. Even in doctrine the lines were hard to draw by the end of the 1850's.

The OS church made some gains in New York State. The original Presbytery of Caledonia in western New York had been divided by the Synod of New Jersey (OS) into Steuben and Wyoming in 1842. The next year the General Assembly combined these two with Ogdensburg to form a Synod of Buffalo to cover the score of OS churches in the bounds of the three exscinded synods. Through the forties and fifties this synod was weak and thinly scattered. In 1844 the Presbytery of Buffalo City was organized and in 1852 that of Rochester City. Then two years later the remains of Steuben and Wyoming were once more consolidated into the Presbytery of Genesee Valley. There were thus three presbyteries chiefly in the bounds of the (NS) Synod of Genesee, and one on the St. Lawrence in Utica bounds.

The OS Synod of Albany had its chief strength, of course, in Albany and the Presbyteries of Albany and Troy. It also sheltered Ogdensburg until that presbytery was attached to the Synod of Buffalo. A Presbytery of Saratoga was cut off from Albany in 1849 and then reunited with it the next year when the Presbytery of Mohawk was set off.

The OS Synod of New York enrolled several African and Asiatic presbyteries — Ningpo, Amoy, Canton, Shantung, West Africa — perhaps because it contained the headquarters of the Foreign Board. The Presbyteries of California and Oregon were also attached to this synod. Within its proper bounds it

[20] Lewis Cheeseman, *Differences Between Old and New School Presbyterians* (Rochester, 1848), Ch. VII.

added the Presbyteries of Connecticut in 1850 and Nassau in 1855. In 1862 Connecticut assimilated Bedford.

The Synod of New York contained in 1861 more churches and ministers than the other two OS synods together, and nearly two thirds of the OS communicants of the state. The OS churches of New York City were particularly distinguished for their wealth and philanthropies. The offices of the Boards of Home and of Foreign Missions were in the city, and their work was generously supported. The First Church of New York was the largest single giver to Presbyterian foreign missions for forty years, and its pastor, Dr. Phillips, was chairman of the Board's Executive Committee. James Lenox, of First Church, was also responsible for the founding of Presbyterian Hospital in 1868 and the Presbyterian Home for Aged Women in 1869, as well as the Lenox Collection in the New York Public Library and other philanthropies.

One of the most interesting episodes in New York OS history was the parochial school movement.[21] Presbyterians had played a major role in building up the free schools in New York, which became the basis of the public-school system. But they were deeply distressed when they found themselves opposed by an alliance of Roman Catholics and secularists who wished to keep religious teaching, and especially the Bible, out of the common schools. In 1869, at the very end of our period, the NS General Assembly was still defending the place of the Bible in public education.

The OS General Assembly appointed a committee on the problem of education, headed by Dr. Alexander, of the Fifth Avenue Church. The recommendation, adopted by the Assembly in 1847, was for Presbyterian parochial schools. Scores of churches opened such schools across the country, often assisted by the Board of Education. Over half the subsidies used nationally came from two New York elders, James Lenox, of First Church, and Silas Holmes, of the Brick Church.

[21] L. J. Sherrill, *Presbyterian Parochial Schools, 1846–1870* (New Haven, Yale University Press, 1932).

By 1853 all the New York City parochial schools were closed except two. Upstate the Geneseo Academy continued, but this was not properly a parish school in the first place. The church had been unable to secure good teachers, and the people were not sufficiently convinced of the policy to support them financially.

3. THE CIVIL WAR AND REUNION [22]

The Old School in the War. The Civil War brought about an internal transformation of the OS church. Founded on a covenant to defend slavery from attack, the church was increasingly embarrassed by the rapid movement of events. The memorable General Assembly of 1861, meeting a month or two after Fort Sumter had been fired on, found it impossible to avoid a stand on secession. To general surprise, the issue was forced by the elderly antiabolitionist, Dr. Gardiner Spring, of the Brick Church in New York City. The New York delegation as a whole, anxious not to alienate the South, preferred the Hodge alternative, and the Spring Resolutions did not receive a majority of the New York votes. The two chief OS pulpits in New York City had a tradition of Southern sympathies. Dr. Spring had had a Southern co-pastor, Dr. Hoge, until 1861. And in that year Dr. N. T. Rice, generally esteemed to be, with Professor Hodge, one of the leading Southern sympathizers in the North, was called by the Fifth Avenue Church from the Seminary of the Northwest. Henry J. van Dyke, of Brooklyn, was usually the most outspoken of all. The Buffalo delegates, however, were disowned by their constituency for supporting the Hodge report. The Synod of Buffalo recorded the view (over the protest of Buffalo City) that the Southern revolt was a sin "against God and the Church," which was to be purged by "repentance and public confession."

The Presbyterian Church of the Confederate States was organized in December, 1861, at Augusta, Georgia, committed to

[22] Cf. L. G. Vander Velde, *The Presbyterian Churches and the Federal Union, 1861–1869* (Cambridge, Harvard University Press, 1932).

the political and military cause of the Confederacy. This schism removed from the OS church the chief pressure for silence on slavery, and at the same time the most irreconcilable opposition to the NS church. The General Assembly still avoided the forbidden subject of slavery until 1863 when the Emancipation Proclamation forced their hand again. Even then the action was simply to reaffirm the declaration of 1818 together with that of 1846. It was not until 1864 that antislavery men at last captured the OS church. The old antiabolitionists gave up as the Assembly condemned slavery almost unanimously and looked forward to its complete abolition. Van Dyke wrote a paper for the minority in the Synod of New York that opposed the Assembly actions.

The Louisville Presbytery also declined to accept the Assembly's deliverance. The Assembly of 1865, further aroused by Lincoln's assassination, then passed a resolution requiring a loyalty test for ministers from the South. The response was defiance in the "Declaration and Testimony" of September, 1865.[23] Van Dyke again defended this manifesto, and indeed, there were reports that it was written in his Brooklyn study.[24] The General Assembly of 1866, however, set drastic penalties on the Louisville Presbytery, driving out two Border State synods and a presbytery. The Synod of New York that year and the next similarly denied a seat to an elder from van Dyke's church who had signed the "Declaration and Testimony."

The New School in the War. The history of the NS church in the war was less complicated than that of the Old. The church had already lost its Southern synods in 1857 over slavery, and there was no basis for sympathy with the purported

---

[23] Summary in *Biblical Repertory and Princeton Review*, July, 1866, pp. 425–432.

[24] T. C. Johnson, *History of the Presbyterian Church in the United States*, American Church History Series, XI (New York, Charles Scribner's Sons, 1894), p. 443, n. 3.

right of secession. And as to the questions raised by Professor Hodge about the right of political action, the New School was consistently more loyal to the theocratic Calvinist tradition than was the Old School. It was generally observed that "political sermons" were much more common in the New School than in the Old. The contrast was dramatic between the tumult of the OS Assembly in 1861 in Philadelphia and the virtual unanimity of the New School in Syracuse. And the Spring Resolutions were restrained indeed when compared with the Syracuse report on the State of the Country. The latter expressed amazement at the wickedness of treason and rebellion in the South and mourned that ministers and professing Christians gave countenance to it. More fervent prayer for the removal of the evil of slavery was urged.

The vigorous support of the federal government pledged by the 1861 Assembly was reaffirmed by each of the following four Assemblies, usually by a unanimous vote. The 1862 report recognized a pacifist sentiment in the church, but only to remark that in the case of rebellion, as against international warfare, all were of one mind. The whole insurrection was by this report "traced to one primordial root, and to one only — African Slavery, and the love of it, and a determination to make it perpetual," and it was taken for granted that the defeat of the South would end the slavery of the Negro.[25] The next year (1863) the Assembly welcomed the Emancipation Proclamation and prayed for the removal of the last vestiges of the system. "Ill-timed complaints and unnecessary criticisms" of the administration were deplored in 1864, on the eve of the presidential election. But while the assassination of the President five weeks before the 1865 Assembly led to language of unprecedented hostility to the South, the report pledged the church at once to support Andrew Johnson in the assurance of political and personal rights to freedmen. The Assembly had the grace to confess that Northern customs and legislation on

[25] *Minutes of the General Assembly*, NS, 1862, pp. 23–27.

this subject (the "black laws") were not above reproach, and admitted responsibility for the correction of these wrongs. "Let it not be said that, as a Church, we have nothing to do with civil legislation. . . . The members of our churches are bound to be Christians, in politics as well as in religion." This Assembly also unanimously adopted a special report on the matter of extending the suffrage to the freed slaves, urging that it was "better to meet the question at once," and encouraging the government to move in this direction.[26]

The most problematical of this series of political declarations came in the year after the war and on the subject of reconstruction policy. The OS Assembly, wrestling with the problem of its Border States' constituency held its peace that year on public issues. But the NS Assembly entered boldly into the conflict between the Congress and President Johnson on the Freedmen's Bureau and the Civil Rights Bill. The Assembly committed itself to the punitive and vindictive policy of the "radicals." With this unfortunate deliverance, the NS church ended its series on the State of the Country.

The synods and presbyteries in New York had behaved much as the earlier attitudes toward slavery would lead one to expect. Albany Synod maintained dead silence on slavery throughout. The western synods and New York (NS), on the other hand, concurred heartily in the Assembly declarations of support for the government and in the identification of slavery as the primal cause of the struggle. The people were urged to pray for victory and for the destruction of slavery. The Emancipation Proclamations of 1862 and 1863 were acclaimed. It was a new thing, to be sure, as the Synod of Geneva put it, "for us to bring companies of soldiers tramping into our churches and give them the sanction of our religious blessing and bid them God speed as they go forth to their work of blood." [27] The regular work of the churches often suffered from the drain of men and money to war purposes. But the judicato-

---

[26] *Ibid.*, 1865, pp. 36–43.
[27] MS. Minutes of the Synod of Geneva, 1862, p. 40.

ries commended the Christian Commission and chaplaincy to the congregations.

In special wartime activities the New School, true to its patriotic tradition, was second only to the more numerous Methodists in the number of chaplains in service in the first year of the war, four times as many as the Old School. By the end of the war the Old School had apparently caught up in the number actually in service, although not in percentages. The newly established agencies of the NS church, on the other hand, could not rival the resources and efficiency of the Old School. The OS Board of Publication, which distributed religious literature in camps, naval vessels, military posts, hospitals, prisons, was, in the whole period of the war, surpassed in such activities only by the Methodists. Similarly, the NS church extension committee was overstrained already with its effort in the West, and never succeeded in accomplishing much for ex-slaves in the South. Work with freedmen proved very difficult and thankless for Northerners in any case; the OS church was not much more successful with it than was the NS.

Presbyterians generally were among the most loyal supporters of the nondenominational United States Christian Commission, which served the material and spiritual needs alike of men in service. Presbyterians also generally endorsed and contributed to the war work of the United States Sanitary Commission and the American Tract and Bible Societies.

Reunion. One effect of the war, which no one would have guessed possible in 1861, was the healing of the breach of 1837 and the reunion in the North and in the South of the divided branches of the church. On the eve of the war there was still, after a quarter of a century, no exchange of fraternal delegates between the General Assemblies, although both maintained standing relations with other church bodies less closely related. The denominational periodicals kept feelings sore with their bickering and sarcasm, and there were irritating conflicts in home missions and church extension. There seemed to be no widespread urge to reunion. The Old School church was already so large and far-flung that it had administrative difficulties, and while the smaller church did not feel this embarrassment, it was at last sufficiently organized to feel content with the situation.

A sudden and remarkable change in this state of affairs was brought about by the war. The Old School was led by events to take the antislavery position, which the New School had held all along. The leaders in this process in the Old School felt their kinship with the New School and sought support there. The war thus undid the OS antiabolitionist alliance of 1837 that had made the excision possible and, instead, divided the church on slavery lines, as had almost happened in 1836. In both the North and South doctrinal differences came to seem less considerable in comparison to moral and political conflicts.

In the war years the overtures to reunion came chiefly from the OS side. Here was the chief instability and tension. The New School was on public issues pretty much of one mind, but the Old School was sharply divided into four parties, the Princeton-Philadelphia axis, the South, the Border States, and the West, especially the old Northwest. It was the last that was most definitely pro-union, antislavery, and consequently more inclined to friendship with the New School than with the Southerners of its own household. This party was strengthened by the course of events, and when the Southern and Border sections finally departed irretrievably, the Princeton-Philadelphia wing had no constructive alternatives to reunion with the New School. They would have preferred reunion with the South, but of this there would be no possibility for decades to come.

The first significant steps to reunion came in the second year of the war. The OS Assembly of 1862 proposed an exchange of delegates with the New School. The action was nearly unanimous, but this did not mean a general sentiment for friendly reunion. The establishment of correspondence with the NS Assembly was rather felt by many to be a way of stabilizing the separation and mutual independence of the two. Thus it was regarded also from the NS side, for instance, by the *New York Evangelist*. The Old School was silent on slavery, as it had been since the bargain of 1837, and was felt to be in a weaker position morally by the New School.

For the next four years the Assemblies received memorials asking for action toward reunion, but no official action was taken until 1866. Delegates were exchanged and cordially received on both sides, beginning in 1863. None of the NS delegates of the first four years advocated early reunion, but every year the OS representatives spoke for it.

New York OS Presbyterians were divided on reunion much as on the issues of the war. The most vigorous proponents were in the Ogdensburg Presbytery, which had proposed reunion to St. Lawrence (NS) Presbytery as early as 1852. The two presbyteries did hold several joint meetings in 1862 and 1863. The Synod of Buffalo, to which Ogdensburg belonged, took favorable notice of the reunion proposals a year or two before Albany and New York Synods, and by 1864 was arranging an exchange of delegates with the NS Synods of Genesee, Geneva, Albany, and, in 1865, Utica. Albany and New York Synods, on the other hand, moved forward with the OS General Assembly, but no faster.

The General Assembly (OS) discussed the matter in 1864 and 1865, declining to take action. In the former year, however, seventy ministers and fifty-three elders convened a reunion conference at the time of the Assembly and published a paper expressing confidence in " the doctrinal soundness and ecclesiastical orderliness " of both churches.[28] And the actions on slavery in 1864 and on reconstruction policy in 1865 showed that the antislavery and pro-reunion party was at last in command of the OS church.

[28] *Presbyterian Reunion: a Memorial Volume, 1837–1871* (New York, DeWitt C. Lent & Co.; Chicago, Van Nortwick & Sparks, 1871), pp. 250–251; hereafter, *Reunion Memorial.*

The strongest theologian of the NS church had in the meantime taken the leadership for reunion on that side. As retiring Moderator, Prof. Henry B. Smith, of Union, preached at the Assembly of 1864 a very influential sermon on " Christian Union and Ecclesiastical Reunion." [29]

The two Assemblies met in 1866 in the same city, St. Louis, and took decisive steps on the basis of the realignment of the preceding years. They met for corporate worship and the sacrament of the Lord's Supper. A joint committee to explore reunion was proposed by the OS and taken up enthusiastically by the NS Assembly. Henry J. van Dyke attempted a diversion in the interests of Southern Presbyterians, but it was clear to all that this was hopeless.

The Joint Committee met in New York City in February and May of 1867. As one might expect, over a third of the NS contingent were New Yorkers, including the NS chairman, W. A. Adams of the Broome Street Church and the secretary, Edwin Hatfield of the North Presbyterian Church and Stated Clerk of the General Assembly. Among the OS committeemen, only two were New Yorkers. The group as a whole was at first dubious of the possibilities and only talked comity. But in May they produced a proposal of reunion on equal terms for the two Assemblies of 1867.

According to the 1867 report, the common Standards were to be the doctrinal and ecclesiastical basis of reunion, the Westminster Confession in " its fair historical sense, as it is accepted by the two bodies in opposition to Antinomianism and Fatalism on the one hand, and to Arminianism and Pelagianism on the other." [30] Imperfectly Presbyterian congregations were to be advised to complete their structure as soon as possible, and no more such were to be received. A three-fourths vote of the presbyteries of each branch would be required within one year of the time when the basis was submitted to them, but to avoid

[29] Henry B. Smith, *Faith and Philosophy,* ed. by G. L. Prentiss (New York, Scribner, Armstrong & Co., 1877), pp. 265–296.
[30] *Reunion Memorial,* p. 257.

any appearance of haste the General Assemblies were not to act until 1868, while the intervening year was to be used for debate and modification of the Basis.

The NS Assembly accepted this report unanimously, but there was a hard core of resistance in the OS Assembly. A minority of sixty-four there wished to attach three conditions: (1) a more definite statement of the doctrinal basis; (2) the exclusion of committeemen from church courts; and (3) recognition of the obligation of presbyteries to examine all ministers admitted.

The most notable of the public discussions of the following months was opened by Charles Hodge, the most influential theologian of the OS church. Hodge contended that however numerous the orthodox individuals in the NS body, that church, "as an ecclesiastical organization, never has and does not now" sincerely receive and adopt all the doctrines essential to the Reformed or Calvinistic system.[31] H. B. Smith of Union replied that the New School adopted the Confession in the Calvinistic or Reformed sense and challenged proof to the contrary.[32]

Just at this time George H. Stuart, former head of the Christian Commission, organized a Presbyterian National Union Convention in Philadelphia. Half a dozen Presbyterian bodies were represented — Old School, New School, United, Reformed Presbyterian, Cumberland, Southern, Reformed Dutch — and unprecedented enthusiasm was generated for organic union of all Presbyterians. Smith, who was active in the deliberations, took the occasion to reassure Hodge and the faction he represented by offering unexpectedly an amendment to the proposed doctrinal basis. The Confession should be received, he moved, "in its proper historical, that is, the Calvinistic or Reformed

[31] "The General Assembly," *Biblical Repertory and Princeton Review*, July, 1867, esp. pp. 503–522.

[32] "The Reunion of the Presbyterian Churches," *Presbyterian Review*, October, 1867.

sense." [33] At the vote, the New School contingent, obviously without coaching, supported the amendment 46 to 2. There could hardly have been a more dramatic or crushing refutation of the charges Hodge had made against the New School, and as Smith wrote, Hodge "relented wonderfully."

When the Joint Committee met in March of 1868 to assess the reaction of the churches and to consider possible revisions, the OS contingent expressed a desire to substitute for the 1867 doctrinal basis that of the Presbyterian Union Convention together with the Smith Amendment. This the NS members would accept provided there was also a clause acknowledging the NS freedom of interpretation. Dr. Gurley, President Lincoln's pastor, finally produced such an amendment. "It is also understood," the amendment went, "that various methods of viewing, stating, explaining and illustrating the doctrines of the confession, which do not impair the integrity of the Reformed and Calvinistic system, are to be freely allowed in the United Church, as they have hitherto been allowed in the separate Churches." [34] The final "terms of Reunion," as presented to the two Assemblies for action in May, 1868, thus were modified chiefly by the Smith Amendment, to define Calvinistic substance, and the Gurley Amendment, to authorize liberty of interpretation within the Reformed tradition.

Besides the doctrinal basis, two other knotty points should be noticed. The "Presbygational" churches, first of all, were to be "counselled and expected to become thoroughly Presbyterian" within five years. [35] The Committee had been led to believe that this counsel would prove not inacceptable to these churches, some of which were considered by their presbyteries as among their most efficient and excellent congregations.

A new article, in the second place, was introduced to reconcile divergent practices with regard to the examination of min-

[33] *Reunion Memorial*, pp. 263–265.   [35] *Ibid.*, p. 276.
[34] *Ibid.*, p. 268.

isters transferring from one presbytery to another. Here was an issue that had accumulated much heat in the 1830's. It was now proposed to resolve it by making examination a right but not an obligation. This article was the least acceptable to the NS Assembly at Harrisburg, as was the doctrinal basis, amendments and all, to the Old School at Albany, but both Assemblies passed the whole plan by large majorities.

Hodge and his supporters, however, were not reconciled, and entered a formal minority "Protest," detailing eight or ten "Arminian" or Pelagian propositions which, they asserted, a minority of NS members held and which that Church as a whole, they alleged, declared to be consistent with the Westminster Confession. The answer to this "Protest" noted that exactly these "errors" had been formally repudiated by the New School thirty years before at the Auburn Convention. "This Assembly," it was now declared, "regards the 'Auburn declaration' as an authoritative statement of the NS type of Calvinism, and as indicating . . . how much liberty they wish." [36] Thus the OS church at last accepted as adequately Calvinistic the theological platform of the Auburn Declaration.

The New York synods and presbyteries, Old School and New, concurred with these advancing negotiations. The Albany Synod (OS) assured other portions of the OS church in 1867 that they had found "brethren in the NS body within our bounds in cordial harmony with us in their teachings and ecclesiastical tendencies." [37] The Synod of New York and New Jersey arranged concurrent meetings and joint celebrations of the Communion with the Synod of New York (OS) in 1867 and with the Synod of New Jersey (OS) in 1868. All three accepted the revised basis of 1868.

The voting in the presbyteries generally, however, became hopelessly confused in 1868-1869. When the Assemblies convened in 1869, consequently, the legal situation was a muddle

[36] *Minutes of the General Assembly*, OS, 1868, pp. 658-665.
[37] MS. Minutes of the Synod of Albany, OS, 1867, p. 142.

and in NS circles there was widespread suspicion of bad faith on the other side.

The Assemblies of 1869 met concurrently in New York City in the Brick Church and the Church of the Covenant. From the beginning they met together for worship, and it was apparent at once that despite the procedural tangle, desire for union was running at high tide. A new joint committee was put to work and produced its report while the Assemblies were still in session. The doctrinal basis was now to be the Westminster Standards, pure and simple. The proposal was that the presbyteries be instructed to vote on the plan if approved by the Assemblies, before October, so that adjourned meetings in November could take appropriate action.

In the Church of the Covenant, Dr. Adams found unanimous approval by the NS Assembly. In the Brick Church, the only clause that evoked spontaneous applause read " each recognizing the other as a sound and orthodox body, according to the principles of the confession common to both." [38] This formula was to be regarded thereafter as the Magna Charta of liberal Presbyterianism. The patriarchal Dr. Spring pleaded for immediate action: " If you postpone this union another year, I shall probably not see it, but shall die a member of a divided Church." [39] In the tally there were only nine nays. And the next day Dr. Spring was able to offer the Eucharistic prayer at a joint Communion, presided over by the two Moderators.

Over the summer and fall the presbyteries voted. Of 144 Old School presbyteries, three voted no — Hudson (New York), Rio de Janeiro, and West Lexington. All of the 113 NS presbyteries voted in the affirmative, and 110 did so unanimously.

The adjourned Assemblies, meeting in the First and Third Churches, respectively, of Pittsburgh, had only to register the decision of the presbyteries and take the necessary steps to prepare for the joint Assembly of the reunited church in 1870. The reunion required the consolidation of the synods and agen-

[38] *Reunion Memorial*, p. 350.   [39] *Ibid.*, p. 349.

cies of the Assemblies. This was the chief business of the Assembly of 1870. Originally, it was planned to establish the boundaries of synods and presbyteries during the Assembly. But after debate it was determined that the Assembly would set bounds only for the synods, and that the latter, when they met, should reconstruct their own presbyteries before July 15, 1870.

Thirty-four synods were established, two of them in Asia. New York State was to have six. Genesee, Geneva, Utica, and Albany retained the bounds of the old NS synods, save that the New England churches were to be detached from Albany and connected with the new Synod of New York. That synod was reduced, on the other hand, by all the New Jersey presbyteries, which now went to the new Synod of New Jersey. And a new Synod of Long Island was erected, including also Staten Island. The new New York Synod included eight New York counties and the New England churches.

VII : *The Reunited Church and the "Higher Criticism,"*

1870–1900

1. CHURCH LIFE IN THE 1870's AND 1880's

In general the churches in the seventies and eighties continued to exhibit the characteristics of the generation before the Civil War. It was an individualistic understanding of Christianity, stressing personal conversion and therefore revivalistic and strongly missionary. Orthodoxy was defined in practice ever less by creeds and confessions than by the current literal reading of the Bible. The denominational organization of church life was taken generally for granted, although in fact the distinctive Presbyterian and Reformed heritage in theology, worship, church order, was progressively receding as a common type of American evangelical Protestantism emerged in most denominations.

The years after the Civil War saw much expansion and activity in the churches of New York. Membership increased, and money was raised and spent on a new level. Single gifts were now much larger than earlier, and the modern charitable "foundation" emerged as a significant factor. In the seventies and early eighties many churches were remodeled and many

175

new ones were erected, now often in pretentious "depot Gothic" style.

These churches had been grouped at the reunion of 1870 into six synods — Genesee, Geneva, Utica, Albany, New York, and Long Island. For a decade this synodical structure endured, with the name of Genesee changed to Western New York, and of Utica to Central New York. Then in 1882 the consolidated modern Synod of New York was authorized and assembled for the first time. The basis of delegation was settled, and the synod was incorporated in 1884. The series of printed annual minutes had begun in 1882.

There was relatively little change thereafter in ecclesiastical structure. The twenty-six presbyteries within the state were reduced by one when the ministers and churches of Genesee Valley were distributed among neighboring presbyteries. There were a few minor adjustments of presbytery bounds, Buffalo gaining the Allegheny and Cornplanter Church from Pennsylvania Synod, Westchester losing five congregations to New York and being compensated at Boston's expense by the churches of Hampden County in Massachusetts, Brooklyn yielding Staten Island churches to New York and gaining five from Nassau.

The New England section developed significantly. Boston Presbytery had 63 ministers and 42 churches on its rolls in 1896. It was overtured that year to change the name to the Synod of New York and New England but the proposal was dropped when it was realized that legislation to change the terms of incorporation would be necessary.

When the Synod of New York was consolidated in 1882 it emerged as easily the largest and wealthiest in the whole Presbyterian Church. Thereafter it normally led the church both in the total amount of its giving and in the size of the average contribution per member. In relation to property, however, New York gifts were less generous than those of some other synods. New York Synod totaled a little less than a quarter of the whole membership of the church and contributed usually a little less than a third of the budgets of the Boards. Within the synod, New York Presbytery gave more than a quarter of the synod's total. If Brooklyn were added to New York Presbytery, nearly 40 percent of the synod giving would be accounted for by these presbyteries of the metropolitan area.

Through the decade of the 1880's, contributions to the Boards steadily increased to a peak in 1888. Thereafter there was a steady decline, most of New York contributions going elsewhere. While the church was gaining slightly in communicants in the 1890's, both benevolences in general and the Boards in particular suffered losses. It may be that the relatively slight giving to Presbyterian causes in this period was related to theological differences between New York Synod and the majority of the General Assembly and to the struggles over Union Seminary and its professors, which must be recounted later.

The various Board causes were promoted at this period by a publication, *The Church at Home and Abroad.* Also a device of "missionary congresses" in relation to synod meetings proved highly successful in presenting the work of the Boards. The first was held at Saratoga in 1893. Synod's committee on systematic beneficence campaigned steadily for a pledge system of giving. Some strong churches did this effectively, but apparently most churches relied on an annual collection for each of the various Boards.

The enduring strength of individualistic evangelicalism in New York Presbyterianism was dramatized by its sympathy for revivalism, which continued into the twentieth century. Dwight L. Moody was at his peak in the 1870's and 1880's and left his mark on the state. Other lesser names appear frequently in the records of New York congregations — B. Fay Mills, J. Wilbur Chapman, Billy Sunday. The last two were themselves Presbyterian ministers whose careers were significantly associated with New York City.

These revivals were of a somewhat different type from those of Finney. They did not generally contribute to the ethical energies of the church but by their premillennialism rather weakened the church's social witness. Their reliance on organizational machinery and psychological manipulation became more evident. Preliminary committees of all kinds, publicity, studied effects musical and dramatic, meetings for special-interest groups — all had become technique. The revival preacher might well be above this in his personal sincerity, but that sincerity became a tool in a calculated propaganda effort. The churches, meanwhile, were gradually placing less stress on revivals as the index of spirituality. They still generally cooperated with organized revivals, but were less pained than previously by the intervals between.

Church Programs. The Sunday schools generally continued the earlier pattern. They had largely replaced the old catechetical instruction by families. They were a nursery of evangelical religion, focusing on conversion, and the chief outlet for the ministry of the laity. In 1889 it was noted that four out of five Sunday school pupils did not attend church. The Sunday school was for them a substitute. By 1890 the Shorter Catechism was rarely used, having been largely replaced by the Board's *Westminster Helps.* Attendance averaged only about 60 percent, and the hold on many children was precarious. In 1895 there were more Sunday schools than churches in the synod, but their quality was poor. Attempts were made periodically to train the teachers, and the use of graded materials was urged, but the Sunday school at the turn of the century was problematical in its effectiveness.

There was much discussion in the 1880's and 1890's over the place of religion in the public schools. The prevailing opinion in the synod was that " basic theism " should be taught in a nonsectarian fashion and that teachers sympathetic to religion should be appointed. A conference of some ten denominations met in New York in 1890 and unanimously advocated moral instruction in the public schools and worship as desired by the community. A League for Moral Instruction in Public

Schools was formed. It was observed, however, that the law gave the school superintendents authority in such matters, and they usually ruled against religious exercises in the schools. Presbyterians followed with interest the heated Roman Catholic debates in these years over such arrangements as those in Poughkeepsie and Faribault. Synod committees submitted extended reports on the whole problem in 1887 and 1892.[1]

A conspicuous new development of the post-Civil War period was the phenomenal growth of lay leadership and activity, especially in the fields of women's work and youth work. The women of New York Presbyterianism became organized in the decade after the Civil War to a high degree. When the synod was put together in 1882 the attempt was made to unify and coordinate the numerous local enterprises. A Woman's Synodical Committee on Home Missions was created, but it proved more difficult to unify the societies for foreign missions. Within a few years, however, both societies were reporting regularly to the synod. There were, for example, 490 local women's foreign missions societies in the churches in 1893. The Woman's Synodical Committee on Home Missions more than doubled its membership and more than tripled its gifts within a generation. They reported supporting 92 teachers for home missions and freedmen's work in 1910.

Another women's organization enlisted strong Presbyterian support in these years, the Women's Christian Temperance Union. Temperance (meaning "abstinence") was probably the most widespread social and ethical concern among Presbyterians at the period.

Another form of specialized ministry that developed largely in this period was young people's work. Presbyterians were active in the Y.M.C.A., which expanded into the "railroad branches" and the colleges after the seventies, and into boys' work a little later. Even more striking was the emergence in the 1880's of the Young People's Societies for Christian Endeavor. These societies enforced a discipline of daily Bible-

[1] *Minutes of the Synod,* 1887, pp. 33–41; 1892, pp. 40–41.

reading and prayer, of missionary giving, the temperance pledge, and "personal holiness." They expanded very rapidly, nowhere more than among Presbyterians. They became established in virtually every congregation in the 1890's and with the Boys' Brigades even outnumbered Sunday schools. In 1899 the synod calculated that seven thousand converts had been made among them in the preceding year, by which they meant full church members. A slump was observed early in the twentieth century, and the denominations took a greater measure of control over the work.

Colleges and Academies. A prominent item on the agenda of New York Synod in this period grew from its relations to various academies and colleges. It was not a period for founding new institutions, but for strengthening and finding adequate support for those in existence, and in this undertaking the synod uniformly failed.

Three institutions of higher education were especially involved — Elmira College, Hamilton College, and New York University. Ingham University and Geneseo Academy had already fallen out of earlier relations with New York Presbyterian bodies. The problems of Adams Collegiate Institute were still repeatedly considered by the synod, at times as part of an ambitious scheme of a system of six academies over the state.

Of these institutions, Elmira College, founded in 1855 as the oldest women's college in America, was the only one directly under the control of the synod, which had inherited it in 1882 from the old Synod of Geneva. The synod elected trustees and printed the financial report of the college in its minutes. It regularly commended the college to the churches, blessing its campaigns for endowment, but never raising any significant money for it. The college almost died in the mid-1890's but was rescued by the promotional energies of President MacKenzie. In 1899 the college still lacked a single endowed professorship, paying salaries out of current income.

The student body usually numbered from one hundred fifty to two hundred. A high proportion of them became teachers.

A proposal was made in 1879 that Hamilton College, like Elmira, be put in direct relation to the Presbyterian Church. The trustees accepted this proposal on condition that the synod raise half a million dollars for endowment. The college had always been essentially Presbyterian, having grown out of the Kirkland Academy for the Indians. Synod failed to raise the money, and when the trustees lowered the terms to $300,000, synod failed again.

The Hamilton student body in this period was about the size of Elmira's. A very high percentage went into the ministry, 35 percent in 1886, 28 percent in 1888, 40 percent in 1889. The college was the chief feeder to Auburn Seminary. In 1902 it was reported that 656 of nineteen hundred alumni were ministers, 430 of them Presbyterian. The president and eight of the eighteen faculty members were Presbyterian, and the catalogue described the college as "neither sectarian nor secular."

With Adams Collegiate Institute, as with Hamilton, there was a scheme to raise an endowment that would put the institution directly under church control. In this case synod was unable to raise $50,000. St. Lawrence Presbytery eventually took over synod's interest in the enterprise.

The University of the City of New York was also essentially Presbyterian but not formally so. Most of its major donors as well as its constituency and much of its management were Presbyterian. The undergraduate division numbered only a hundred or so about 1890. The university possessed the first graduate school of pedagogy. Its medical school charged no tuition, and had prepared more medical missionaries than any other medical school. Biblical languages and comparative religion were taught. The synod urged support of this institution as "the only Presbyterian university in the East." (It was Presbyterian in the sense that Columbia was Episcopalian, Chicago was Baptist, and Boston and Syracuse were Methodist.)

But the Presbyterian relation meant no responsible support for the institution.

Missions and Public Morals. Foreign missions remained the chief extraparochial interest of most Presbyterian congregations, as it had been before the Civil War. In fact there was a perceptible increase in missionary interest in the 1870's. A certain shift in motivation can also be detected as imperialist ambitions appeared. The Spanish-American War, largely incited by two New York newspapers, swung most church opinion, as it did President McKinley himself, to a benevolent imperialism. The missionary activities of the American churches in the Philippines and elsewhere drew more attention. New York Synod had also urged the president to protect the lives and property of American missionaries in Turkey at the time of the Armenian massacres of 1896. The contemplated exclusion from the United States of Armenian refugees was vigorously protested. Then again, the Boxer Rebellion and the later Chinese Republic engaged much interest, mingling economic, cultural, and religious aspects.

Missionary interest in New York was heightened by the synod's ties with missionary presbyteries in Persia, Siam, Chile, and after 1904, Puerto Rico. Affairs in these regions were brought before the synod periodically in the regular course of business.

New York City was the scene of the great ecumenical missions conference of 1900, the immediate predecessor of that Edinburgh Conference of 1910 from which the International Missionary Council sprang and which is usually taken as the beginning of the modern ecumenical movement. New York Presbyterians were conspicuous in both conferences.

Home missions in the narrower sense was now concerned chiefly with various special groups in the population — freedmen, Indians, Mexicans, Alaskans. Within the bounds of New York State there were significant numbers of Indians, four fifths of them in Buffalo Presbytery. That Presbytery twice printed reports on the subject.[2] The Onondagas were largely under care of Methodists and Episcopalians, the Mohawks of the Roman Catholics, but the bulk of those in the four reservations of Cattaraugus, Allegany, Tonawanda, and Tuscarora looked to the Presbyterians for help. The Presbyterians had inherited the old Seneca mission of Asher Wright and his wife.[3]

What was most needed was some form of vocational training to equip the Indians to live in white society when the reservation system was given up. There were a few state schools of little efficiency. In 1893 the synod proposed an industrial school at Lewiston, near Tuscarora. A legacy was available on a matching basis. The synod, however, had its usual experience in raising funds for educational purposes, and the legacy had to be returned. At least the representations of the synod contributed to gaining for New York Indians the privileges of the federal schools at Hampton and Carlisle.

Throughout the generation after the Civil War two concerns dominated the social ethics of New York Presbyterians — temperance and Sabbath observance. In 1883, synod voted that each presbytery should have a standing committee and each church a temperance society. Pastors were to preach on the theme at least annually. The permanent committee of synod observed in 1887 that with its cider, hop, barley, malt, and beer production, New York State was "the imperial seat of the liquor interest of this country." Sentiment for legal prohibition was growing, although not all pastors agreed on it. The General Assembly commended total abstinence and discouraged even wine-drinking. In 1895, it ruled that unfermented grape juice could be considered "wine" in the New Testament sense (but recommended against the use of individual cups in place of the common cup).

[2] *Report of Special Committee on Indians of Buffalo Presbytery,* April 9, 1889; *Second Report to the Presbytery . . . Indians of Western N. Y.,* April 14–16, 1890.

[3] Cf. Harriet S. Caswell, *Our Life among the Iroquois Indians* (Boston and Chicago, Congregational Sunday-school and Publishing Society, 1892).

New York Presbyterians had less success in the maintenance of the Sabbath, whether as a matter of personal discipline or of legislation. Excursions by railroad and steamboat were a major grievance, and pressures were brought on such enterprises to discontinue Sunday activities. Sunday mails were questioned. The Sunday newspaper was deplored by the General Assembly and the Synod of New York. The Chicago World's Fair remained open on Sunday despite protests but the New York exhibit was closed. A thoughtful and sensible report was adopted in 1896, questioning the value of "hopeless expostulations" or wholesale vetoes of Sunday recreation.[4] But the prevailing attitude was legalistic. As the 1903 report put it, "Even in heaven we shall still be face to face with the duties and privileges of Sabbath observance."[5]

2. Theological Readjustment

The American Protestant churches, it has been said, were confronted about 1890 by a twofold challenge, on the one hand to their inherited habits of thought and on the other to their social structure and procedures.[6] This thesis is illustrated forcibly by the developments of the period in New York Presbyterianism.

The last decade of the nineteenth century struggled through the second great theological controversy of American Presbyterian history. New York State again provided the most important arena and many of the leaders. Two intrinsically unrelated debates now became inextricably entangled in church actions, the issue of revision of the Westminster Confession on the one hand, and the meaning for the faith of the new historical interpretation of the Bible on the other. In both matters the thinking of the church was undergoing changes of momentous scope.

[4] *Minutes of the Synod of New York,* 1896, pp. 20–22.
[5] *Ibid.,* 1903, p. 38.
[6] A. M. Schlesinger, "A Critical Period in American Protestantism, 1875–1900" *Mass. Hist. Soc. Proc.,* LXIV.

Revision of the Confession. Seen in the historical perspective, the movement to revise the Confession was a continuation of the New School tendency of the 1830's. It represented a reaction against the predestinarian aspects of the inherited doctrine. As such it was common to all the major Reformed churches of the English-speaking world. For a time, indeed, it had seemed possible that they might meet the problem together. When the World Alliance of Reformed Churches held its first council in 1877 at Edinburgh, Philip Schaff, of Union Theological Seminary, urged in an address published as " The Harmony of the Reformed Confessions" that a "consensus creed" be undertaken. He was made chairman of a committee to develop this proposal. The third pan-Presbyterian council at Belfast in 1884, however, defeated the proposal by the combined votes of those who wished more and those who wished less change. The several churches then perforce addressed themselves to the problem more or less independently. The Church of Scotland, being established in civil law, could not change its Confession without Parliamentary action. The only feasible procedure was to loosen the terms of the subscription. The Scottish Free Church and the United Presbyterians preferred a revision on the one hand and a "declaratory statement" on the other. The English Presbyterians, the English Congregationalists, and the American Congregationalists proceeded to draft new confessions altogether. What would the American Presbyterians do?

American Presbyterians by and large no longer believed in several of the best-known affirmations of the Westminster Confession and Catechisms. Schaff challenged the whole Presbytery of New York in 1889 with the declaration that he knew no Presbyterian minister who preached reprobation or preterition.[7] The church at large no longer accepted reprobation or a limited atonement or the damnation of nonelect infants or of the non-Christian world generally. If a minister still held to

[7] P. Schaff, *Creed Revision in the Presbyterian Churches* (New York, Charles Scribner's Sons, 1890), pp. 13-14.

these views, his congregation would refuse to listen to them. Presbyterians generally had come to believe in God's intent to save all men, and wished to join to the affirmation of his free grace in election more recognition of human responsibility than the Confession allowed. This generation was also perhaps the most missions-minded in American history, and wished an explicit acknowledgment of God's concern for every creature as the basis of the missionary obligation. Many doubted whether there was adequate Biblical warrant for the predestinarian parts of the Confession.

These theological changes had come about gradually and inconspicuously and more extensively than almost any realized at first. The first attempts to open the issue came from the New York area. The *New York Evangelist* published a series of articles pro and con in 1887. Then the Presbytery of Nassau sent an overture to the General Assembly, and in 1889 fourteen other presbyteries joined it in requesting a study of the advisability of revision. The General Assembly, meeting in New York that year, requested the presbyteries to express their views.

This request launched the great debate across the land. New York State presbyteries voted for revision by twenty-two to two, only Genesee and Long Island opposing, and Albany abstaining. The debate of the Presbytery of New York in the Scotch Church continued twelve days, with nearly a hundred speeches. Schaff considered it " the greatest doctrinal discussion held in America " to that time.[8] The vote for revision was overwhelming. The report of the committee set to draft a proposal, however, was restrained, recommending that only the third and tenth chapter of the Confession, those with the most explicit predestinarian declarations, be revised. The third chapter was the chief focus of dissatisfaction throughout the church. Cayuga Presbytery returned a complete draft of a new

[8] P. Schaff, *Creed Revision in the Presbyterian Churches* (New York, Charles Scribner's Sons, 2d edition, enlarged, 1890), p. 69.

short confession, based on the Westminster Confession and Catechisms, drafted by two Auburn professors. It was clear that the great majority of presbyteries desired revision of some sort, and the General Assembly of 1890 set up a committee to prepare specific proposals that would not impair the Reformed system of doctrine.

The Committee had a draft ready for the Assembly of 1891, and that Assembly decided to circulate the draft among the presbyteries for criticism. The final report was thus presented in 1892 in the form of twenty-eight overtures. The Assembly adopted the report. But when the presbyteries then voted, no one of the twenty-eight overtures secured the necessary two-thirds vote. On the other hand, all but two of the overtures won substantial majorities of all the presbyteries in the church. The great body of the church was evidently in favor of the Committee's work but not, apparently, a sufficient proportion for Constitutional changes. The strength of the revision movement was in New York Synod and that part of the old Northwest Territory that shared the same New School tradition. The opposition was strongest in Pennsylvania, the South, and Princeton.[9]

The Briggs Case and Union Seminary. By the time the revision proposals came to a vote in 1892 and 1893 the church generally was preoccupied with another issue, the trial for heresy of Prof. Charles Briggs of Union Theological Seminary. Although he had not been converted to revision until 1889, Briggs then became one of its leading advocates, and the suspicion of his unsoundness was very damaging to the revision cause. He and others, in fact, charged that his accusers deliberately pressed his case to stop the revision movement. In any case it worked out that way. The embattled minority on the re-

[9] Cf. the geographical analysis in L. A. Loetscher, *The Broadening Church* (Philadelphia, University of Pennsylvania Press, 1954), pp. 44–45.

vision issue could readily command a majority and take the offensive against the "higher criticism" with which Briggs was associated.

Charges were preferred against Briggs before the Presbytery of New York in 1891, and the General Assembly of that year voted against confirming his transfer to the new professorship of Biblical theology in Union Theological Seminary. Charles Briggs had been on the Union faculty for seventeen years and was perhaps the most conspicuous "higher critic" in America. He had for years rejected the literalist conception of Biblical inspiration and had shown sympathy for the views of Wellhausen and Robertson Smith. He affirmed "plenary" but not "literal" inspiration. He had taken the leading part in the 1880's in bringing the new historical and textual studies of European and British scholars before the American churches, especially in a series of articles in the *Presbyterian Review* in which he and Prof. Henry Preserved Smith of Lane had defended the historical method against the conservatives of Princeton.[10] Personal attacks on him had been widely circulated in the religious press, and a student spy had undertaken to collect evidence of his heretical teaching. When the Union Directors transferred him from Hebrew to a new chair of Biblical theology an inaugural address was called for. At the request of the donor of the chair Briggs devoted the inaugural to the key issue of the "Authority of Holy Scripture." Exasperated by the treatment he had received, he adopted a provocative and defiant tone, which his colleagues deplored and which provoked overtures from sixty-three presbyteries to the General Assembly of 1891.

To understand the tragedy that followed one must remember the prevailing views on the Bible about 1890. American evangelicalism had always been Biblicist. Where there was less reliance on the Confessions as guides to Biblical interpretation the authority of the Bible as read by private judgment was all

[10] 1881–1883.

the greater. American Presbyterianism, however, was largely influenced by the type of scholasticism known as the Princeton theology, which inculcated a view of Biblical inerrancy unknown to the Reformation and held by no other major Reformed church. New School theology was as literalist as the Old School. Few churches were as ill-prepared to cope with the historical understanding of the Bible as the American Presbyterians at the end of the nineteenth century. The confrontation would inevitably be violent.

The conflict was from another viewpoint a struggle in theological method. American Presbyterian theology had hitherto been dominated by confessional systematics. But now this kind of theology was challenged by the new disciplines of Biblical theology and historical theology. In the persons of Schaff and Briggs, Union Seminary had acquired two of the most distinguished masters of these disciplines in America. The historical method was in principle as dangerous to rigid confessionalism as to Biblical literalism, and Briggs's and Schaff's historical studies of Reformed theology were as damaging to scholastic orthodoxy as were the new Biblical researches. To be sure, Union also had in Shedd a confessional dogmatician, whose *Dogmatic Theology* (1888, 2 volumes) was at least as strictly orthodox as Hodge. But Princeton lacked able representatives of the historical method and was wholly committed to the old rationalistic orthodoxy. Princeton was losing to Union the intellectual as well as the financial leadership of Presbyterian seminaries, and Princeton men were conspicuous in the attack on Union. Institutional and personal rivalries thus embodied and heightened the struggle of theological disciplines and methods.

When the Briggs case was brought before the General Assembly in 1891 the Assembly would have done well to postpone action by agreement with the Directors of Union. Judicial action had already been initiated in New York Presbytery, and for the Assembly to act was inevitably to prejudge the case. But the case was assigned to a committee composed of oppo-

nents to Briggs and headed by President Patton of the College
of New Jersey. This Committee gave no opportunity to the
Union Directors to explain their position and took no notice of
the written clarification of his views that Briggs had supplied
to the Directors. The recommendation was that the Assembly
veto Briggs's transfer without giving reasons. This amounted
to a verdict without a hearing, on the basis of common fame,
while the formal trial was still in process. The Assembly was
stampeded into adopting this recommendation, thus impeach-
ing Briggs's orthodoxy and the competence of the Union Directors.

This intervention by the General Assembly had not been anticipated by the Directors of Union Theological Seminary, nor
did it seem to them adequate grounds for taking action against
Briggs. The basis for the Assembly's action was an agreement
dating from 1870 at the time of the reunion of the two
churches. At that time Princeton Seminary, fearing New School
influence in the reunited General Assembly, had sought to re-
strict the control of the Assembly over seminaries. By constitution Princeton must remain under Assembly control, but now
it was proposed that the faculty be elected by Directors, leaving to the Assembly only the right of veto. In contrast to
Princeton, Union had always been governed by its Directors,
with no direct supervision from any church judicatory. To
oblige Princeton and in the interest of uniformity in the
united church, Union agreed in 1870 to the procedure of giving the General Assembly the right of veto. This right had
never been exercised at Union in the twenty years since, and
the Union Directors had never been forced to consider its im-
plications.

After the veto of 1891, however, the Union Directors con-
ferred with a committee of the Assembly. The two groups discovered that they disagreed on the status of the 1870 agreement. For one thing, no new appointment was involved in the
Briggs case; it was simply a transfer from one chair to another,
such as had been done three times with Schaff. The Directors

doubted that the right of veto applied to a transfer. More fundamental was the fact that the 1870 agreement was now seen to contravene the charter of the seminary, which placed the government of the seminary in the hands of the Directors.[11] Either the charter or the 1870 agreement must be changed. The Directors were bound by law to the charter and preferred its policy. They memorialized the General Assembly of 1892, consequently, requesting that the agreement be abrogated and expecting that the Assembly would concur with them.

The charges against Briggs, meanwhile, were brought before the Presbytery of New York. The presbytery investigated them and dismissed them. In New York State generally the church evidently did not believe that Briggs was a heretic. When the committee which had presented the charges in presbytery appealed to the Assembly of 1892, the New York Synod commissioners voted two to one against entertaining the appeal. The vote in the whole Assembly, however, was overwhelming on the other side, and the Presbytery of New York was ordered to conduct a formal trial.

The Assembly also expressed its mind on the point at issue in a paragraph that came to be known as the Portland Deliverance. The crucial sentence, " Our church holds that the inspired Word, as it came from God, is without error," [12] illustrated in its naïve ambiguity the prevailing state of mind.

The same Assembly declined the request of the Union Directors to annul the agreement of 1870. The Assembly Committee would have preferred legislation to change the seminary charter. The Directors in consequence regretfully abrogated the agreement unilaterally as contrary to their charter and therefore illegal.[13] They affirmed the undiminished loyalty of Union Theological Seminary to the doctrine and government of the Presbyterian Church, and its desire to return to its status

[11] G. L. Prentiss, *The Union Theological Seminary . . . Another Decade* (Asbury Park, New Jersey, 1899), p. 225; cf. 232-233.
[12] *Minutes of the General Assembly*, 1892, p. 179.
[13] Prentiss, *op. cit.*, pp. 281-283.

of the period from 1836 to 1870. Its professors were held to ordination vows and were subject to the discipline of their presbyteries. But there was to be no direct administrative control of the seminary by any church court. In support of this action four Directors from Presbyterian churches in New York City presented the chairman of the Board with a gift of $175,000. The Synod of New York that fall also " cordially commended " Union Theological Seminary to its churches.[14]

There were eight charges in the trial before the Presbytery of New York. The most important were the assertions that Briggs taught that inspiration did not preclude errors in matters of fact in the Bible, even in the original manuscripts, and that he denied the Mosaic authorship of the Pentateuch and the literary unity of The Book of Isaiah. Briggs acknowledged these positions as his own and denied that they were contrary to the Standards of the church. The presbytery judged in January, 1893, that no one of the eight charges was sustained.[15]

The prosecution appealed again to the General Assembly, and the main business of that body in 1893 was to hear and adjudicate the appeal in the Briggs case. Briggs had offered to resign his post and withdraw from the church, but was overruled by his friends. He went through the painful business of the trial, where the conclusion was foregone in the light of the Portland Deliverance. A court of five or six hundred men, mostly incompetent in the subtle issues under debate, and subject to all kinds of pressure, dealt to Briggs much the same sort of justice Socrates received from the Athenian demos. They voted to suspend Briggs from the ministry. It is notable that once again the majority of the New York Synod commissioners voted against sustaining the appeal (42 to 29).

The Washington Assembly of 1893 published the ground for its verdict in a clarification of the Portland Deliverance. " The original Scriptures of the Old and New Testaments," it was

---

[14] *Minutes of the Synod,* 1892, p. 18.

[15] J. J. McCook, ed., *The Appeal in the Briggs Heresy Case* (New York, John C. Rankin Co., 1893).

now defined, "being immediately inspired of God, were without error." This recourse to the "original" manuscripts was a defensive maneuver of dubious utility invented in the preceding decade at Princeton. Nevertheless, the Assembly proceeded to declare what was patently untrue, that it "had always been the faith of the Church taught in the Westminster Confession." [16]

This Hodge-Warfield speculation about the "original autographs" was then challenged in a "Protest" signed by eighty-seven commissioners to the Assembly.[17] It was, as they pointed out, outside the Standards of the church, beyond verification one way or the other, and in effect disparaging to the only Bible we have. The Assembly then improved its position by unanimously declaring that the *existing* Bible, when freed from all errors of translators, copyists, and printers is "wholly without error." [18] This opinion at least, although not stated in the Westminster Standards, had in fact been the prevailing view in the American Presbyterian Church. In the theological panic of the 1890's many or most supposed it an indispensable bulwark of the doctrine of inspiration. It was a preposterous and impossible position from which the church would later have to climb down.

The Washington Assembly also took note of the action of the Directors of Union Theological Seminary with regard to the 1870 agreement. They disavowed all responsibility for the teaching of Union Seminary and declined to receive any report from its Board until relations satisfactory to the Assembly should be established. They enjoined the Board of Education from giving financial aid to students in seminaries not approved by the Assembly.[19] Two years later the Assembly attempted to instruct the Presbytery of New York not to ordain Union graduates, but it was recalled in 1897 to the Constitu-

---

16 *Minutes of the General Assembly*, 1893, p. 163.
17 *Ibid.*, pp. 167–168.
18 *Ibid.*, p. 169.
19 *Ibid.*, p. 161.

tion of the church, which places authority over ordination in the hands of the presbyteries. The quarrel was bitter and endured well into the twentieth century. It did great damage to the loyalty of many Presbyterian laymen of New York, whose respect for the wisdom of the General Assembly was sorely tried. The net effect was also unnecessarily to alienate to a degree what had become the most distinguished theological faculty in the church and probably in the nation.

Another development that probably reflected the feud between Union and the Assembly was the sudden expansion at Auburn, the other seminary in the synod. In the 1880's, Auburn usually enrolled about 50 students, Union from 125 to 140. From 66 students in 1893 Auburn leaped to 105 in 1894, and the registration remained over the 100 mark through the decade.

There was considerable restiveness in the New York churches after the Assembly of 1893. The decision in the Briggs case would have gone the other way if the vote of the New York commissioners had decided it (and the Presbyterian Church would have been saved the grief and shame of having falsely condemned Charles Briggs as disloyal to his ordination). A third (32) of the New York commissioners had signed the "Protest" against the new doctrine concerning the original manuscripts of Scripture. Now as the Synod of New York came to review the records of the presbyteries it felt called to declare that it disapproved any presbytery actions questioning the deliverances of the General Assembly.[20] Cayuga Presbytery, where the Auburn faculty were located, had expressed itself as opposed to the erection of new dogmas by General Assembly majorities. North River, Niagara, Rochester, recorded similar opinions. The Synod of 1893 and the Assemblies of 1893 and 1894 maintained the dubious proposition that these definitions were not new doctrines and tests but merely interpretations of the old.[21]

[20] *Minutes of the Synod,* 1893, p. 49.
[21] *Minutes of the General Assembly,* 1893, p. 163; 1894, p. 45.

A conference was held in Cleveland in 1893 of Presbyterians disturbed by the Briggs case. Their manifesto carried the signatures of hundreds of ministers and elders. A Presbyterian League of New York was also organized the following spring. It sought the reversal of the heresy verdict, claimed more theological liberty, and desired confessional revision.

H. P. Smith, G. F. Moore, A. C. McGiffert, and Revision Completed. For the moment, however, blind reaction was in the saddle. The General Assembly of 1894 heard the appeal of Prof. Henry Preserved Smith of Lane against his suspension by the Presbytery of Cincinnati. The issue was again the denial of the Princeton theory of inerrancy of the original autographs. The Assembly rejected Smith's plea even more emphatically than it had Briggs's. This time the majority even of the New York commissioners opposed Smith's appeal, although New York also gave him nearly half the total votes for the appeal. Another distinguished scholar on the rolls of New York Synod, Prof. George Foot Moore of Andover, decided that the verdict made it impossible for him to remain in the Presbyterian Church. Thus, wrote Smith, "the church lost from its ministry the leading Old Testament scholar of this country." [22] Professor Smith was to end his own career as librarian of Union Theological Seminary and as a Congregationalist.

The only Lane colleague who had supported Smith was Prof. A. C. McGiffert. McGiffert had studied church history with Harnack and was called to Union to succeed Philip Schaff in 1893. In 1897 he published a *History of Christianity in the Apostolic Age,* which qualified him for the third famous Presbyterian "case" of the decade. The Assemblies of 1898 and 1899 considered the problem, the second of these referring the case to New York Presbytery. That Assembly of 1899 also unanimously declared four doctrines to be "fundamental," including the inerrancy of the Scriptures, the inerrancy of all

[22] Henry P. Smith, *The Heretic's Defense* (New York, Charles Scribner's Sons, 1926), p. 113.

statements made by Jesus Christ, the belief that Jesus himself instituted the Lord's Supper.[23] The Presbytery of New York condemned some of McGiffert's views but declined to prosecute him formally. When a private prosecutor appeared and appealed to the General Assembly, McGiffert withdrew from the church to prevent further litigation. He became a Congregationalist and remained for years the most popular lecturer at Union Seminary. It is interesting that Professor Briggs was with difficulty restrained from formally protesting to the Directors against McGiffert's teaching on the virgin birth.

Before the McGiffert case was finally disposed of, the issue of revision of the Confession emerged again rather unexpectedly. The majority of the church was not to be frustrated indefinitely on this matter. Nearly forty presbyteries overtured the Assembly of 1900 to resume the discussion. A Committee of Fifteen was appointed to report in 1901. That year the Assembly moved decisively. A Committee of Twenty-five under the chairmanship of Henry van Dyke of Brick Church, New York, was instructed to amend Chs. III and X with regard to reprobation, Ch. XVI on the works of the unregenerate, Ch. XXII on oaths, and Ch. XXV with reference to the papacy. The revision was to be accomplished either by modification of the text or by a supplementary declaration. In addition, a brief and nontechnical statement of the church's faith was to be prepared. This last was largely drafted by Dr. van Dyke, and made no reference either to reprobation or to inerrancy. In addition, his committee revised the text at three points and also produced a declaratory statement. The whole report went through the Assembly of 1902 in less than two hours, a startling contrast to the furious struggle of 1889–1894. All the proposals found support in two thirds of the presbyteries, and the Assembly of 1903 could call the revision done. The Cumberland Presbyterians, who had earlier separated in part over "Calvinistic fatalism," could now consider reunion, and the bulk of them did reunite in 1905 and 1906. One might also say

[23] *Minutes of the General Assembly*, 1899, pp. 96–98.

that New School theology had captured the church.

The church at large had finally caught up to New York Synod with regard to the eternal decrees. But in the matter of Biblical inspiration New York was still a generation ahead of the church at large. The General Assembly majorities had repeatedly asserted the Princeton theory of inerrancy and in its name had driven from the church four of her most gifted theological scholars. Union Theological Seminary remained "outside the church" and suspect to many. To be sure, a substantial section of the ministry were on record as declining to accept the Assembly's doctrine, and no attempt was made to discipline them. And the slow and careful work of rethinking the meaning of inspiration proceeded without much relation to majority votes in Assemblies. No doubt, too, the painful process of the trials served to disseminate and in time strengthen in the church at large such views as those of Briggs. But these consequences would scarcely be observable until after the First World War.

The Book of Common Worship. The decade of the 1890's marked a significant change in public worship as well as theology. Up to that time the evangelical stress on immediacy and individualism had predominated, often to the loss of distinctive Reformed practices. The chief changes were in hymnody, in which a revolution was effected between 1860 and 1890 with regard both to hymns and to musical settings. There was a Presbyterian hymnal for the reunited church as early as 1874, but of poor quality. The most active hymnologist in the church in this period was the New York City pastor, Charles S. Robinson, who published some fifteen collections between 1862 and 1892. He was not, however, a creative molder of standards.

The 1890's saw numerous experiments in the "enrichment" of worship in liturgical forms as well as church music. Despite Baird's *Eutaxia*, there was little general knowledge of the Reformed liturgical tradition, and most experiments in this direction consisted of borrowing from the Episcopalians. St. Peter's Church in Rochester had been one of the earliest of these. Large city churches especially felt the need of more dignity in worship. In the nineties the most important leader of the church in this matter was perhaps Henry van Dyke of the Brick Church in New York, also, as we have seen, a leader in the movement for confessional revision.

The Synod of New York appointed a committee in 1898 to study the growing and confusing diversity in forms of worship. After four years the committee produced a long and careful report.[24] Despite the experimentation, a remarkable uniformity in the order of the preaching service was reported. About two thirds of the churches now read the psalm responsively. There were usually three hymns in addition, and often Old Hundredth at the opening. A few used the "Glory be to the Father" after the psalm. There was usually only one reading, almost always from the King James version. About half used the Lord's Prayer. The "general prayer" usually came before the sermon rather than after. The Apostles' Creed was used by some at the Communion, the Nicene rarely. Most of the recent elaborations were musical, instrumental, or vocal. A wide variety of manuals — a dozen or more — were used by ministers, and many expressed the wish that the General Assembly would provide model services or a manual for voluntary use as was being done by many other Reformed churches.

The synod overtured the Assembly of 1903 to supply such forms. That Assembly appointed a committee and the synod committee put at its disposal the materials already gathered in New York. Henry van Dyke and Louis Benson made the chief contributions to *The Book of Common Worship*, which was finally approved and published by the Assembly of 1905.

3. Sociological and Ethical Reorganization

The second great challenge to the churches, which reached a climax about 1890, was sociological.

[24] *Minutes of the Synod*, 1902, pp. 31–35.

Town and Country. The rolls of the synod registered gains in these decades, but these were qualified by serious losses. The leakage in town and country churches, which had appeared even before the Civil War, remained a vexing problem. Scores of churches that at one time had flourished now lost ground, and sometimes became feeble and vacant as their people emigrated.

Only a little over half the churches of the synod had settled pastors in the 1880's. Over a hundred churches were vacant altogether, and over two hundred were served by stated supplies, which meant little continuity of ministry. In 1892, for example, of 832 churches in New York and New England (here 31), 355 had less than 100 members, 179 less than 55, 49 less than 25 members. Only about 500 of the 832 were effective self-supporting congregations.

A synodical superintendent, James Crocker, was appointed in 1885 to work with presbytery committees to support the vacant and feeble congregations. The national Board of Home Missions had urged two years before that the wealthier eastern synods should take care of their own home missions problems. New York Synod, along with New Jersey and Pennsylvania, undertook this. It was not anticipated that the needs would increase rather than decrease. The scheme was that each presbytery would raise an assessment for its own weak churches and in addition contribute to the Board for home missions work elsewhere. In the 1890's however, the New York presbyteries were raising only a third to a half of the New York needs.

At the end of the century a new scheme of Synodical Missions was adopted, whereby the Board was to aid only the Indian work in New York, the rest being handled locally, either by the synod or by presbyteries independently. The first full year of the plan was 1899, and the Board again had to make up the deficit in the local quotas.

The countryside and its churches were losing. Urban population (4,000 and over) increased 36 percent from 1890 to 1910 in New York, but the rural population actually decreased.

Town and country churches were being left on the sands by this receding tide. A net loss was reported in 1905 in the presbyteries of Steuben, Genesee, Rochester, Columbia, Buffalo, Lyons. Synod as a whole had gained 1 percent while the Presbyterian Church nationally gained 2.4 percent. Between 1885 and 1905 New York Synod gained 39 percent. Indiana gained 70 percent in the same period. The church nationally was growing more rapidly than the population, but New York Presbyterianism was losing, both in the church nationally, and in the population of its own state.

Another symptom of trouble was the decline in candidates for the ministry, which became a subject of comment at the turn of the century. In 1907 there were one third fewer men studying for the Presbyterian ministry than ten years earlier.

The Urban Challenge. But while the church seemed withering on the vine in its old strongholds, new peoples were pressing into the state by the millions. New York had always been a chief port of entry for immigration, but from 1890 this flow reached even new levels and changed in character. Hitherto, immigration had come chiefly from northern and western Europe, but now came the Italians and Poles, the Russian and Lithuanian Jews, the variegated peoples of the Austro-Hungarian Empire. They congregated in New York City, Buffalo, Rochester, Syracuse, Utica, in large colonies more alien to American culture and to Protestantism than any previous element of the population. A traditionally Protestant society was swamped by Roman Catholics and Jews. City churches found their neighborhoods suddenly alien and unresponsive. Even rural areas filled up with non-Protestant Europeans. In the mid-nineties there were nearly a million people in the state who did not speak English. In the following decade the foreign-born went up 60 percent in the Hudson River tier of counties, 51 percent in the southern tier, 91 percent in the central tier.

In the early years of the twentieth century it came to be

widely realized that the most urgent frontier for the church was no longer in the West, but in the great urban concentrations. Work among the foreign-born was developed in many presbyteries, first in Buffalo, New York, North River, St. Lawrence, Troy, Westchester. A synod secretary was assigned to the enterprise in 1911.

But the problem was deeper than merely a relocation of energies. Much in the procedure and tradition of the church was suddenly revealed to be ineffective in this new situation. When Dwight L. Moody campaigned in the New York City working class areas he failed conspicuously. The city mission type of program could not reach these people effectively. The great majority of Presbyterian ministers had been raised in town and country churches, and their individualist outlook, their worries about drink and Sabbath-breaking evoked little response in the emerging urban culture of the twentieth century. Parkhurst and Crosby fought commercialized vice and corrupt politics in New York City, but something more constructive was needed also.

One response was the development of "institutional churches" and settlement houses. Thomas Beecher of Elmira had pioneered in this as early as 1875. Union Seminary Settlement in New York City was an institution whose influence reached many future ministers. At Auburn, similarly, these new methods were considered in the curriculum before the turn of the century.

The most striking individual figure in the church in meeting the new society was probably the "son of the Bowery," Charles Stelzle. Stelzle was perhaps the most effective mediator between industrial labor and the Protestant Church in his day. He was called to found a new Department of Church and Labor in the Board of Home Missions in 1903 and became the first paid secretary in this field in any denomination. When the Federal Council was formed a few years later the Presbyterians loaned him to perform a similar function there. Stelzle founded Labor Temple in New York in 1910. But the ease with which conservative interests ousted him from his post a few years later showed how little the Presbyterian Church generally comprehended the new world of the twentieth century.

An effective response to the religious and ethical needs of the city could not be made on the basis of denominational autonomy. The church unity movement developed in close relation to the efforts to make an effective Christian witness in the new society. New York Presbyterians were active in the Open and Institutional Church League (1894) and the Federation of Churches and Christian Workers of New York City, which fathered the Federal Council of Churches of 1908.

VIII : *The Twentieth Century and Fundamentalism, 1900–1930*

1. ORGANIZATION AND PROGRAM

Ecclesiastical Boundaries. The synod as formed in 1882 contained the Presbytery of Boston, whose territory was the United States east of the State of New York. In 1911 at the request of this presbytery, the synod asked the General Assembly to form a new synod covering the six New England states, to be known as the Synod of New England. The General Assembly in 1912 erected this synod, comprising the Presbyteries of Boston, Newburyport, Providence, and Connecticut Valley. This last consisted of ministers and churches of Connecticut and western Massachusetts taken from the Presbytery of Westchester. The churches were Bridgeport First, Darien, Greenwich First, Stamford First, Thompsonville.

In 1904 the Presbytery of Puerto Rico was transferred by the General Assembly from the Synod of Iowa to the Synod of New York. Thus the synod gained a territory from which many people were to come to New York City and an important mission field under the care of the Board of National Missions.

The Presbyteries of Brooklyn and Nassau were joined as Brooklyn-Nassau in 1917, and in 1929 the Presbytery of Columbia was joined to that of Albany. These consolidations were the first of several such actions caused by growing de-

sire that presbyteries be more effective. In 1917 the names of
the Presbyteries of North Laos and Siam were changed to
North Siam and South Siam. In 1929 the synod's presbyteries
outside the state were these two, and Chile, Eastern Persia,
and Puerto Rico.

Home Missions. Early in the century the reports of the
synod's Committee on Synodical Missions show the synod
awakening to two urgent and not new conditions. One of these
was the decline of country and village churches, caused by the
movement of population to the cities, which had been going
on for some time, but rapidly since 1890. The other was the
incoming to cities and also to the country of thousands of immigrants, what the reports called "foreign-speaking people,"
among whom there was crying need for Christian teaching.

Under a new chairman, George P. Conard, the synod's committee took on new vision and energy. A new plan for its operation was adopted in 1908, embodying the principle of its
predecessor, that the synod should maintain its own home missions, but more efficiently organized. The ministry to foreign-
speaking people was vigorously pushed. Already in 1908 there
were ten churches and nineteen missions, mostly for Italians,
also for Hungarians and Slavs. Most of this had been done by
the Presbyteries of New York and Brooklyn, independently of
the synod. By 1911 work for the foreign-born had been established in nine other cities throughout the synod, and was projected in several more, and an associate secretary of the committee, Arthur H. Allen, had been appointed to supervise this
part of its service. In 1912 the problem of the country church
was grappled with. In that year U. L. Mackey entered on his
long and fruitful service to the synod. He first came to the
Committee on Synodical Home Missions to carry on financial
promotion, to foster the spirit of benevolence in the churches
and assist the weaker among them toward self-support, and
also to stimulate evangelism. Out of this grew a notable general
service of inspiring and guiding the smaller churches, espe-

cially those in the country and village. In 1912 he became Superintendent of Synodical Home Missions, succeeding J. Wilford Jacks, who had served faithfully since 1897. In the same year a ministry to the men in the Adirondack lumber camps was begun by the committee under the care of Aaron W. Maddox, who long served there.

In 1923, when in the reorganization of the church the Board of Home Missions became the Board of National Missions, the synod's committee took this name, and its work was more closely integrated with the Board's. Dr. Mackey's title was changed to that of Executive of the Committee, and as Associate Executive he had Arthur J. Dean, who had been working for the committee for several years. Before and after the reorganization the service of the committee was steadily enlarged and diversified, so that through it the synod became an efficient body for the strengthening of its churches. In 1924 the committee reported a staff of five general workers. By their care many churches were benefited in better provision of pastors, stronger administration of finances, wiser policies, and higher morale. Grants in aid were made to weaker churches from the Board's treasury on the recommendations of presbyteries and the committee, continuing the synod's policy of long standing. In the grants, regard was had to the principles of interdenominational comity adopted by the synod as early as 1914 and confirmed by agreement with the Home Missions Council in 1928, so as to avoid denominational competition and duplication. Efforts were made by the synod's staff and the presbyteries to unite weaker churches, in order to make stronger fields.

Work for the foreign-born increased. In 1926 there were twenty-seven enterprises, churches and community centers, speaking Italian, fourteen using Hungarian, and four of other tongues. The mission to the lumber men grew until in 1928 a "very large number of camps" were being reached in a varied ministry by three workers who led adventurous lives. In 1924 there was celebrated the centennial of Presbyterian missions to the Indians of western New York. In the present period this work was largely supported by the committee's funds derived from the Board of National Missions, and administered by the Presbytery of Buffalo. On the Cattaraugus Reservation, where there had been a Presbyterian establishment, there was in 1928 a cooperative arrangement, a Baptist Indian missionary being maintained partly by Presbyterian funds. On the Allegany Reservation, where there were about one thousand Indians in a tract forty miles long, the Presbyterians had a clear field and were responsible. Presbyterian work was carried on at four organized churches. The old mission to the Shinnecock Indians on Long Island was under the guidance of the synod's committee, but supported mainly by the Indians.

The synod's committee gave other valuable services. It acted as a committee on vacancy and supply for the synod generally, lessening the number of pastoral vacancies. It furthered evangelism in the churches under its care and in the presbyteries. It promoted contributions to the Board of National Missions. Its staff cooperated in various undertakings of the General Assembly, such as the "every member plan" of giving to benevolences and the New Era Movement, later to be described. Thus the synod through its Committee on National Missions proved itself an efficient organ for strengthening its churches and the work of the whole church.

One measure of the growth of this part of the synod's work is that the budget of the Committee on Synodical Home Missions in 1901 was $30,895; the budget of the National Missions Committee in 1928 was $78,942, of which $61,150 was for aid to fields. In 1927 the National Missions Committee reported 125 churches aided and nine community centers among the foreign-born.

Religious Education. In the early years of the century, Sunday school work was carried on in the churches faithfully but conventionally. No considerable progress appeared except some use of graded lessons and some teacher-training. In 1912 a sign of increased interest was the synod's establishment of the Committee on Religious Education, to cover the field of this name in Sunday schools and young people's societies, and its urging presbyteries to form such committees. Despite some improvement, the committee in 1918 reported that "the Sunday-school situation is steadily growing more serious," that there were losses in membership, in the teaching force and in attendance.[1] In 1919 there was reported a loss in membership of forty thousand. In that year the committee under the leadership of Nevin D. Bartholomew undertook a vigorous effort to realize "the principle that the Sunday-school is a school," to hold up educational standards and to raise morale.[2] Two years later an important step toward these ends was taken when David H. Craver was appointed Superintendent of Religious Education for the synod, and brought a new spirit into Sunday school work. In 1925 the Commission on Religious Education was able to report that the ministry and the church had become much more alive to the need of "educational standards, organization and methods."[3] On Dr. Craver's lamented death in 1928 he was succeeded by J. Elmer Russell, with the title of Superintendent of Christian Education. Largely because of their active travels among the churches and their wise, inspiring leadership, in 1929 there had come about in the synod a substantial educational awakening, shown in the erection by churches of educational buildings, the introduction of graded Sunday schools, the advance of worship in the schools, the strengthening of teacher-training in Presbyterian organizations and interdenominationally, the increase of weekday religious education and daily vacation Bible schools, the enlarged attendance at young people's summer conferences, emphasizing Bible study and training for teaching. With all this there came a real spiritual awakening.

In the early years of the century the synod had a Committee on Young People's Societies, which had been formed in 1895. This was replaced in 1912 by the Committee on Religious

[1] *Minutes of the Synod,* 1918, p. 14. [3] *Ibid.,* 1925, p. 24.
[2] *Ibid.,* 1919, pp. 22–23.

Education, which, as has been said, had oversight of young people's organizations as well as Sunday schools. In this decade the young people's work was carried on zealously, but it was said to be on the whole not in very progressive condition, though summer conferences flourished, with large attendance and enthusiastic spirit. In 1927 the Superintendent of Christian Education reported that the young people's work was "far from what it ought to be." [4] A decided revival was to come after 1930.

Educational Institutions and Work for Students. In this period the synod's relationship to educational institutions, which constitutes a rather inglorious chapter of its history, came to an end. In 1910–1912 the synod discontinued appointing visitors to Hamilton College, New York University (the University of the City of New York), and Elmira College. With Hamilton and New York University, neither the synod nor any of its predecessors had ever had organic connection. The attempt to form such a connection with Hamilton, unsuccessful because the synod did not provide the necessary endowment, has been narrated. The synod inherited the very strong interest always felt by New York Presbyterians in the college, and witnessed to this by its appointment of visitors, whose reports constantly emphasized its bonds with Hamilton. The visitors to New York University likewise repeatedly dwelt upon the large part played by Presbyterians in its history and management, and urged support of it. But their appointment ceased because the synod had no official responsibility for the institution. In 1908 the Trustees of Elmira College, who had been appointed by the synod, on its initiative became self-perpetuating in order to qualify for a Carnegie gift. This was after a last futile effort by the synod in 1901 to raise money for the college. The history of the synod's relation to colleges is largely a history of failures to secure funds for institutions with which it was naturally allied.

<hr>

4 *Ibid.,* 1927, p. 34.

In the years 1901–1912, the synod, as it and its predecessors had done, appointed visitors to Auburn Theological Seminary. Their very favorable reports were expressive of the synod's cordial attitude toward the institution. In 1912 this appointment was discontinued, not because of any change in this attitude, but because the synod, like its predecessors, had never had organic relations with the seminary, whose ecclesiastical ties had always been with the presbyteries that elected its governing boards.

An important educational activity of the synod began when in 1907 it took a step that resulted in the appointment in 1910 of the Committee on Student Work, authorized to have oversight of Presbyterian students in non-Presbyterian institutions, and to begin work in Ithaca. Ever fewer Presbyterian students were attending church-related colleges. They sought instead the institutions strongest academically. At Cornell there were in 1907 probably more Presbyterian students than at Hamilton and Elmira together. In 1913 a contract was drawn among the synod, the Assembly's Board of Education, and the First Presbyterian Church of Ithaca, under which the synod would employ a student pastor for Presbyterian students in the institutions in Ithaca, principally Cornell, of whom there were then more than a thousand, the Board would provide his salary, the Board and the synod would cooperate in securing a residence for him and an endowment for it, and the church would give the use of its building for the work, continuing what it had been doing. In 1914, Herbert M. Moore became Presbyterian Student Pastor. After successful service, he was succeeded in 1919 by Hugh Moran. A house was obtained for a residence and to be a center of activities. In 1920 the synod appointed a special committee for the Cornell work, which gave energy and direction and secured large financial support from the churches. In the years following, the Cornell enterprise developed rapidly in power and usefulness under the leadership of Dr. Moran. Early in the 1920's work of the same kind was begun by the synod in Columbia University, Herbert Evans being Student Pastor. In 1925 the synod directed the Board of Christian Education to allocate from funds contributed by the churches of the synod $7,500 for the work at Cornell, and for Columbia, $4,500, soon enlarged to $7,500. The student pastorates at these institutions were maintained with increasing success through this period. These undertakings were the beginning of the later Westminster Foundation work for students.

Synodical Reorganization. A new type of organization was formed by the synod in 1908, when it appointed an Executive Commission "to work along the lines of the Executive Commission of the General Assembly," that is, to be a permanent body of reference and leadership.[5] Its principal function concerned the benevolent contributions of the synod, under a new plan according to which the General Assembly sent down to the synods budgets of amounts to be raised, as will be described in the later section on Benevolent Finances. In 1918, when the synod held no meeting because of the influenza epidemic, the Commission discharged the necessary business.

In 1918, as the end of World War I was expected, the church felt new ambition. The General Assembly instructed a committee "to prepare a plan for a united movement of the whole church, to cover a period of five years." The program was to "embrace within the scope of its suggestions, the work of the local congregations, the Presbyteries and Synods, the Boards and other agencies of our church, with special reference to family religion, evangelism, education, missions, social service and stewardship." The Committee was authorized to put the plan into operation and was made responsible for promoting the "every member plan" for benevolent contributions. The name "The New Era Movement of the Presbyterian Church in the U.S.A." was adopted.[6] The synod heartily endorsed the Movement and appointed a committee to further it. This com-

[5] *Ibid.,* 1908, p. 56.
[6] *Minutes of the General Assembly,* 1918, pp. 67–68.

mittee under the Rev. John Lyon Caughey organized the Movement thoroughly in the synod and the presbyteries and led in action during the period. It promoted the budget system of supplying funds for the benevolent agencies of the church, bringing about the adoption of budgets by presbyteries and churches, and in connection with this the expansion of the "every member plan." It stimulated missionary education by holding schools in churches for this object, and awakened the churches to the duty of evangelism. In the reorganization of 1923 its functions were transferred to the new Committee on Program and Field Activities.

In 1923 there was consummated by the General Assembly a general reorganization, the principal features of which were the establishment of the General Council, having large supervisory powers in the church, the inclusion in the Office of the General Assembly of several agencies hitherto separate, the consolidation of eighteen boards and organizations of the Assembly into four Boards, those of National Missions, Foreign Missions, Christian Education, and Ministerial Relief and Sustentation (later the Board of Pensions), and the adoption of plans for the operation of the new Boards. This required a reorganization of the synod, which was adopted in 1923. There were established a Synodical Council and five principal committees and a Commission on Religious Education. These took over the functions of ten former committees and agencies of the synod, the Synodical Council replacing the Executive Commission; the Committee on National Missions succeeding the Committees on Synodical Home Missions, Missions to Freedmen, and the Board of Church Erection; the Committee on Christian Education replacing the Committees on Education, Temperance, Men's Work, and Sabbath Observance; the Committees on Foreign Missions and Ministerial Relief and Sustentation succeeding the former committees of these names. The Commission on Religious Education succeeded the former committee of this name and corresponded to the Department of Home, Church, and Community of the new Board of Christian Education. A new Committee on Program and Field Activities was to have oversight of all matters of benevolent giving.

The new plan made more effective the working of the organization of the synod. The Synodical Council soon became a trusted organ, giving leadership and administrative direction. At the same time with the reorganization the synod voted that in its meetings "the inspirational and educational phases of the program be emphasized." [7] The carrying out of this direction resulted in a considerable improvement in the character of the meetings.

Benevolent Finances. During this period the synod had a variety of organizations for furthering the giving of the churches for benevolent causes. In 1901 the Committee on Systematic Beneficence, formed in 1885, was in existence. In that year the committee was highly encouraged, after several lean years caused by financial depression. It reported gifts to all benevolent causes of $830,226 and to the Boards of the church of $371,482, against $644,025 and $352,802 in 1900. In the years following there were ups and downs, but no falling away to the levels of the previous decade. The churches largely depended on an annual collection for each Board of the church, though there was some use of annual pledges toward the Boards. In 1908 the Executive Commission undertook the administration of benevolent giving, acting on the new plan under which the General Assembly apportioned to synods amounts to be raised. The Commission prepared a plan, which was widely followed in the synod, for the securing of the apportionment by pledges for weekly payments. In 1913 the personal canvass for benevolent gifts was made a policy of the church by the General Assembly's appointment of the Committee on the Every Member Plan. The promotion of this Plan in the synod was taken over by the Synodical Home Missions

[7] *Minutes of the Synod,* 1923, p. 41.

Committee, with the result of a large increase in the giving of the churches.

In 1916 the General Assembly introduced a scheme for the support of its Boards by a budget of contributions providing an amount for each organization, thus putting the giving of the church on a more businesslike basis. The New Era Committee of the Assembly in 1919, just formed, was made responsible for work for the attainment of the budget. Accordingly, the New Era Committee of the synod undertook the supervision of plans for the adoption of particular budgets of contributions by the synod, the presbyteries, and the churches, and the further-ance of the Every Member Canvass. Such a canvass was carried through in a large number of churches. In the reorganization of 1923 the functions of the New Era Committee of the synod were transferred to the Committee on Program and Field Activities. To this committee there fell, with other things, the promotion of everything that concerned the benevolent giving of the churches. This was carried on through 1929.

Organizations for Women and Men. In 1901 the Woman's Synodical Committee on Home Missions submitted to the synod its nineteenth annual report. This committee often called itself and was often called the Woman's Synodical Society of Home Missions. For a few years the members of the Woman's Committee were elected by the synod on nomination of a synodical committee, but from 1906 the nominations are recorded as made by a committee of the Woman's Synodical Society, so that the Committee or Society became practically self-perpetuating, but it continued to report to the synod. Through its presbyterial auxiliaries and the societies in the churches the Woman's Synodical Society supported the Women's Board of Home Missions and its Department of Work for Freedmen, having special responsibility for schools and hospitals. It also had oversight in missionary matters of young people's societies, and stimulated missionary education in them as well as in the women's organizations. A measure of its activity and growth is that in 1901 its contributions to Home Missions and Work for Freedmen were $60,559 and at its reorganization in 1921 they were $135,360. Meanwhile, the women of the synod had expressed their interest in foreign missions by support of the Women's Board of Foreign Missions of New York, which was related to the women's presbyterial societies.

In 1921 all women's missionary work in the synod was united under the name of the New York Women's Synodical Missionary Society, which was auxiliary to the Women's Boards of Home Missions and Foreign Missions. When at the same time the Synodical Council was established, it was provided that it should have three women members, nominated by the Synodical Society, and that the same thing should be true of each of the five new principal committees of the synod.

The undenominational Laymen's Missionary Movement appeared in 1905 with the purpose of strengthening the support for foreign missions. It was broadened into the Men and Religion Forward Movement in 1911, to interest men in all aspects of the church's work, especially the "five points": Bible study, boys' work, evangelism, social service, missionary extension. Presbyterians were prominent in these "crusades," and New York City was the center for many of them. The synod urged Presbyterian support of the Men and Religion Forward Movement in 1911.

In 1909 the Synod's Committee on the Presbyterian Brotherhood, formed the year before because of a movement initiated by the General Assembly, reported that in at least eighty churches of the synod there were brotherhoods or men's societies. A Brotherhood Conference in 1910 brought together three hundred men and planned to further men's work. In 1913 the synod advised that Brotherhoods be formed in every church and that they carry on the Every Member Canvass for benevolences and church support. From 1916 there was an increasing growth of men's organizations and of interest and activity. In 1923 the Synod's Committee on Men's Work, as it had become, was discontinued, but the men's organizations maintained their life.

Public Morals. The strong concern for social righteousness in New York Presbyterianism found expression in the proceedings of the synod in this period regarding only two principal subjects. Their traditional opposition to the evil of alcoholic drink was vigorously sustained in the annual reports of the Committee on Temperance. These, while emphasizing education and personal abstinence, showed increasing reliance on legal restraints. The synod declared in 1903 that "the Presbyterian Church stands for abstinence and prohibition." [8] In 1905 the committee reported that "religious and temperance people . . . are devoting . . . almost exclusive attention to prohibition." [9] In 1910 the synod on recommendation of the committee urged the attainment of prohibition by local option and endorsed the Anti-Saloon League, which was working for this object,[10] and it continued to support the League. In 1917 it petitioned the President and Congress to bring about statutory national prohibition of the "manufacture, sale and importation of all kinds of alcoholic liquors for beverage purposes," and petitioned the New York members of the House of Representatives to bring about the passage of the prohibition amendment recently passed by the Senate.[11] After the adoption of the Eighteenth Amendment in 1918 the synod for several years urged the retention and enforcement of prohibition.

In 1912 the Committee on Temperance became the Committee on Temperance and Moral Welfare. Its province was enlarged to include other causes of social morals, but it confined its attention to the safeguarding of prohibition. In the reorganization of 1923 this committee was discontinued, and its interests were taken over by the Committee on Christian Education, representing the Department of Moral Welfare of the new Board of Christian Education.

[8] *Ibid.*, 1903, p. 19.
[9] *Ibid.*, 1905, p. 47.
[10] *Ibid.*, 1910, p. 49.
[11] *Ibid.*, 1917, p. 34.

The other principal traditional concern in public morals of the synod was the observance of Sunday. In this period, as long before in the New York synodical organizations, there was a Committee on Sabbath Observance, which made annual and usually long reports. On its recommendations the synod regularly took uncompromising positions. Several historical expositions provided occasions for organized pressure, with varying success. While strict personal observance of the day was enjoined on the people of the synod, here also the chief interest was in matters of law. The synod favored the enactment of more rigid laws and opposed relaxation of those in force. It sought legal prevention of baseball, motion pictures, theatrical performances, and business on Sunday. It disfavored the Sunday newspaper. In some of its utterances the synod was mindful of the interests of workers, and in general, while negative, they were motivated by concern for social welfare. In 1923 the Committee on Sabbath Observance was discontinued.

The deep concern felt by New York Presbyterians over World War I in its early stages and the strong sympathies excited among them find curiously little reflection in the proceedings of the synod. In 1915 the synod voted " that all our churches be urged to earnest prayer . . . that God in His mercy might bring to an early close the awful world-crisis which is now shaking the very foundations of our civilization." [12] Nor after the United States entered the war were the strong convictions of the people of the churches about the justice of the war and their determined support of it much expressed by the synod. A committee report of 1918, approved by the synod, said, " Every resource of America is pledged to help win the war . . . the supreme task of the day, winning the war." [13] There was no such questioning of the moral character of war as appeared later. In 1924 the synod concurred in action of the General Assembly condemning war, favoring participation by the United States in the Permanent Court of

[12] *Ibid.*, 1915, p. 33.   [13] *Ibid.*, 1918, p. 14.

International Justice and disarmament by international agreement, and calling on the churches to unite for securing " complete machinery for peace." [14]

Interdenominational Action. In 1914 the synod accepted the principle of comity in its aid to weak churches. It disapproved aid to a Presbyterian church in a community of five hundred or less where another evangelical body recognized by the Federal Council was better able to minister.[15] Presbyteries were advised to apply this rule not only to new churches but also to existing ones.

The New York County Church Council was formed in 1915 by representatives of five denominations, including the Presbyterians. Under its auspices a survey of religious conditions in Madison County was made, out of which grew an evangelistic campaign that covered the county and from which two thousand conversions were reported. In 1917 a like survey was made in Onondaga County, the synod's Committee on Synodical Home Missions participating in its support. This was a late manifestation of the spirit of interdenominational cooperation that had been strong in the synod for many years and had found expression in many local actions.

In 1922 at a meeting of delegates of denominational bodies of the state, including delegates of the synod, steps were taken toward the formation of the New York State Council of Churches. The Council at length having been formed, in 1927 the synod elected representatives to its membership and the next year voted a contribution of $2,000. Thus began the synod's permanent membership in the Council.

In 1928 the Synodical Council was directed to make a study of town and country churches, especially in view of the principles of comity approved by the synod. Next year the Council reported that under the guidance of the Home Missions Council and with the assistance of the New York State Council of

[14] *Ibid.*, 1924, p. 58.   [15] *Ibid.*, 1914, p. 44.

Churches a survey of thirteen eastern counties of the state had been made and a large amount of information assembled. An interdenominational committee, formed to consider these results and initiate action, held two meetings, but no outcome was reported to the synod.

2. THE FUNDAMENTALIST CONTROVERSY

The Five Points of Fundamentalism. The Synod of New York was involved in the occasion that proved to be the debut of the Fundamentalist controversy in the official actions of the Presbyterian Church. A judicial case was brought before the General Assembly of 1910, arising from complaints against the Presbytery of New York for licensing and ordaining certain students of Union Theological Seminary. The complaint was dismissed by both the synod and the General Assembly. But the Assembly went on in its last session, after a majority had left, to adopt a theological declaration. Five doctrines were specified as essential to the Bible and the Confession of Faith.[16] These were the inerrancy of the Scriptures, the virgin birth of Christ, his physical resurrection, his substitutionary atonement, and his miracles as changing the order of nature. These were the "five points" which were to play a great part in the subsequent history of the effective creed of the Fundamentalist movement. The assembly also directed that presbyteries should see to it that all candidates for licensure declared their assent to these doctrines.

In 1916 another similar complaint against the Synod of New York was before the Assembly, which had a like issue. This Assembly reaffirmed the doctrinal declaration of 1910 and repeated the direction to the presbyteries.[17] These directions were largely disregarded, as before, as many presbyteries stood on their Constitutional rights in licensure.

These actions of the Assemblies were the outcome of a con-

[16] *Minutes of the General Assembly,* 1910, pp. 272–273.
[17] *Ibid.,* 1916, pp. 132–133.

servative theological movement which had been rising in the Presbyterian Church and other churches since the late nineteenth century. This was compounded of several strong bodies of thought. There was opposition to liberal views of the Bible, which had been gaining ground since the 1890's. There was opposition to the evolutionary view of the origin of man. There was opposition to the rising social interpretation of Christianity. With this theological conservatism there was mingled millennial expectation. All this thought was expressed in a series of twelve pamphlets entitled *The Fundamentals*, of 1909–1910, which were very widely circulated gratis, especially in the Presbyterian Church, by two wealthy California laymen. Hence originated the name Fundamentalism applied to this strong conservative movement.

The Postwar Fundamentalist Campaign. During a few years after World War I, New York Presbyterianism was involved in the Fundamentalist controversy much more than it had been previously. The war was followed in American Protestantism by a marked strengthening of the rigorous theological conservatism and the millenarian expectation that had arisen earlier in the century. This appeared in the World Conference on Christian Fundamentals held in Philadelphia in May, 1919, attended by six thousand people of many denominations from almost all the states, and also from Canada and seven foreign countries. At this meeting the movement of Fundamentalism was organized for aggression. A "Doctrinal Statement" was adopted, containing, with the standard Christian beliefs, the tenets hitherto emphasized by the Fundamentalists and adding the imminent return of Christ. Throughout the conference, opposition to the teaching of the evolutionary origin of man was expressed. A many-sided program of propaganda and action was planned, the ultimate object of which was to gain control of the organizations of the important denominations and form them on the Fundamentalist pattern.

The first attack was directed against the Northern Baptist

Convention in 1922. In anticipation of this, a sermon entitled "Shall the Fundamentalists Win?" was preached in the First Presbyterian Church of New York by Dr. Harry Emerson Fosdick, the most influential leader of liberalism, a Baptist minister who was a regular preacher in this church. In the sermon he stated the views of Fundamentalists and liberal evangelicals regarding three matters in dispute — the virgin birth, the inspiration of the Bible, and the Second Coming of Christ — and urged that room be given in the churches for both kinds of thinking. Dr. Fosdick did not formally express his opinions, but showed frankly where his sympathies lay and spoke against the intolerant exclusiveness of Fundamentalism. The sermon was widely distributed and aroused much interest. It was thus that Fundamentalism became a matter of newspaper publicity and general discussion. Thus also the storm center of the Fundamentalist controversy was moved into the Presbyterian Church, and New York Presbyterianism was drawn into it.

In the General Assembly of 1923 a charge was brought by the Presbytery of Philadelphia against the preaching in the First Church of New York as being "in open denial of the essential doctrines of the Presbyterian Church in the U.S.A." [18] The Assembly directed the Presbytery of New York to require that the preaching in this church conform to the Confession of Faith, and to report to the next Assembly; and it also reaffirmed the doctrinal declaration of 1910, containing the five points of Fundamentalism. This action of the General Assembly toward a presbytery made the matter a question for the whole church. Now the propaganda seeking to establish the five points as the church's effective creed and to make the church Fundamentalist, which had been intense ever since Dr. Fosdick's sermon, was redoubled and much embittered. In periodicals, pamphlets, sermons, addresses, all who dissented from the five points or were known to hold liberal theological views were accused of opposition to Christianity. It was asserted that many ministers of the church were so opposed, that

[18] *Presbyterian*, October 26, 1922, pp. 6–7.

among missionaries on the field there were men of the same spirit, and that in some theological seminaries there was teaching hurtful to Christianity.

After several months of this campaign there appeared a proposal designed to accomplish its ends. In March, 1924, the Presbytery of Philadelphia sent to the General Assembly an overture asking that the Assembly require that all representatives of the church in the Boards, the General Council, the theological seminaries, and other agencies reaffirm their adherence to the doctrinal Standards of the church, particularly as these were interpreted in the deliverances of the General Assemblies containing the five points.[19] This involved giving to certain utterances of the Assemblies an authority equal to that of the church's creed. The intent of the overture was that all who had places in the general organization of the church should be Fundamentalists.

The " Auburn Affirmation." Meanwhile, those in the church who inherited the historical Presbyterian tradition of freedom had been moving. A group drew together, the leaders largely from the Synod of New York. The result was the publication in January, 1924, of *An Affirmation Designed to Safeguard the Unity and Liberty of the Presbyterian Church in the United States of America.* As first published, this was signed by one hundred and fifty ministers. At its second publication, in May, 1924, just before the meeting of the General Assembly, it bore the names of almost thirteen hundred, of whom three hundred and fifty were of the Synod of New York. In the *Affirmation* the signers protested their loyalty to evangelical Christianity and their adherence to the Confession of Faith, as given at their ordination. From its history and law they showed that the church assured to its ministers liberty in the interpretation of the Confession and the Scriptures. They characterized the General Assembly's censure of the preaching in the First Church of New York as " out of keeping with the law and spirit of our

[19] *Ibid.,* March 13, 1924, p. 12.

church." They maintained that when General Assemblies declared, as was done in the deliverances containing the five points, that certain doctrines were "essential," they acted unconstitutionally, since for declaration of the doctrine of the church the concurrence of the presbyteries was required by the Constitution. They gave this positive testimony: "We all believe from our hearts that the writers of the Bible were inspired of God; that Jesus Christ was God manifest in the flesh; that God was in Christ, reconciling the world unto Himself, and through Him we have our redemption; that having died for our sins He rose from the dead and is our ever-loving Savior; that in His earthly ministry He wrought many mighty works, and by His vicarious death and unfailing presence He is able to save to the uttermost." To this they added: "Some of us regard the particular theories contained in the deliverance of the General Assembly of 1923 as satisfactory explanations of these facts and doctrines. But we are united in believing that these are not the only theories allowed by the Scriptures and our standards as explanation of these facts and doctrines of our religion, and that all who hold to these facts and doctrines, whatever theories they may employ to explain them, are worthy of all confidence and fellowship. . . . We hope that those to whom this Affirmation comes will believe that it is not the declaration of a theological party, but rather a sincere appeal, based on the Scriptures and our standards, for the preservation of the unity and freedom of our church, for which most earnestly we plead and pray."

The General Assembly of 1924 decided that the additional doctrinal tests proposed by the Philadelphia overture to be imposed on representatives of the church were unconstitutional, as the *Affirmation* contended. It also voted — on a complaint against a favorable report by the Presbytery of New York on Dr. Fosdick's preaching — that his position as a Baptist minister serving as a regular preacher in a Presbyterian church was "an anomaly," and that the Presbytery of New York be instructed to take up with him the question of whether he wished to enter the Presbyterian Church.

The *Affirmation*, sent in May, 1924, to every Presbyterian minister, aroused great interest in the church and beyond. It at once strongly counteracted Presbyterian Fundamentalism by showing that many men who were not Fundamentalists were evangelical believers, who had a right in the church. Its influence lasted long as a vindication of liberty in the church and a defense of its unity.

Meanwhile, the controversy continued through judicial proceedings originating in the Synod of New York. The synod of 1924 had before it a complaint against the Presbytery of New York for licensing two candidates who could not affirm belief in the virgin birth of Christ. The complaint was dismissed on the ground of the presbytery's final authority in licensure. The General Assembly of 1925 sustained the complaint, holding that the presbytery erred in giving the licenses, and remanded the matter to it "for appropriate action." The Assembly did not revoke the licenses, but came near enough to this to imperil the sole right of the presbyteries in licensure, a cherished Constitutional liberty of the church. It also asserted the Assembly's authority to prescribe doctrine for the church. This decision brought on a storm and crisis in the Assembly. For the Presbytery and the Synod of New York, statements were read declaring their purpose to maintain the right of presbyteries in licensure. The atmosphere in the Assembly was so charged with danger of revolt and schism that the Moderator took the floor and proposed the appointment of a special commission to consider "the causes of unrest in the church."

As soon as possible after this decision a similar case was brought to the Synod of New York. The synod of 1925 had before it a complaint against the Presbytery of New York for its licensing a candidate and its receiving into membership a Baptist minister. These men, it was alleged, had on their examinations given unsatisfactory answers regarding several doctrinal matters, four of the celebrated five points. The synod in 1926 dismissed the complaints on the ground that there was nothing

in the presbytery's record to support them. Complaint against
the synod being taken to the General Assembly of 1927, the
Permanent Judicial Commission of the Assembly rendered a
judgment sustaining the synod. When this was presented to
the Assembly, there ensued a disorderly scene and an inconclusive result. But by this time the Special Commission of
1925 had made its reports to the General Assembly, in 1926
and 1927.[20]

These reports, learned in the history and law of the church,
convincing in substance and tone, sustained the major contentions of the liberals of the church and of the *Affirmation*.
They upheld the authority of the presbyteries in licensure and
ordination. They discouraged the promulgation of "essential"
doctrines by General Assemblies. They emphasized the provision in the Constitution of the church for difference of opinion, and denied the existence of any such defection from Christianity as Fundamentalism had alleged. The adoption of the
reports in General Assemblies by overwhelming majorities established in the church the liberties that had been contended
for, and marked a notable increase in the church of the spirit
of unity and mutual confidence. In this result the Synod of
New York, as has been seen, had played a considerable part.

[20] *Minutes of the General Assembly,* 1926, pp. 62–87; 1927, pp. 58–
86.

IX : *The Religious Depression and After, 1925–1960*

It has been observed that a religious depression was well under way in American Protestantism before the financial crash of 1929.[1] This was the case with Presbyterianism in New York State, where one might compare the two decades from 1925 to 1945 with the experience of the colonial Old Side church and that of the separate New School church in the 1840's and 1850's. It was a time of low religious vitality, of decreased giving and curtailed missionary programs, of static or relatively decreasing membership, of shrinking Sunday schools, of inadequate replacements in the ranks of the ministry. There were a few signs of new vigor in the late 1930's, and the giving of the church recovered during the Second World War, but on the whole the end of the slump should probably not be dated before 1945.

1. THE RELIGIOUS DEPRESSION

Church Membership. The New York State communicants of this period increased, but just barely. From 1925, when 241,000 were reported, they rose to 269,000 in 1949, an annual gain of ½ percent. At a time of substantial population growth this

[1] R. T. Handy, "The American Religious Depression, 1925–1935," *Church History*, March, 1960, pp. 3–16.

meant a continued dwindling of the Presbyterian section of the whole community.

Sunday Schools. Even more startling as an indication of spiritual ill-health was the decline of the Sunday school. It was observed at the semicentennial of the synod in 1932 that while the number of communicants had increased 95 percent in fifty years, Sunday school students had remained at the same level. In 1882 there had been more Sunday school students than church members; in 1932 there were only slightly more than half as many. The decline was steady from 1926 with its 146,000 students to a low ebb of 98,000 in 1945. To be sure, budgets had been cut severely and staff much reduced. But the deeper problem was theological. The Sunday school had arisen in the days of revivalist evangelicalism. Then it had come to embody the kind of liberal theology that was in rapid disintegration in the thirties. The one church school activity that seemed to prosper was the summer conference for young people.

Ministerial Vocations. There was an increasing problem also of recruiting for the ministry, another significant index of lack of religious vitality. It was reported at the end of the thirties that New York Synod had not been producing its share of ministers. After 1932 it had imported fifty-nine more ministers from out-of-state presbyteries than it had dismissed to such presbyteries, and it had received forty-five more ministers from other denominations than it had transferred to such denominations. Over a hundred more ministers had been brought in from elsewhere to fill New York vacancies than had moved in the other direction.

It was also reported that, as generally throughout the church, more men were being lost year by year by death or retirement than were being ordained. The year 1947, with its postwar bulge of seminarians, was the first time in fifty years that more ministers were ordained than buried. The average

age for ministers was then fifty-five.

The Committee on Ministerial Relations was inclined to suspect the chief explanation was lack of religious interest, although disappointment in the church as an institution, and finances were also noted as factors.

Contributions for Benevolences. New York Presbyterians began to taper off their contributions to national and foreign missions from 1926 onward, at a time of great financial prosperity. There was a brief improvement in 1929, then the decline was even more rapid. By 1933 the field staff of national missions had been cut from seven men to one, Dr. Mackey, and his salary had been reduced and his duties extended. The decline was 59 percent in seven years. Contributions to foreign missions likewise fell inexorably year by year to 1935, when a single gift of about three millions by C. Sidney Shepard, of Buffalo, changed the pattern on the graph. But by that year the 1,606 missionaries of 1926–1927 for the church at large had been reduced to 1,344, and their native helpers from 9,285 to 8,000. Two years later the roster of missionaries was down to 1,262. Decreases in contributions progressed cumulatively year after year until 1939–1940, more markedly in New York than in the church generally. Only in the war did the tide of giving again begin to rise and Boards begin again to renew their depleted personnel.

General economic conditions explain this story in part, but only in part. Even before the depression it was observed in New York Presbyterianism that the rank and file of laymen were neither informed about nor vitally interested in the world mission of the church. The missionary societies in the congregations were largely composed of older women; the younger women and the men knew little about the matter. Widespread resistance to the missionary responsibility was indicated by the use of promotion materials " covering the possible objections," [2] and the provision for " knockers " to raise difficulties at confer-

---

[2] *Minutes of the Synod of New York,* 1932, p. 31.

ences. In 1937 the synod committee proposed it as a goal to interest at least a majority in the church in foreign missions. That goal was never reached.

Public Affairs. The sense of national crisis was reflected in the erection in 1930 of a Special Committee on Social Service to inform the synod about social issues and the application of the Christian gospel to them. This Special Committee was then made one of the standing committees and under the chairmanship of Cameron Hall returned some striking reports in the great questioning of the depression era. The reports reflected the widespread and unprecedented dissatisfaction with the traditional assumptions of the American economic order and its consequences in mass unemployment and social injustice. They attacked the profit motive and the great inequality of wealth in America. In 1933 they welcomed state intervention in economic affairs, the abolition of child labor, the elimination of the sweatshop, the establishment of minimum wages and maximum hours, the recognition of labor's right to organize and bargain collectively. They supported the payment of relief to strikers. They affirmed that the payment of a "just wage" was a primary obligation on industry and approved such aims of the New Deal as Social Security programs. The church, it was held, should stand with those who wished to organize economic life more effectively for the welfare of all.

It is hard to believe that these views represented fairly the mass of Presbyterian laymen. That the synod would accept such reports year after year is indicative of the intellectual revolution then in process. The name of the committee was changed to Social Education and Action in 1936, and organization on the presbytery level was pushed. Such regular consideration of public affairs has continued ever since.

Some of the traditional social concerns of the church were also voiced, as with problems of divorce and the liquor trade. The committee reported a widespread disillusionment with attempts to regulate the latter. They also urged in 1932 that a study should be made of means for realizing racial equality in the synod, the General Assembly, and other corporate gatherings of the church.

The most insistent preoccupation, however, and increasingly from 1934, was with war. The reports of the 1930's were predominantly pacifist in sentiment. They opposed the Naval building program and Naval maneuvers, supported the Disarmament Conference of 1932 and American entry into the World Court. They urged a "break with the war system" and put war in a category with adultery, theft, and murder. It was apparently the student protest against compulsory military training at Cornell that led the committee to urge that Presbyterian conscientious objectors be given the same status as Quakers, and excused from military training without official censure. An effort was made to modify the Westminster Confession to give explicit expression to pacifist convictions. The committee supported the League against the Italian assault on Ethiopia, but urged a neutral attitude to the Spanish Civil War and commended the Munich agreement with Hitler. When the European war broke out the committee opposed peacetime conscription. The majority of the committee were still pacifists, but recognized that the church at large was not. Not until 1942 did the report, finding no national alternative, pledge the church to work and pray for a righteous victory.

Weakened Congregations. The old problem remained of the local church in the area of dwindling population. In 1937 only 321 of the 812 congregations in the synod were located in the centers of more than 5,000 population where the overwhelming mass of people in the state lived; 214 churches were in communities of less than 500 population; and 421 churches — over half the total — had less than 200 members at a time when the average size of a church was over 300. It was noted that over half the 200-some churches of less than 100 members had no accessions on profession of faith in 1937. In 1939, 240 churches reported no gain in membership. These were often the churches that could not afford to pay a minimum salary and they were reconciled, in many cases, to never having a settled pastor.

Among these churches there was a higher mortality than was always realized. The number of churches in the synod decreased from 826 in 1930 to 776 in 1949. This seemed to be a loss of only 50, but in fact 96 churches had disappeared; 34 had merged into 17, 6 had transferred to other denominations, and 73 had been dissolved. Meanwhile 48 new churches had been organized. It was the obvious need to care for small leaderless churches that led the synod finally to secure an associate executive with this responsibility.

While some churches had become superfluous, new areas of need were also emerging. In 1940 three counties were reported as, respectively, 62 percent, 66 percent, and 68 percent unchurched. In some areas the expanding cities suddenly converted village churches into suburban churches. Then in the inner city, population movements left old churches as starved as in the depopulated countryside.

National Missions. Akin to the weakened congregations in their need for special help were the various groups on the national missions list. With the virtual cessation of immigration, the language congregations gradually disappeared as such. As late as 1943, however, there were thirty-five foreign-language churches in the synod, using ten languages. The Italians had twenty-six churches in 1937 and were the chief body. Then there were half a dozen or more congregations of Indians on the seven and a half Indian reservations. An increasing number of Negro congregations were receiving help. Throughout this period migrant farm labor constituted a growing problem, especially among Indians, Italians, Poles, Negroes, French Canadians. In the pressure of the war, lumber camps increased 50 percent, and the synod maintained two missionaries to the lumberjacks, constituting a " Northeastern Lumber-camp Parish " in New York and New England. This increase, however, disappeared again with the loss of the military market for lumber at the end of the war.

Reorganization in Synod. The synod sought in various ways to meet the problems of national missions and struggling congregations. Among them were some statesmanlike measures, in particular the creation of synod executives, the reorganization of presbytery bounds, comity arrangements, and the Maintenance of the Pastorate Fund.

The office of Synod Executive arose in 1934 under the pressure of dwindling budgets. Dr. Mackey, the Director of National Missions, was assigned also the responsibilities of Vacancy and Supply, and Program and Field Activities. Dr. Howard Yergin succeeded him and served fourteen years as executive, until succeeded in 1950 by Dr. MacInnes. The office of Associate Executive was created in 1942, with especial responsibility for churches with little supervision, and Dr. Schubert Frye served in this capacity.

In 1928, meanwhile, the synod appointed a committee to study presbytery boundaries with a view to improving their effectiveness. Population movements and the general use of the automobile had significantly shifted the social relationships for which the existing pattern had been devised. It was generally felt that to be effective working units, especially in church extension, the presbyteries should be larger — some said large enough to support a presbytery executive. Also the committee sought to follow county lines where possible in order to expedite interdenominational cooperation on a county basis.

The report was in part adopted by the synod in 1930, but the General Assembly, receiving protests from some quarters, returned the whole matter to the synod. The proposals for the Utica-Syracuse-Binghamton area bogged down. But some consolidations took place. Niagara was divided in 1932 between Rochester and a new Buffalo-Niagara Presbytery. Steuben-Elmira emerged in 1933 out of a merger of those two presbyteries. Another recommendation, the merger of Geneva and

Lyons, was finally voted by the synod after the war in 1945 at the petition of both.

Three presbyteries, those of Utica, Troy, and New York, were also strengthened in 1936 by fifteen churches from the former Welsh Synod of New York and Vermont.

Comity. The New York State Council of Churches, with which the New York State Council of Religious Education was merged in 1933, was increasingly effective in these years. The synod had appointed delegates from the time of its organization in 1922, and in 1928 had decided to contribute funds if other denominations would also do so. The amounts, as one might expect, were considerably reduced in the next two years, but some contribution was made. From the end of the 1930's the annual report of the General Secretary was regularly printed in the synod minutes.

In 1928 the synod had indicated to the State Council of Churches that its chief interest was in comity, in doing away with unnecessary existing churches and in preventing the organization of such. The synod entered into an agreement not to subsidize such new churches. Maintenance of the Pastorate grants were not to be made in such situations. It turned over its National Missions list to enable the State Council of Churches to draw up in 1935 a master list of communities where denominational home missions might be unprofitably competitive. By 1939 New York State was said to have the best record in the nation for rural comity.[3]

By 1943 some form of interdenominational cooperation was in operation in some eighty local communities. The synod preferred federated churches retaining denominational connection to community churches without any. There were also cases of interdenominational mergers where one denomination relinquished its claims. Such arrangements could be made so as to match gains and losses, at least in some degree. In many

[3] *Ibid.,* 1941, p. 11.

cases this was the only hope of an effective Protestant ministry in a community.

Minimum Salaries. The synod recommended the establishment of a minimum salary for ministers in 1936. A committee studied the experience of the Free Church of Scotland and the Presbytery of Chicago and proposed a scheme for a " Maintenance of the Pastorate Fund." They calculated that by raising about $10,000 from the stronger churches and individuals it should be possible to subsidize the lowest salaries and secure a minimum of $1,200 and manse ($1,500 and manse in larger cities). The scheme was approved by the synod and most presbyteries and put into operation in 1938. In its first year the plan admitted 31 claims, and paid them to the extent of 65 percent. By 1942 payments had reached 100 percent and the floor was raised to $1,600. By 1946 it was $2,000 and manse, by 1950 $2,400 and manse, by 1960 all but two presbyteries had adopted a minimum of $4,500, manse and pension. In its first decade the plan averaged only about 30 claims a year, but for these men it made a substantial difference. The demonstration of solidarity in the church, moreover, went far beyond what the statistics might suggest.

Overseas Presbyteries. This generation saw large transfers from missions to new national churches all over the world. Some of these affected the number of missionary presbyteries that belonged to New York Synod. The Presbytery of Siam, for example, had been enrolled in the Synod of Albany (OS) by the General Assembly of 1859. After belonging for a year to the Synod of China, which received two Chinese presbyteries from the Synod of New York (OS) in 1870, the Presbytery of Siam was reassigned to the Synod of Albany in 1871, from which it was inherited by the united Synod of New York. In 1884 it was divided into the presbyteries of North Laos and Siam, or, as they were renamed in 1917, North Siam and South

Siam. Now in 1932 these two Siamese presbyteries were cordially encouraged by the synod to become independent in order to join in the formation of a national Christian church. The Church of Christ in Siam was formed in 1934 of communities gathered by Baptists, Presbyterians, the Christian Alliance, and others.

The Persian Presbytery had a similar history. As the Presbytery of Oroomiah it was attached to the Synod of Western New York in 1873, and inherited by the consolidated Synod of New York. It was divided in 1889 into Eastern Persia and Western Persia, but in 1897 Western Persia was dissolved. In the year in which the Church of Christ in Siam was formed, Eastern Persia requested that it might be released to unite with other churches to form two presbyteries in the Church of Persia. The synod supported this action, and it was effected in 1935. Thus were achieved the hopes and desires of the New York Synod for these missionary presbyteries. After 1935 only Chile and Puerto Rico were left on the roster.

The Ministry to Students. Some of the first signs of a more positive interest generally in the Christian faith appeared on college and university campuses in the late 1930's. Presbyterian student pastors had been at work all through the decade at Cornell, Columbia, and Syracuse. Alfred University was then added, and the synod contributed to the support of the SCM secretaries traveling about the institutions where there were no Presbyterian pastors. It was noted in 1940 that in the country at large there were six times as many Presbyterian students in fifty-two non-Presbyterian institutions as in the fifty-two Presbyterian colleges. The work was extended during the war to Rensselaer Polytechnic Institute and later to New York University, Buffalo, Albany, and Fredonia State Teachers Colleges. The Presbyterians led in this whole development of ministry to college and university students in New York State. Other denominations then came to emulate them.

Just as World War II broke out the church awakened to a

long-neglected opportunity. Some three thousand students from lands to which American missionaries were assigned were studying in American colleges and universities along with thousands of other foreign students. In New York colleges and universities alone there were counted five hundred thirteen students from the sixteen countries where Presbyterian missions were at work, and fifteen hundred others in 1941. Out of the synod's effort to meet this missionary opportunity came an Interdenominational Committee on Work with Foreign Students in the State of New York (1942).

2. THE POSTWAR RECOVERY

The Seminaries and Theological Revival. Among the casualties of the depression years was the theological enterprise at Auburn. Various possible consolidations upstate were explored and finally the seminary was moved to New York City for a kind of merger with Union. Auburn continued its corporate existence with its own funds. But it conducted no separate academic program and had no separate student body at Union. Auburn became, as it were, the explicitly Presbyterian organization within the now interdenominational structure of Union. The Presbyterians of the Union faculty were elected as Auburn professors and were active in extension work. The dean of Auburn worked with the Presbyterian third of the Union students. Auburn was also more directly related to the synod as the number of presbyteries was reduced to the point where every presbytery in the synod could be represented by a director. From 1954 the annual report of the Auburn Directors was printed in the synod minutes.

Union, meanwhile, had become, under the leadership of President Henry Sloane Coffin, and with the teaching of Reinhold Niebuhr and Paul Tillich, the most eminent theologians in the country, America's foremost theological faculty. It was the most important single center of that "neo-orthodox" current of theology which from the 1930's increasingly took the initiative from the older liberalism. Thus once again as with the New School modifications of predestinarianism, and with the historical approach to the Bible, New York led the church at large into fresh theological paths. Students were drawn in significant numbers from abroad, especially from Great Britain, to study theology and social ethics at Union, and the seminary on Morningside Heights became one of the world's greatest theological centers.

Moral Man and Immoral Society (1932) is usually taken as the signal for Niebuhr's new theological turn. He was reacting from the naïve moralism of the liberal social gospel, and in the process led in the rediscovery of classical doctrines of sin and grace, judgment and forgiveness. By the end of the thirties he was acknowledged to be the most discerning and influential theological analyst of American political life. Paul Tillich's more philosophical and systematic orientation won its wide public during and after the war. The churches began to feel the impact of this new direction in the fifties as the students of these teachers became pastors.

New Vigor in Church Life. The church came out of the war with new energies. Benevolent giving had already begun to recover, as we have seen. The synod had raised its full quota for the Wartime Services Commission. In 1946 the national church launched its Restoration Fund, a campaign of unprecedented dimensions. New York Synod lagged slightly behind the national average in meeting its quota, but had reached 89 percent by the General Assembly of 1948. Thereafter the direction was upward in contributions of various sorts.

The relentless decay of the Sunday school received a check in 1945. Then the " New Curriculum " was presented to the churches in the course of 1948. This curriculum was an ambitious effort to equip the church with educational materials it could defend theologically and intellectually. Sums were spent at unprecedented levels and authors of real competence en-

gaged. The curriculum was, on the whole, well received in
1949, and largely used. Despite the fact that the old wineskins
were severely strained in many places, Sunday school enroll-
ment actually increased. The curriculum was used in other denominations and won recognition as probably the best available. In 1960 the Synod Executive reported that in the last
decade church schools had grown twice as fast as communicant memberships.

The growth of membership had held almost even with the
growth of population generally in New York in the 1950's. This
was not a sensational gain, but it was more impressive than
the long years when the synod had lost ground in relation to
the population. Most of the two millions added in New York
had come in the eight metropolitan areas of the state, where
four out of five New Yorkers now lived. The town and country
districts (and their churches) were generally static or decreasing. About twenty-five new congregations had been organized
in the decade.

The new situation with regard to church finances was reflected in the appearance of the buildings. "Whereas, ten
years ago properties were in need of paint and repairs" reported the Synod Executive in 1960,[4] "today most properties
are in good repair; new additions have been built, sanctuaries
have been modernized; and entirely new church edifices have
been erected." The increase of contributions for this purpose
was the largest, about 166 percent, while the increase for benevolences was 100 percent.

Ministerial Supply. Some eighty ministers had gone into the
chaplaincy from New York Synod. This movement much wors-
ened a shortage already serious among the smaller churches.
In 1943, 102 pastors left churches in the synod. In the war
years there was an average of 75 churches a month seeking
pastors.

After the war, vacancy remained a problem, though not so

desperate. General Assembly statistics tended to show 150 to 200 vacancies, but a number of these were being supplied in fact by students, laymen, ministers of other denominations. The number of congregations desiring and seeking settled pastors ran about 45 to 55 month by month at the end of the forties. These were almost always charges which paid a bare subsistence salary and promised little possibility of development in any way. In 1947, for example, of the 44 churches or yoked fields seeking pastors, only 8 offered a salary of as much as $3,000, while a quarter named less than $2,000. Less than a third of those listed as vacant in General Assembly statistics had as many as 250 members.

The Maintenance of the Pastorate Fund was now stronger. In 1958 half the presbyteries had a minimum of $4,200 with manse and pension. Most of 33 grants from the Fund for the next year were for children's allowances to men already receiving the minimum.

Late in the fifties the inner city church problem was growing. Nearly 100 churches were reported in New York and Brooklyn presbyteries with operating budgets of less than $20,000 each.

Public Affairs. During the war and thereafter, meanwhile, there had developed a program of weekday religious education of some dimensions. These differed from Sunday schools in being usually interdenominational and staffed by professional teachers. When well conducted they maintained the standards of good public education. From 50,000 students in 1939 they leaped to 200,000 in New York by 1943. The State Council of Churches pushed the program and endeavored to set and maintain standards in order to keep the respect of public-school administrators. In 1938 and 1939 the Council had arranged hearings and claimed much credit for the Coudert-McLaughlin Bill which made such programs possible in any community desiring it. The Supreme Court ruling in the Champaign case of 1948, however, cast doubt on the constitutionality of the undertaking. It was clearly illegal now to conduct such classes in school buildings, a practice widely followed previously in New York. Just what was Constitutional in this direction was not certain.

Social Education and Action was now effectively rooted in the presbyteries and more oriented to local situations than in the 1930's. The synod's committee, to be sure, urged the immediate cessation of testing of nuclear bombs in 1958, but most of the concerns were more local, the problems of migratory farm labor, of "open occupancy" in housing, of birth-control facilities in hospitals, of public schools, bingo and pari-mutuel betting, civil rights, alcohol. At the end of the decade came the sit-ins and Freedom Rides. For many of these issues the State Council of Churches was now providing coordination of Protestant efforts, especially when it was a matter of legislation or other political action. This activity was still, however, almost entirely confined to the clergy, and church sessions and the laity were generally unaware of the declarations of the higher courts of the church. This gap was dramatized at the end of the decade when the National Council of United Presbyterian Men indicated sympathy for policies radically contrasted to those advocated by the General Assembly and synod.

Missionary Presbyteries. The island presbytery of Puerto Rico was brought closer to the synod in this period, partly because of the large Puerto Rican immigration to New York and partly because of American interest in the extensive economic reorganization of "Operation Bootstrap." The fiftieth anniversary of Presbyterian work on the island was celebrated in 1949. There were 48 churches, 50 ministers and about 5,000 communicants in 1960, a hospital, a seminary, an Inter-American University in San German and a farm at Guacio conducted on a work-camp basis with young people from the continent as well as the island. All the pastors and nearly all the teachers, doctors, and nurses were Puerto Ricans. In 1957 every presbytery in the synod was represented on a preaching mission in Puerto Rico.

With Chile, where the Presbyterian enterprise was about half the dimensions of that in Puerto Rico, relations were much less close. Toward the end of the 1950's the Presbytery of Chile was considering the formation of a national church.

Merger. The merger in 1958 of the Presbyterian Church U.S.A. with the United Presbyterian Church of North America changed the basis for statistical comparisons. But in that year the Presbyterian Church U.S.A. was in flourishing condition. Its membership and benevolences were at the highest point in its history and its Sunday schools had reached the highest level since 1934.

The realignment of presbytery boundaries to provide more effective oversight was now resumed. Albany and Troy were merged into one and discussion proceeded on a consolidation of Hudson, North River, and Westchester. The merger itself argued for reconsideration of boundaries at some points. The old United Presbyterian Church brought to the merger some 73 churches with 18,763 communicants in New York State, making the merged synod the second largest in the united church, with a total of 940 churches and 323,000 members. A committee set up to consider presbytery boundaries reported that it would urge a reduction of presbyteries to ten or eleven in the state. Such a reduction would make possible an executive staff in every presbytery.

Bibliography

I. OFFICIAL RECORDS

A. Minutes and Records of the Synods and Presbyteries in the Bounds of New York State in the Eighteenth Century

Records of the Presbyterian Church in the U.S.A., 1904, contains minutes of the Presbytery, from 1706 to 1717, the Synod, from 1717 to 1745, the Synod of New York (New Side), from 1745 to 1758, the Synod of New York and Philadelphia, from 1758 to 1788. The manuscripts of all these are located in the Presbyterian Historical Society (PHS).

The minutes of the New York State area presbyteries of the eighteenth century are as follows:

1. Long Island, 1717–1738   Lost
   Merged in 1738 with East Jersey to form:
2. New York, 1738–1775   Lost
       1775–1809   Presbytery of Newark
                 copies in PHS, and Presbytery of New York
3. Suffolk, 1749–1789
   Dissolved 1790, largely succeeded by: PHS
4. Long Island, 1790–1900   PHS
5. Dutchess County, 1766–1790
   Name changed to:
   Dutchess, 1790–1795   Lost

Resolved in 1795 into:
6. Hudson, 1795–   Middletown
7. Albany, 1790–   Schenectady
8. Associate Reformed Presbytery of New York,
    1786–1796   PHS
9. Presbytery of Morris County, 1780–ca. 1821
    Name changed to Associated Presbytery
    of Morris County   Lost
10. Associated Westchester Presbytery, 1792–1830   PHS
11. Northern Associated Presbytery of State of New York,
    1794–ca. 1821   Lost

The last three presbyteries held no official connection with the regular presbyterian organization, but there was considerable overlapping and movement back and forth of ministers and churches.

B. Minutes of the New York State Synods Under the Undivided General Assembly, 1788–1837

(Those in the possession of the synod are deposited at Union Theological Seminary [UTS].)

1. New York and New Jersey, Vol. I, 1788–1823   UTS
    Reconstituted in 1823, New Jersey being separated, as:
2. New York, 1823–1836   UTS
3. Albany
    Vol. I, 1803–1811   UTS
    Vol. II, 1812–1828   UTS
    Vol. III, 1829–1837   Lost
4. Geneva, Vol. I, 1812–1835   UTS
5. Genesee, Vol. I, 1821–1838   UTS
6. Utica, 1829–   Lost

C. Minutes and Records of the New School Church in New York, 1838–1870

1. New York, 1838–1839, and in the same volume
2. New York and New Jersey, 1840–1855   UTS

Vol. II, 1856–1869   UTS
(*Also in print*)
3. Albany, 1838–1868   UTS
4. Geneva, Vol. II, 1836–1860   UTS
    Vol. III, 1861–1881   UTS
5. Genesee, Vol. II, 1839–1850   UTS
    Vol. III, 1851–1869   UTS
6. Utica   Lost
7. Susquehanna, 1853–1869   UTS
8. Onondaga, 1855–   Lost

D. Minutes and Records of the Old School Church in New York, 1838–1870

1. New York
    Vol. III, 1837–1856   UTS
    Vol. IV, 1857–1869   UTS
2. Albany, 1838–1858   Lost
    Vol. III, 1858–1869   UTS
3. Buffalo, 1843–1869   UTS
4. New Jersey also held some western New York OS
    presbyteries   PHS

E. Minutes and Records of the Synods as Reconstituted at Reunion, 1870

1. Long Island, 1870–1881   PHS
2. New York, 1870–1881   UTS
    (*Also in print*)
3. Albany, 1870–1881   UTS
4. Geneva, Vol. IV, 1861–1881   UTS
5. Genesee
    Name changed in 1870 to Western New York,
    1870–1881   UTS
6. Utica
    Name changed in 1873 to Central New York,
    1870–1881   Lost

In 1882 these six synods were combined into the Synod of New York. The minutes have been printed ever since.

II. REGIONAL AND PRESBYTERY HISTORIES AND RECORDS

A large amount of church history is to be found in county, city, and town histories generally. There are also a few regional church histories.

N. S. Prime, *A History of Long Island from its First Settlement . . . with special reference to its ecclesiastical concerns.* New York, 1845, 420 pp., map.

B. F. Thompson, *History of Long Island,* 3d ed. New York, 1918, 4 vols.

G. P. Disosway, *The Earliest Churches of New York and its Vicinity.* New York, 1865.

J. Greenleaf, *A History of the Churches of All Denominations in the City of New York from the First Settlement to 1850.* New York, 1850, 429 pp.

T. F. Savage, *The Presbyterian Church in New York City.* 1949, 259 pp.

W. C. Swartz, "The Presbyterians of the Lower Hudson Valley during the Colonial Period, 1680–1775" (STM thesis, typescript UTS), 1942, 92 pp., map.

A. S. Moffatt, *Old Churches of Orange County.* 1928.

P. H. Fowler, *An Historical Sketch of Presbyterianism within the Bounds of the Synod of Central New York.* Utica, 1877, 722 pp.

James H. Hotchkin, *History of the Purchase and Settlement of Western New York, and of the rise, progress, and present state of the Presbyterian Church in that section.* New York, 1848, 600 pp.

Manual of the Churches of Seneca County . . . 1895–1896. Seneca Falls, 1896, 240 pp.

O. J. Price, *Significance of the Early Religious History of Rochester.* Rochester, 1924, 23 pp.

F. De W. Ward, *Ecclesiastical History of Rochester, N.Y.* Rochester, 1871, 184 pp.

Along with the printed histories of presbyteries are listed some manuscript histories deposited in the library of the Presbyterian Historical Society. Most of the presbytery minutes that have not been lost are in the care of the stated clerks of the respective presbyteries, but those deposited in the Presbyterian Historical Society and at Union Theological Seminary are listed below.

A. Miller and J. Coe, "History of the Presbytery of Albany," 1790–1802. *JPHS,* III, 224–235.

J. A. Miller, "Angelica Presbytery: Historical Notes, 1828–1856" (MS., PHS).

J. B. Scouller, *History of the Presbytery of Argyle.* Harrisburg, 1880, 158 pp.

B. C. Smith, *A Few Chapters . . . Presbytery of Bath. . . .* New York, 1857, 64 pp.

J. A. Miller, "Bath and Steuben Presbyteries: 1817–1896" (MS., PHS).

"Minutes of the Presbytery of Bath," 1817–1866 (MS., PHS).

D. D. Gregory, *Historical Sermon . . . Binghamton Presbytery. The Planting and Growth of Presbyterianism in Broome and Tioga Counties, N.Y.* 1873, 46 pp.

J. S. Pattengill, *History of the Presbytery of Binghamton, N.Y.* 1877, 46 pp.

—— *Continued History of the Churches of Binghamton Presbytery, 1876–1888.* Walton, New York, 1890, 18 pp.

"Minutes of the Presbytery of Binghamton," 1870–1895, 4 vols. (MS., UTS).

T. Stillman, *Fifty Year History of the Presbytery of Buffalo.* 1867, 51 pp.

W. Waith, *Historical Sketch of the Presbytery of Buffalo.* 1887, 23 pp.

"Minutes of the Presbytery of Caledonia," 1838–1853 (MS., PHS).

L. M. Hopkins, "History of the Presbytery of Cayuga, N.Y.," 1889 (MS., PHS).

J. Q. Adams, ed, "Records of the Middle Association . . . 1806–1810." *JPHS*, X, 217–230, 258–284; XI, 20–39, 49–69.

E. A. Bulkley, *Historical Sketch of the Presbytery of Champlain*. Plattsburgh, 1877, 16 pp.

P. T. Myers, "Sketch of the History of the Presbytery of Champlain, N.Y.," 1887 (MS., PHS).

"Minutes of the Presbytery of Chemung," 1836–1933 (MS., PHS).

"Historical Report of Chemung Presbytery," 1888 (MS., PHS).

"Minutes of Chenango Presbytery," 1826–1870 (MS., PHS).

G. C. Yeisley and B. Parsons, *History of the Presbytery of Columbia, N.Y. 1802–1888*. 32 pp.

"Minutes of the Presbytery of Cortland," 1825–1870, 2 vols. (MS., UTS).

"Records of the Presbytery of Delaware," 1831–1870 (MS., PHS).

J. E. Nassau, "History of the Presbytery of Genesee, N.Y.," 1888 (MS., PHS).

"Minutes of the Presbytery of Genesee," 1819–1923 (MS., PHS).

J. A. Miller, "Genesee Valley Presbytery, 1859–1886, Historical notes" (MS., PHS).

"Minutes of the Presbytery of Genesee River (OS), 1853–1870" (MS., PHS).

J. J. Porter, *History of the Presbytery of Geneva*. 1889, 62 pp.

G. R. H. Shumway, *Fifty Years of Geneva Presbytery*. Lyons, 1857.

C. H. Dayton, "Early History of Geneva Presbytery," 1946 (MS., PHS).

C. H. Dayton and J. G. Dayton, *Brief History of the Presbytery of Geneva*. Shortsville, New York, 1955, 67 pp.

J. B. Coleman, "Some Early History of the Geneva Presbytery." *Yesteryears,* No. 3 (Feb., 1958), pp. 8–11; No. 4 (July, 1958), pp. 34–37.

H. A. Harlow, *A History of the Presbytery of Hudson, 1681–1888.* Middletown, New York, 1888, 252 pp.

J. Johnston, "Early Presbyterianism on the East Line of the Hudson," 1844, ed. with notes by E. H. Gillett. *American Presbyterian and Theological Review,* VI (1868), 609–620.

E. Whitaker, *Presbyterianism on Long Island.* 1906, 13 pp.

C. E. Craven, *The Presbytery on Long Island.* 1916, 16 pp.

G. Nicholson, *The Story of Long Island Presbytery and Churches.* 1956, 32 pp.

" Minutes of the Presbytery of Long Island (including Suffolk and Long Island Second)" 1747–1900 (MS., PHS).

" Records of the Presbytery of Lyons," 1857–1934 (MS., PHS).

J. G. Symes, *Historical Sketch of Monmouth Presbytery and its Churches.* Trenton, 1877, 50 pp.

A. Miller, *The Presbytery of Montrose.* Harrisburg, 1873, 30 pp.

" Historical Records of Nassau Presbytery," 1855–1887 (MS., PHS).

J. B. Scouller, *History of the Associate Reformed Synod of New York* and

J. Harper, *History of the United Presbyterian Synod of New York.* Philadelphia, 1877, 70 pp.

S. D. Alexander, *The Presbytery of New York, 1738–1888.* New York, 198 pp.

D. R. Fox, ed., " Minutes of the Presbytery of New York, 1775–1782." *New York State Historical Association Proceedings,* XVIII (1920).

" Records of the Presbytery of N.Y.," 1775–1936, 27 vols. (MS., PHS).

" Minutes of the Second Presbytery of N.Y.," 1838–1871 (MS., PHS).

" Records of the Third Presbytery of N.Y.," 1831–1870 (MS., PHS).

" Minutes of the Fourth Presbytery of N.Y.," 1846–1870 (MS., PHS).

Minutes of the Presbytery of New York and Vermont (Welsh), 1885–1932.

E. P. Marvin, *The Presbytery of Niagara, 1824–1874.* Lockport, New York, 1875, 24 pp.

E. P. Marvin, R. Norton, M. D. Babcock, *History of the Presbytery of Niagara, N.Y. 1824–1887.* Lockport, 1887.

J. K. Wight, *Historical Sketch of the Presbytery of North River.* Poughkeepsie, 1881, 24 pp.

H. N. Baird, *Presbytery of Utica, centennial 1843–1943.* 132 pp.

J. R. Page, . . . *Historical Sermon . . . Presbytery of Ontario.* 1867.

H. H. Allen, "History of the Presbytery of Otsego, N.Y.," 1871 (MS., PHS).

W. Thrush, "The Presbytery of Otsego, its beginnings and early history," 1952 (mimeograph).

"Minutes of the Presbytery of Otsego," 1819–1946 (MS., PHS).

A. C. Shaw, "History of the Presbyterian Church of Wellsboro, Pa., Presbytery of Pennsylvania — Presbytery of Wellsboro, 1844–1888 " (MS., PHS).

C. P. Bush, "Historical Discourse," in *Half century celebration of the Rochester Presbytery.* 1869.

L. Parsons, ed., *History of Rochester Presbytery.* 1889, 319 pp.

J. A. Miller, *History of the Presbytery of Steuben, N.Y.,* including that of all the other presbyteries to which the churches of Steuben and Allegany Counties have belonged. Angelica, 1897, 92 pp.

"Minutes of Steuben Presbytery," 1867–1933 (MS., PHS).

C. C. Corss, *Presbytery of Susquehanna.* 1875, 48 pp.

"Records of Susquehanna Presbytery, 1817–1828, with Articles of Faith, etc., of the Luzerne Association " (MS., PHS).

W. M. Booth, *History of the Syracuse Presbytery 1796–1938.* 1938, 175 pp.

"Minutes of the Presbytery of Tioga," 1829–1870, 2 vols. (MS., UTS).

J. H. Noble, *Historical Discourse* [Troy Presbytery]. 1871, 45 pp.

J. Boyce, ed., *Centennial of Utica Presbytery, 1843–1943*. 132 pp.

"Records of Utica Presbytery," 1843–1888 (MS., PHS).

W. J. Cummings, *History of Westchester Presbytery 1660–1889*. Hartford, 1889, 229 pp.

C. W. Baird, "Historical Account of Presbyterianism in the Field Embraced by the Presbytery," in *Abstracts of the Minutes of the Presbytery of Westchester*, I (1876), New York.

B. H. Everitt, *History of the Presbytery of Westchester*. Brooklyn, 1962, 101 pp.

A. T. Chester, *Historical Sermon . . . semi-centennial of the Synod of Western New York*. Buffalo, 1871, 24 pp.

"Minutes of the Presbytery of Wyoming," 1842–1853 (MS., PHS).

III. Printed Histories of Particular Congregations

(Not including accounts published only in local newspapers.)
Since local histories often contain references to neighboring congregations, the following list is arranged geographically to assist those interested in a particular locality. The regions used in the list may be located on the endpaper maps.

A. Long Island

E. Whitaker, *History of Southold, Long Island, Its First Century, 1640–1740*. Southold, 1881.

C. E. Craven, ed., *Whitaker's Southold*. Princeton, 1931, 194 pp.

The Celebration of the 250th Anniversary of the Formation of the Town and the Church of Southold, Long Island. Southold, 1890, 220 pp.

E. H. Palmer, *Tercentenary Celebration, 1640–1940, First Presbyterian Church of Southold, L.I., N.Y.* New York, 1940, 47 pp.

The 250th Anniversary of the Village and Town of Southampton, 1640–1890. Sag Harbor, 1890, 105 pp.

A. F. Halsey, *First Presbyterian Church, Southampton, Long Island, 1640–1940* (in part reprinted from *In Old Southampton*). 13 pp.

H. P. Hedges, "Historical Address" in *Bi-Centennial of the Presbyterian Church in Bridge-Hampton, New York, 1686–1886.* Sag Harbor, 34 pp.

S. L. Mershon, *The Church of the Colony and Town of East Hampton, Long Island, 1649–1861.* 22 pp.

K. W. Strong, *First Presbyterian Church in Brookhaven, at Setauket.* Bay Shore, 1942, 20 pp.

R. Scharff, *History of Setauket Presbyterian Church, 1660–1960.* 28 pp.

T. R. Bayles, *History of the Middle Island Presbyterian Church, 1766–1954.* 18 pp.

G. Borthwick, "History" in *200th Anniversary, South Haven Church (Presbyterian) 1740–1940.* 39 pp.

C. E. Craven, *History of Mattituck, Long Island, N.Y.* 1906, 400 pp.

J. E. Mallmann, *Historical Papers on Shelter Island and its Presbyterian Church.* New York, 1899, 332 pp.

F. M. Kerr, *Souvenir of the 250th Anniversary of Christ's First Presbyterian Church, Hempstead, Long Island.* Hempstead, 1895, 72 pp.

——— *Fifty Years of Ministry.* 63 pp.

R. Davidson, *Historical Discourse on the Bi-centennial Commemoration of the Founding of the First Christian Church in the Town of Huntington, L.I.* Huntington, 1866, 64 pp.

Records of the First Church in Huntington, L.I., 1723–1779, Being the Records Kept by the Rev. Ebenezer Prime. Huntington, 1899, 144 pp.

The 250th Anniversary, First Presbyterian Church, Huntington, Long Island, 1658–1908. 19 pp.

Old First Church, Huntington, Long Island, 1658–1933. 76 pp.

L. C. Lockwood, *The Presbyterian Church of Melville, L.I.* 1876, 11 pp.

J. W. Eaton, ed., *History of the First Presbyterian Church of Babylon, L.I., from 1730–1912.* Babylon, 1912, 65 pp.

O. L. Daley, *Historical Sketch of the Presbyterian Church of Islip, 1857–1932.* 31 pp.

The Minutes of our Years. 1857–1957. The Presbyterian Church, Islip, N.Y. 24 pp.

T. F. Burnham, *Record of the Memorial Services of the First Presbyterian Church of Freeport, L.I.* Rockville Center, 1875.

R. H. Kiely, *History of the First Presbyterian Church of Port Jefferson, L.I., N.Y., 1870–1945.* 11 pp.

H. S. Manley, *No Man's Land, Long Island. Historical data concerning the founding of the Presbyterian Church among the Shinnecock Indians at Canoe Place, L.I.* 8 pp.

For Jamaica, Newtown, and churches in Brooklyn and Queens through 1940, see WPA Historical Records Survey, *Inventory of the Church Archives of New York City, Presbyterian Church.* Since 1940 have appeared:

G. W. Winans, *First Presbyterian Church of Jamaica, New York; 1662–1942, A Narrative History of its Two Hundred and Eighty Years of Continuous Service.* Jamaica, 1943, 248 pp.

R. F. Weld, *A Tower on the Heights, the Story of the First Presbyterian Church of Brooklyn.* New York, 1946, 169 pp.

B. New York City

See WPA Historical Records Survey, *Inventory of the Church Archives in New York City, Presbyterian Church.* New York City, 1940, 160 pp. Since 1940 have appeared:

A. W. Courtney, *Our Father's Faith and Ours, An Historical Account of the First Presbyterian Church, University Place*

Presbyterian Church, Madison Square Presbyterian Church. 1949, 26 pp.

Don Bogardus, *This House with Glory, a History of the Rutgers Presbyterian Church.* New York, 1948, 62 pp.

W. M. Van Norden, *The Fatness of Thy House.* New York, 1953, 243 pp.

G. T. Peck, *A Noble Landmark of New York. The Fifth Avenue Presbyterian Church, 1808–1958.* New York, 1960, 174 pp.

The One Hundredth Anniversary of Dry Dock Mission, Emmanuel Chapel, and Emmanuel Presbyterian Church, 1852–1952. New York, 1952, 80 pp.

J. M. Howard and G. H. Howard, "And Thy Neighbor, The Story of How a City Church Learned to Discover and Serve its Neighborhood, 1905–1926, from Notes and Memoranda of H. S. Coffin and W. R. Jelliffe" (UTS typescript), 1956, 111 pp.

H. D. Burcham, "The Presbyterian Church in Queens Borough, 1920–1946" (STM thesis, UTS), 1947.

C. The Lower Hudson Valley

P. B. Heroy, *Brief History of the Presbyterian Church at Bedford from the Year 1680.* New York, 1874, 34 pp.

C. W. Baird, *History of the Bedford Church.* New York, 1882, 140 pp.

M. A. Clark, ed., *Bedford Presbyterian Church, 1681–1936.* 55 pp.

C. W. Baird, *Quarter Century Sermon, Rye.* New York, 1886, 27 pp.

E. C. McKay, *A History of the Rye Presbyterian Church.* Lancaster, 1957, 260 pp.

A. R. Macoubry, *175th Anniversary of the Beginning of Presbyterianism in White Plains, 1722–1897.* White Plains, 1900, 51 pp.

J. Heermance, *Sermon . . . Presbyterian Church of White*

Plains, N.Y. New York, 1884, 21 pp.

J. H. Robinson, *Sermon . . . White Plains and its Two Hundred and Twenty-fifth Anniversary.* 1908, 20 pp.

Presbyterian Church, Port Chester, New York, 1852–1952.

E. R. Burkhalter, *Historical Sketch of the Presbyterian Church of New Rochelle.* New York, 1876, 28 pp.

H. M. Lester and A. B. Lindsay, *The First Presbyterian Church of New Rochelle, 1688–1946.* 18 pp.

R. E. Prime, "History," in *Jubilee Year Book 1852–1902. First Presbyterian Church, Yonkers.*

R. E. Prime, Jr., "Historical Sketch," in *The 75th Anniversary of the Founding of the First Presbyterian Church in Yonkers, 1852–1927.* Yonkers, 1927.

A. R. Macoubry, *Historical Sermon, South East Centre Presbyterian Church.* New York, 1877, 32 pp.

J. A. Webster, *Brief History of the Presbyterian Church of South Salem, New York, 1752–1902.* Elizabeth, New Jersey, 1902, 74 pp.

W. J. Cumming, *Historical Sermon, Yorktown Presbyterian Church.* Peekskill, 32 pp.

—— *Supplement to an Historical Sermon.* 1879, 5 pp.

E. J. Foster, *Historical Sketch of the Gilead Presbyterian Church, Carmel, N.Y. 1745–1898.* Morristown, New Jersey, 45 pp.

C. C. Wallace, *Historical Sermon, Presbyterian Church at Mahopac Falls, New York (formerly Red Mills).* Peekskill, 1878, 30 pp.

W. H. Ewen, *History of the South Presbyterian Church in Greenburgh, 1825–1950* [Dobbs' Ferry]. 40 pp.

H. W. Terry, *The First Presbyterian Church of Ossining, N.Y., 1763–1948.* 1949, 63 pp.

The Semi-centennial Anniversary of the Presbyterian Church of Peekskill, N.Y. 1876, 69 pp.

S. R. Knapp, "Historical Sketch" in *Seventy-Fifth Anniversary . . . First Presbyterian Church, Peekskill, N.Y. 1826–1901.* 63 pp.

C. F. Chapman, *History of the Presbyterian Church of Mount Kisco, New York, 1852–1902.* Katonah, 1902, 48 pp.

History of the Presbyterian Church, Irvington, N.Y. 1876, 8 pp.

J. B. Platt, Historical Sketch in *Year Book of the First Presbyterian Church, Poughkeepsie, N.Y.* 1900, 74 pp.

W. D. Hasbrouck, *A History of the First Presbyterian Church of Poughkeepsie, N.Y.* 1928, 61 pp.

J. S. Gilmor, *History of the Presbyterian Church of Freedom Plains, N.Y. 1828–1878.* Poughkeepsie, 34 pp.

A. B. Pritchard, " Historical Sermon," in *Manual of the Presbyterian Church, Pleasant Valley, New York.* Poughkeepsie, 1882.

W. N. Sayre, *Forty Years' Ministry . . . Pine Plains, N.Y.* Fishkill, 1873, 8 pp.

A. James, *Smithfield Presbyterian Church, 1742–1942.* 11 pp.

R. E. Barlow, *History of the South Amenia Presbyterian Church of Union Society, 1759–1959.* 98 pp.

Memorial, the Presbyterian Church, Goshen, N.Y. Goshen, 1874, 35 pp.

R. B. Clark, *The First Presbyterian Church, Goshen, New York, 1700–1895.* New York, 1895, 79 pp.

M. P. Seese, *A Tower of the Lord . . . First Presbyterian Church, Goshen, N.Y., 1720–1945.* Goshen, 1945, 183 pp. and index.

D. M. Maclise, *Historical Discourse . . . Goodwill Presbyterian Church, Montgomery, N.Y.* 1865, 31 pp.

J. M. Dickson, *A Discourse Historic of the Goodwill Presbyterian Church, Montgomery, New York.* New York, 1877, 64 pp.

——— *The Goodwill Memorial; or the First One Hundred and Fifty Years of the Goodwill Presbyterian Church, Montgomery, Orange County, New York.* Newburgh, 1880, 163 pp.

First Presbyterian Church 1841–1941 Washingtonville, N.Y.

S. W. Mills, *The Scotchtown Memorial, 1796–1896.* Newburgh, 41 pp.

Manual, Presbyterian Church of New Windsor. Poughkeepsie, 1841.

A. C. Niven, ed., *Centennial Memorial of the A. R. Presbyterian Church, Little Britain, New York.* New York, 1859, 251 pp.

J. S. King, *The Sketch of the History of the Associate Reformed Congregation of Little Britain, New York (The Presbyterian Church), 1765–1915.* Newburgh, 1915, 33 pp.

R. H. Wissler, *History of the Presbyterian Congregation of Florida, New York, 1741–1941.* 31 pp.

J. M. Price, *One Hundred and Fifty Years of the First Presbyterian Church of Ridgebury, N.Y., 1792–1942.* 24 pp.

A. Seward, *History of the First Presbyterian Church in Middletown, Orange County, N.Y.* Middletown, 1876, 18 pp.

G. A. Boyd, *Centennial History of the Webb Horton Memorial Presbyterian Church.* Middletown, 1954, 170 pp.

R. H. McCready, *The First Presbyterian Church, Chester, New York, 1798–1888.* Chester, 1889, 111 pp.

S. B. Cole, " First Presbyterian Church, Nyack." *The Microtin,* July 10 and 11, 1878.

A. S. Freeman, *Our Silver Wedding . . . Central Presbyterian Church, Haverstraw, N.Y.* Haverstraw, 1871, 20 pp.

—— *Sermons . . . Central Presbyterian Church of Haverstraw.* Haverstraw, 1891, 18 pp.

100th Anniversary Central Presbyterian Church, Haverstraw, N.Y. 1846–1946. 32 pp.

Centennial of the Presbyterian Church, Monticello, N.Y., 1810–1910. 130 pp.

T. Brittain, *Historical Sketch of Cochecton Presbyterian Church, Sullivan County, New York.* 1871. 16 pp.

The First Presbyterian Church of Jeffersonville, N.Y. 1845–1945. 30 pp.

C. T. Feagles, *They Went to Church in Amity, 1796–1896.* 1949 [?], 95 pp.

J. MacInnes, *History of the Unionville Presbyterian Church, 1803–1910.* 18 pp.

R. Lambert, *First Presbyterian Church, Unionville, N.Y. 1803–1953*. 20 pp.

W. K. Hall, *Centennial Celebration of the First Presbyterian Church, Newburgh, New York, 1784–1884*. Newburgh, 1884, 47 pp.

The Union Church, Newburgh, New York. 1902, 32 pp.

S. H. Jagger, *Centennial Discourse . . . Presbyterian Church of Marlborough, N.Y.* Newburgh, 1867, 36 pp.

J. N. Kugler, *A Brief History of the First Presbyterian Church of Marlborough, N.Y. 1764–1914*. Newburgh, 31 pp.

I. Clark, *Historical Discourse [Rondout Presbyterian Church]*. Kingston, 1876, 23 pp.

I. Magee, *Semi-centennial Celebration of the Rondout Presbyterian Church, Kingston, New York, 1833–1883*. Albany, 1884, 82 pp.

C. S. Stowitts, *Historical Sermon. Rondout Presbyterian Church*. 1895, 8 pp.

A History of the Rondout Presbyterian Church, Kingston, N.Y. 1936, 42 pp.

D. The Old Albany Synod

J. M. Blayney, *A History of the First Presbyterian Church of Albany, New York*. Albany, 1877, 124 pp.

H. C. Stanton, *The Origin and Growth of Presbyterianism in Albany*. 1886, 27 pp.

V. H. Paltsits, " The Beginnings of Presbyterianism in Albany," in *The First Presbyterian Church of Albany*. Albany, 1909 (cf. also, *JPHS*, V, 155–203).

W. B. Sprague, *Sermon . . . Sketches of the History of the Second Presbyterian Church and Congregation, Albany*. Albany, 1846, 43 pp.

—— *Sermon [24 years of Pastorate]*. 1854, 40 pp.

—— *Discourse . . . Fiftieth Anniversary of the Dedication of the Second Presbyterian Church*. 1865, 41 pp.

—— *Discourse [40th Anniversary of Pastorate]*. 1869, 32 pp.

The Second Presbyterian Church of Albany, New York, Centennial Celebration, 1813–1913. Albany, 1915, 16 pp.

One Hundred Years of the Fourth Presbyterian Church of Albany, New York, 1829–1929. Albany, 1929, 32 pp.

R. C. James, *A Collection of Historical Records of the State Street Presbyterian Church of Albany, New York, 1861–1911.* Albany, 1911, 93 pp.

E. A. Huntington, *Last Words . . . with a History of the Third Presbyterian Church of Albany.* Albany, 1855, 102 pp.

H. N. Dunning, *Lest We Forget. The Lives and Labors of Those Who Have Served as Pastors of the Third Presbyterian Church of Albany, New York.* Albany, 1950, 47 pp.

W. Durant, "Historical Sketch," in *Manual of the 6th Presbyterian Church.* Albany, 1882.

E. P. Sprague, *Historical Sketch of the Presbyterian Church in Salem, Washington County, New York.* Salem, 1876, 49 pp.

F. H. Williams, *Centennial Celebration of the U.P. (The Old White) Church Building, Salem, Washington County, New York, 1797–1897.* New York, 1898.

W. C. Mitchell, *Brief History of the East Presbyterian Society of Hebron, N.Y.* (mimeographed, 27 pp.).

E. H. Tilford, *The United Presbyterian Church, Argyle, New York, 1792–1943.* Hudson Falls, 16 pp.

L. Kellogg, *Sketch of the History of Whitehall.* 1847, 16 pp.

J. R. Cronkhite, *Historical Survey, First Presbyterian Church, Hudson Falls, N.Y. 1803–1953.* 24 pp.

A. S. Hoyt, *An Historical Sketch of the Presbyterian Church of Ballston Center, N.Y.* 1876, 71 pp.

A Brief History of the Presbyterian Church at Ballston Center, N.Y., 1775–1950. 39 pp.

J. Dooly, *Historical Discourse, Presbyterian Church of West Milton, Saratoga Co., N.Y.* 1897, 16 pp.

J. G. K. McClure, *History of New Scotland Presbyterian Church.* Albany, 1876, 45 pp.

Sesquicentennial of the Schoonmaker Memorial Presbyterian Church, Stillwater, Saratoga County, N.Y., 1791–1941.

R. H. Stearns, *Historical Sketch of the Freehold Presbyterian Church, Charlton, Saratoga Co., N.Y.* Albany, 1886, 51 pp.

R. W. Beers, *The Last Century. First Presbyterian Church, Waterford, N.Y., 1804–1904.* 73 pp.

P. Stryker, "Historical Discourse, First Presbyterian Church of Saratoga Springs," in *Manual,* 1880.

J. T. Backus, *The History of the Presbyterian Church of Schenectady during its First Century.* Albany, 1869, 32 pp.

M. J. Thompson, ed., *Souvenir of the First United Presbyterian Church, Schenectady, N.Y.* 1908, 36 pp.

C. W. Backus, *Historical Sketch of the First Presbyterian, Church of Princetown, Schenectady County, N.Y.* Schenectady, 1884, 24 pp.

S. M. Ramsey, *Historical Sermon* [Duanesburgh, N.Y.]. Cincinnati, 1877, 12 pp.

M. S. Goodale, *Historical Discourse of the Presbyterian Church of Amsterdam Village.* Albany, 1851, 22 pp.

R. A. Ketchledge, *Sermon. Early History of First Presbyterian Church, Johnstown, N.Y.* 1935, 5 pp.

G. Harness, *Kingsboro, New York, Presbyterian Church. Historical.* Gloversville, 1876, 87 pp.

The Parsons Memorials to . . . the Pioneers of Kingsborough. Gloversville, 1932, 90 pp.

E. H. Miller, *Historical Manual of Kingsborough Avenue Presbyterian Church, Gloversville.* 1932.

History of the Mayfield Central Presbyterian Church, 1626–1926. 19 pp.

G. N. Webber, "The History of the Presbyterian Church of Troy," in *Manual of the First Presbyterian Church, Troy, New York.* 1877.

M. I. Townsend. "History," in *Proceedings of the Centennial Anniversary of the First Presbyterian Church, Troy, New York.* Troy, 1892.

W. Irvin, "Centennial Sermon," in *History and Manual, Second Presbyterian Church, Troy, New York.* 1876.

—— *Fifteen Years . . . Second Presbyterian Church, Troy, N.Y.* Troy, 1882, 21 pp.

W. H. Hollister, Jr., *The Second Presbyterian Church of Troy, New York, Historical Sketch.* Troy, 1917, 69 pp.

B. Y. Woodward and others, *One Hundredth Anniversary, Second Presbyterian Church, Troy, New York, 1826–1926.* Troy.

C. E. Robinson, *Historical Discourse. Second Street Presbyterian Church, Troy, N.Y.* 1876, 22 pp.

G. Van Deurs, *The Chronicles of the Oakwooders, Historical Discourse. Oakwood Avenue Presbyterian Church, Troy, New York.* Troy, 1876, 32 pp.

W. Hawthorne, "Historical Narrative," in *Seventy-fifth Anniversary, Oakwood Avenue Presbyterian Church, Troy, N.Y.* 1943, 16 pp.

L. A. McMurray, *A History of the Sunday School of the First Presbyterian Church, Lansingburgh, N.Y. 1816–1874.* Troy, 1874, 35 pp.

A. M. Beveridge, *A Historic Sketch of the First Presbyterian Church of Lansingburgh, N.Y. 1792–1876.* 1876, 29 pp.

Souvenir. The Old First Presbyterian Church, Lansingburgh, N.Y. 1908, 37 pp.

One Hundred and Fiftieth Anniversary. First Presbyterian Church of Lansingburgh, Troy, N.Y. 1942, 12 pp.

H. Neill, *Discourse . . . History of the Presbyterian Church, Schaghticoke, N.Y.* Troy, 1876, 24 pp.

J. O. Gordon, *An Historical Sermon on the Presbyterian Church, Rensselaerville, New York.* Albany, 1875, 52 pp.

S. G. Spees, *Memorial Address . . . Celebration, Greenville, N.Y.* 1871, 60 pp.

H. M. Dodd, *The Centennial of the Old First Congregational Church, Windham, New York, 1803–1903.* Windham, 1903, 64 pp.

Seventy-fifth Anniversary, Hunter Presbyterian Church, 1822–1897. Albany, 48 pp.

G. A. Howard, *Christ's Church, Catskill.* 1875, 40 pp.

Manual of Christ's Church, Catskill, N.Y. 1903.

G. C. Yeisley, *Historical Discourse. First Presbyterian Church, Hudson, New York, 1790–1890.* Hudson, 21 pp.

A. C. McMillan, *Saint Peter's Church, Presbyterian, Spencertown, N.Y.* 1941, 16 pp.

A. J. Fennel, "Centennial Historical Discourse," in *Manual of the Presbyterian Church of Glen's Falls, New York.* 1876, 73 pp.

Commemoration of the Dedication of the Presbyterian Church in the City of Glen's Falls, 1929.

J. H. Noble, "Sketch History" in *Report of the Caldwell Presbyterian Church.* Albany, 1872.

C. W. Blake, *History of the Caldwell Presbyterian Church.* Glens Falls, 1909, pp. 24.

Historical Manual of the Presbyterian Church, Sandy Hill, N.Y. 1877.

J. Thompson, "Historical Essay," in *Centennial, First Congregational Church, Keeseville, New York, 1806–1906.* 63 pp.

Cyrus Offer, *Centennial Historical Sermon of the First Presbyterian and Congregational Church of Chazy, New York* (*Plattsburgh Sentinel,* July 9, 1876, supplement).

A Short History of the Presbyterian Church, Chazy, N.Y. 1805–1955. Champlain, 1955, 7 pp.

Centennial Anniversary, 1797–1897, First Presbyterian Church, Plattsburgh, N.Y. 127 pp.

J. Gamble, "History," in *One Hundred Fiftieth Anniversary, 1797–1947, First Presbyterian Church, Plattsburgh, N.Y.* 32 pp.

C. F. Nye, *Address . . . Centenary . . . First Presbyterian-Congregational Church . . . , Champlain, N.Y.* 1928, 27 pp.

B. Merrill, *Historical Discourse . . . Ausable Forks, N.Y.* Plattsburgh, 1876, 14 pp.

C. H. A. Bulkley, *Twenty Years . . . Presbyterian Church, Port Henry, N.Y.* 1880, 26 pp.

E. The Old Utica Synod

H. V. Swinnerton, *An Historical Account of the Presbyterian Church at Cherry Valley, New York.* Cherry Valley, 1876, 40 pp.

P. F. Sanborne, *Memorial Discourse, First Presbyterian Church of Springfield, N.Y.* Cherry Valley, 1876, 22 pp.

Manual of the Presbyterian Church of Richfield Springs. 1891–1892.

First Presbyterian Church, Delhi, N.Y., 1805–1958. 40 pp.

S. H. Moon, *History of the First Presbyterian Church of Gilbertsville, N.Y.* 1876, 21 pp.

The Federated Church, Masonville, N.Y., 1919–1960. Sidney, 9 pp.

B. F. Willoughby, *Centennial Discourse . . . Presbyterian Church, Sauquoit, 1776–1876.* Utica, 1876, 24 pp.

O. A. Kingsbury, *Centennial Day of the Presbyterian Church, New Hartford, New York, 1791–1891.* Utica, 1891, 73 pp.

T. B. Hudson, *The Centennial Anniversary of the Installation of Rev. A. S. Norton.* Clinton, 1893, 32 pp.

Exercises, Clinton Presbyterian Church, 1878. Utica, 1878, 62 pp.

Brief History of the First Presbyterian Church and Society in Utica. 1829, 10 pp.

P. H. Fowler, *Reminiscences of Fifteen Years of the History of the First Presbyterian Church of Utica, New York.* 1866, 31 pp.

First Presbyterian Church, Utica, N.Y., 1852–1902. 80 pp.

Fiftieth Anniversary of the First Presbyterian Church Sunday School, Utica, N.Y. 1867, 243 pp.

Centennial . . . First Presbyterian Sunday School of Utica, N.Y., 1816–1916. 71 pp.

Moriah Presbyterian Church (Welsh), Utica, N.Y., 1830–1930. 72 pp.

E. S. Hurd, *A Century in Westminster. Westminster Presbyterian Church, Utica, New York.* 1955, 100 pp.

Olivet Presbyterian Church of Utica, N.Y., 1887–1937. 43 pp.

G. O. Phelps, *Historical Sketch. Memorial Presbyterian Church, Utica, New York, 50th Anniversary.* Utica, 1918, 24 pp.

F. Gage, in *History . . . South Trenton Union Church, 1858–1958.* 8 pp.

J. W. Dodge, *History of the First Presbyterian Church & Society of Verona, N.Y., 1803–1900.* 77 pp.

B. J. Dodge, *Forty Year History of the First Presbyterian Church of Verona, N.Y., 1901–1940,* 23 pp.

C. B. Austen, *Historical Discourse . . . Presbyterian Church, New York Mills, N.Y.* Utica, 1877, 29 pp.

Exercises of Dedication of the Walcott Memorial Church, New York Mills. Utica, 1882, 57 pp.

W. E. Knox, *Semi-Centennial Sermon . . . First Presbyterian Church, Rome, N.Y.* 1851, 32 pp.

J. H. Taylor, *Historical Discourse. First Presbyterian Church, Rome, New York.* Rome, 1888, 29 pp.

E. M. Evans, *The First One Hundred and Fifty Years. 1800–1950. First Presbyterian Church, Rome, New York.* Rome, 1950, 143 pp.

W. B. Parmelee, in *Memorial of the 80th Anniversary of the First Presbyterian Church of Westernville, New York.* 1898, 26 pp.

The Semi-centennial of the Presbyterian Church of Oneida, New York, 1844–1894. Oneida, 1894, 88 pp.

E. N. Manley, *Historical Discourse, First Presbyterian Church of Camden, New York.* Camden, 1876, 9 pp.

—— *Fifteenth Anniversary . . . First Presbyterian Church, Camden, N.Y.* Camden, 1882, 23 pp.

H. M. Dodd, ed., *One Hundredth Anniversary . . . Presbyterian Church, Augusta, N.Y., 1797–1897.* Deansboro, 61 pp.

R. W. Condit, *A Discourse on the 50th Anniversary of the First Presbyterian Church of Oswego, New York.* Oswego, 1867, 15 pp.

A. P. Burgess, *The Old Pratham Church.* Syracuse, 1877, 56 pp.

D. L. Roberts, A *Centennial Celebration, First Presbyterian Church, Mexico, New York.* Watertown, 1910, 120 pp.

Centennial Celebration. First Church, Watertown, New York, 1803-1903. Watertown, 1903, 96 pp.

D. L. Eastman, *First Presbyterian Church, Watertown. The Outline of its History 1805-1928.* 15 pp.

F. N. Kimball, *Years of Faith. A History of the First Presbyterian Church of Watertown, New York, 1803-1953.* Watertown, 1953, 160 pp.

D. L. Eastman, *History of Stone Street Presbyterian Church, Watertown, 1831-1931.* 30 pp.

J. S. Root, *Historical Sketch of the Adams Presbyterian Church.* 1885, 25 pp.

One Hundredth Anniversary, First Presbyterian Church, Carthage, N.Y., 1851-1951. 40 pp.

L. Williams, *Historical Sermon . . . Forest Church, Lyons Falls, N.Y.* Lowville, New York, 1876. 16 pp.

L. M. Miller, "Historical Discourse" in *Manual, First Church of Ogdensburg.* 1865.

—— *Twenty-five Years in Ogdensburg, New York.* Ogdensburg, 44 pp.

A. D. Harsanyi, *One Hundred and Fifty Years of the Presbyterian Church in Ogdensburg.* Boonville, New York, 1955, 154 pp.

R. S. Witherhead, "History" in *125th Anniversary . . . Second Presbyterian Church of Oswegatchie, 1823-1948.* Ogdensburg, 23 pp.

N. J. Conklin, *Centennial Historical Discourse, First Presbyterian Church, Gouverneur, New York.* Gouverneur, 1876, 16 pp.

W. H. Stubblebine, ed., *Historical Sketch of the First Presbyterian Church, Canton, N.Y., 1807-1907.* 65 pp.

J. D. Taitt, *Early History of Ox Bow and the Scotch Settlement, Rossie, N.Y., 1820-1921.* 23 pp.

F. The Old Geneva Synod

S. Lines, *One Hundred and Twenty-five Years of the Western Presbyterian Church, Palmyra, N.Y., 1817–1942.* 10 pp.

C. M. Creighton, *The Park Presbyterian Church, Newark, N.Y., 1825–1925.* Newark, 31 pp.

A. A. Wood, *Sketches of the History of the First Presbyterian Church, Lyons, N.Y.* 1876, 6 pp.

One Hundred and Fifty Years of the Presbyterian Church, Lyons, N. Y., 1809–1959. 51 pp.

Sesquicentennial, First Presbyterian Church, Marion, N.Y., 1808–1958. 4 pp.

L. H. Clark, *History of the Churches of Sodus.* 1876, 70 pp.

V. N. Yergin, *The Clyde Presbyterian Church.* 1898, 25 pp.

W. S. Carter, "Historical Account" in *75th Anniversary of the Presbyterian Church, Waterloo, New York, 1817–1892.*

H. Winslow, *The Former Days. History of the Presbyterian Church of Geneva.* Boston, 1859, 40 pp.

E. A. Bronson, "Historical Discourse" in *Centennial Celebration, First Presbyterian Church, Geneva.* 1900, 40 pp.

L. L. Van Slyke, *Historical Narrative. One Hundred Twenty-fifth Anniversary. First Presbyterian Church, Geneva, N.Y.* 1925, 29 pp.

R. S. Breed, ed., *An Historical Review, 1800–1950.* Geneva, 1950, 61 pp.

E. C. Grosh, "Historical Address" in *Century of Service, Seneca Castle, 1828–1928.* Seneca Castle, 1928, 60 pp.

E. H. Hammond, "The Presbyterian Church of Oaks Corners" in *Centennial . . . 1804–1904.* 35 pp.

A. C. Rippey, *Historical Sketches . . . Presbyterian Church of Seneca, Ontario County, N.Y., 1807–1907.* Canandaigua, 58 pp.

C. C. Thorne, *Historical Sermon. First Presbyterian Church of Manchester, Shortsville, N.Y.* Canandaigua, 1876, 18 pp.

First Presbyterian Church, Shortsville, N.Y., 1860–1960. 24 pp.

N. T. Clarke, "History" in *Directory, First Presbyterian Church, Canandaigua, N.Y.* 1915.

R. E. Moody, "The Pioneer Church 1802–1952" in *The First Congregational Church, Rushville, N. Y. Sesquicentennial.* 34 pp.

The First Presbyterian Church of the Town of Hector, 1809–1959. 52 pp.

F. B. Boyer and C. V. V. Golding, *History of the Lodi Presbyterian Church, 1800–1950.* 8 pp.

F. Starr (1864), J. L. Lewis (1873), D. H. Palmer (1898), C. K. Imbrie (1923), Historical Addresses in *Centennial Record. First Presbyterian Church. Penn Yan, New York, 1823–1923.* 55 pp.

S. P. Merritt, *History of the Presbyterian Church, Prattsburg, New York, 1804–1954.* 17 pp.

B. Bosworth, *Historical Sermon, Presbyterian Church, Hammondsport, N.Y.* 1882, 14 pp.

C. N. Frost, *Centennial Sermon, First Presbyterian Church, Bath, N.Y.* 1908, 19 pp.

S. W. Parker, *The Reverend John Niles, 1775–1812.* [Bath], 1958, 80 pp.

S. M. Campbell, *Sermon . . . Campbell, Steuben County, N.Y.* Corning, 1868, 23 pp.

S. W. Pratt, *Sermon . . . Fiftieth Anniversary . . . Presbyterian Church of Campbell, Steuben County, N.Y.* Corning, 1881, 10 pp.

One Hundred Fortieth Anniversary, 1812–1952, First Presbyterian Church, Corning, N.Y. 20 pp.

First Presbyterian Church, Elmira, New York, 1795–1955. 18 pp.

History of the First Hundred Years of the First Presbyterian Church, Hornell, N.Y., 1832–1932. 40 pp.

Semi-centennial . . . Presbyterian Church of Hornellsville, N.Y. 1882, 41 pp.

W. M. Stuart, *History of the First Presbyterian Church, Canisteo, N.Y.* 1936, 52 pp.

I. L. Jenkins, *Historical Discourse, Presbyterian Church of Jasper, 1829–1879.* 10 pp.

R. H. Massecar, *125th Anniversary Rock Stream Presbyterian Church, 1833–1958.* 6 pp.

J. E. Close, *The First Presbyterian Church of Jordan, Onondaga County, New York.* Syracuse, 1877, 145 pp.

Port Byron, N.Y. First Presbyterian Church. 1801–1911.

Historical Souvenir of the Presbyterian Church of Union Springs, 1801–1901. 16 pp.

G. P. Sewall, *History of the Presbyterian Church of Cayuga, New York, 1819–1876.* Auburn, 1876, 40 pp.

C. Hawley, *History of the First Presbyterian Church in Auburn.* Auburn, 1876, 87 pp.

—— *The First Presbyterian Church, Auburn, New York, Pastorate of Rev. C. Hawley, 1857–1882.* Auburn, 1883, 82 pp.

M. MacPhail, *History of the First Presbyterian Church, Auburn, New York.* Auburn, 1936, 79 pp.

W. J. Beecher, "History" in *The Central Church Semi-centennial 1861–1911.* Auburn, 1912, 157 pp.

J. S. Jewell, *Seventy-Fifth Anniversary of the First Presbyterian Church of Genoa, Northville, Cayuga Co., N.Y.* Auburn, 1874, 24 pp.

C. Ray, *History of Presbyterian Church of Wyoming, N.Y., 1817–1868.* Moravia, 1877, 30 pp.

Centennial Celebration of the First Presbyterian Church of Genoa, King Ferry, New York, 1798–1898. 33 pp.

One Hundredth Anniversary . . . United Church of Fair Haven, Presbyterian, 1847–1947. 14 pp.

E. W. Rice, *Historical Sketches of the Presbyterian Church of Hannibal, Oswego County, N.Y., 1816–1916.* 21 pp.

G. R. Smith, *History of the First Eighty Years of the First Presbyterian Church of Marcellus, New York.* Canandaigua, New York, 1883, 123 pp.

The Centennial Exercises of the First Presbyterian Church of Baldwinsville, 1813–1913. 38 pp.

A. H. Fahnestock, *History of the Presbyterian Church in Sa-*

lina, 1810–1910. Syracuse, 42 pp.

L. H. Reid, *Salina in Olden Times. An Address on the occasion of the semi-centennial celebration of the Sunday School of the First Ward Presbyterian Church, Syracuse, New York.* Syracuse, 1868, 30 pp.

Manual, First Church of Syracuse. 1895, 144 pp.

A. J. Northrup, "History" in *Seventy-fifth Anniversary of the First Presbyterian Society in the Village of Syracuse, 1824–1899.* Syracuse, 1899, 163 pp.

100th Anniversary of the First Presbyterian Society, Syracuse, 1824–1924.

First Presbyterian Church, Syracuse, N.Y., 1906–1956. 16 pp.

Fifty Years in the Life of Park Church, Syracuse, N.Y. 1896, 88 pp.

D. Torrey, *History of the Presbyterian Church, Cazenovia, New York.* Cazenovia, 1876, 43 pp.

S. E. Persons, *The Twelve Apostles of the Church of Cazenovia, an historical address.* Cazenovia, 1898, 96 pp.

Presbyterian Church, Otisco, N.Y., 1803–1953. 24 pp.

D. W. Van Hoesen, *History of the Presbyterian Church of Preble, N.Y., 1810–1915.* 13 pp.

T. Street, *Historical Discourse . . . Semi-centennial Anniversary, Presbyterian Church, Cortland, N.Y.* 1875, 18 pp.

E. D. Blodgett, "Historical Essay" in *One Hundredth Anniversary, First Presbyterian Church, Cortland, New York, 1825–1925.* 77 pp.

G. Bayless, *Historic Discourse of the Presbyterian Church of McGrawville, N.Y.* Cortland, 1876, 12 pp.

The Centennial History of the First Presbyterian Church of Dryden, 1808–1908. Dryden, 1908, 112 pp.

W. Wisner, *Half Century Sermon. Presbyterian Church in Ithaca.* 1866, 18 pp.

J. F. Fitchen, ed., *History of the First Presbyterian Church of Ithaca, New York, 1804–1904.* 163 pp.

Book of Remembrance. Presbyterian Church, Spencer, N.Y., 1815–1915. 32 pp.

155th Anniversary. The Story of the Presbyterian Church of Windsor, New York, 1793–1948. 4 pp.

A. C. Mackenzie, *Retracing Old Paths, or an Historical Sketch of the First Presbyterian Church and Society of Owego, New York.* Columbus, Ohio, 1895, 56 pp.

G. N. Boardman, *Historical Discourse . . . Fiftieth Anniversary of the First Presbyterian Church of Binghamton.* New York, 1868, 39 pp.

P. Lockwood, *Remarks . . . at the Fiftieth Anniversary of the First Presbyterian Church in Binghamton.* Binghamton, 1870, 30 pp.

G. P. Nichols, *Historical Sketch of the First Presbyterian Church of Binghamton, N.Y.* 1909, 24 pp.

S. Dunham, *Retrospect . . . West Presbyterian Church, Binghamton, N.Y.* Binghamton and New York, 1914, 259 pp.

History of the Union Presbyterian Church, Endicott, N.Y., 1822–1922. 18 pp.

G. The Old Genesee Synod

W. R. McNair, *Historical Sketch. Presbyterian Church, Lima, Livingston County, 1795–1895.*

C. W. Backus, *An Historical Sketch of the First Presbyterian Church of Victor, New York.* Rochester, 1888, 122 pp.

G. W. Heacock, *Sermon . . . at installation of G. P. Folsom . . . Second Presbyterian Church, Geneseo, N.Y.* 1859, 39 pp.

G. P. Folsom, *History of the Second Presbyterian Church of Geneseo, New York.* Geneseo, 1868, 30 pp.

J. Mitchell, *Centennial Discourse . . . First Presbyterian Church of Geneseo.* Livonia, 1876, 14 pp.

Centennial Celebration, Geneseo Village Presbyterian Church. 1910.

Historical Narrative of the Central Presbyterian Church, Geneseo. New York, 1876, 11 pp.

D. Chichester, *Discourse . . . Mount Morris.* Geneseo, 1855, 21 pp.

Centennial, First Presbyterian Church, Livonia, New York, 1806–1906. 46 pp.

W. H. Millham, *Historical Sermon. Presbyterian Church, Livonia Center, N.Y.* 1876, 13 pp.

Centennial of the Presbyterian Church, Dansville, N.Y., 1825–1925. 40 pp.

Sesquicentennial of the First Presbyterian Church, Caledonia, New York. 1955, 33 pp.

W. S. Stone, *Centennial History of the First Presbyterian Society, Leroy, New York, 1812–1912.* Leroy, 1912, 46 pp.

Schism the Offspring of Error. Historical Sketches, Presbyterian Church of Warsaw, Genesee Co., N.Y. Buffalo, 1841, 26 pp.

J. E. Nassau, "Historical Address," in *The Seventy-fifth Anniversary of the Presbyterian Church of Warsaw, New York.* Warsaw, 1885, 16 pp.

G. S. Corwin, *History of a Country Church for Forty Years and of a Pastorate for Twenty-five Years.* [Elba] Rochester, 1870, 16 pp.

T. Edwards, *Discourse . . . First Presbyterian Church, Rochester, N.Y.* 1837, 39 pp.

C. M. Robinson, *First Church Chronicles, 1815–1915.* Rochester, 1915, 206 pp.

J. B. Shaw, *Twenty-Fifth Anniversary . . . Brick Church, Rochester.* 1865, 36 pp.

—— *Fiftieth Anniversary of the Brick Church, Rochester, New York. Thirty-fifth Anniversary of the Pastor.* Rochester, 1876, 59 pp.

G. B. F. Hallock and Maude Motley, *A Living Church, the First Hundred Years of the Brick Church in Rochester.* 1925, 274 pp.

Brick Presbyterian Church, Rochester, New York, 1825–1950. Rochester, 1950, 48 pp.

A Century with Central Church, 1836–1936. Rochester, 1936, 274 pp.

W. G. Wildes, *Third Presbyterian Church, 1827–1952*. Rochester, 31 pp.

J. R. Page, *History of the Brighton Church*. Rochester, 1877, 60 pp.

W. A. Fox, "Historical Sermon" in *Manual of the Presbyterian Church in Ogden*. Ogden, 1866.

J. B. Funnell, ed., *Historical Papers . . . Ogden Presbyterian Church, Spencerport, N.Y., 1811–1911*. Rochester, 51 pp.

J. Copeland, *Semi-centennial Discourse on the Organization of the Presbyterian Church at Holley, New York*. Rochester, 1869, 23 pp.

A. E. Sears, *Historical Sketch of the First Presbyterian Church of Albion*. 1895.

The Anniversary Proceedings of the Founding of the First Presbyterian Church of Lockport, New York. Lockport, 1898, 78 pp.

W. K. Tully, *Historical Sermon, First Presbyterian Church. Medina, New York*. 1876, 22 pp.

E. T. Williams, "History" in *Official Souvenir . . . First Presbyterian Church of Niagara Falls, N.Y., 1824–1924*.

G. H. Todd, *Pierce Avenue Presbyterian Church, Niagara Falls, N.Y., 1893–1943*. Niagara Falls, 1943, 18 pp.

H. Kimball, "Lewiston, Niagara County, First Presbyterian Church," *Yesteryears*, Vol. 3, No. 10 (January, 1960), pp. 16–24.

W. Clarke, *The First Church in Buffalo. Half Century Discourses*. Buffalo, 1862, 92 pp.

T. Farnham, *The First Presbyterian Church of Buffalo*. Buffalo, 1884, 48 pp.

R. V. Hunter, *Historical Address . . . Central Presbyterian Church, Buffalo*. 1907, 16 pp.

Historical Sketch of the Central Presbyterian Church, Buffalo, New York, 1835–1935. Buffalo, 1935, 72 pp.

A. T. Chester, *History of the North Presbyterian Church for Twenty-five Years*. Buffalo, 1873, 69 pp.

R. M. Graves, *The North Presbyterian Church, Buffalo, N.Y.,*

1847–1922. Buffalo, 1922, 95 pp.

W. M. Knight, *Manual, Catalogue and History of the Lafayette Street Presbyterian Church of Buffalo, New York.* Buffalo, 1876.

One Hundredth Anniversary, Lafayette Avenue Presbyterian Church, 1845–1945. 27 pp.

I. Riley, *Historical Discourse, Westminster Church, Buffalo.* 1876, 58 pp.

100th Anniversary, Westminster Presbyterian Church, Buffalo, 1854–1954. 36 pp.

W. Waith, *50th Anniversary of the Presbyterian Church in Lancaster.* Buffalo, 1868, 49 pp.

Reunion . . . First Presbyterian Church, Fredonia, N.Y. 1874, 42 pp.

C. Burgess, *Historical Discourse. The Presbyterian Church of Silver Creek, N.Y.* Buffalo, 1876, 30 pp.

Semi-centennial . . . First Presbyterian Church of Panama, N.Y., 1830–1880. Jamestown, 22 pp.

C. B. Gardiner, *Sermon, the First Presbyterian Church of Ripley, N.Y.* 1903, 23 pp.

C. Simpson, *Historical Address . . . Fiftieth Anniversary . . . Presbyterian Church of Sherman, N.Y.* 1877, 19 pp.

Historical Sketch of the First Presbyterian Church of Cuba, New York, 1827–1927. 32 pp.

C. Sheldon, *History of the First Presbyterian Church, Allegany, New York, 1858–1958.* 16 pp.

Index